Wordcraft

Chicago Guides to Writing, Editing, and Publishing

Writing for Social Scientists
Howard S. Becker
The Craft of Research
Wayne C. Booth, Gregory G. Colomb, Joseph M. Williams, Joseph Bizup, and William T. FitzGerald
The Chicago Guide to Fact-Checking
Brooke Borel
Writing Fiction
Janet Burroway, with Elizabeth Stuckey-French and Ned Stuckey-French
Writing Abroad
Peter Chilson and Joanne B. Mulcahy
Immersion
Ted Conover
The Business of Being a Writer
Jane Friedman
The Chicago Guide to Grammar, Usage, and Punctuation
Bryan A. Garner
Legal Writing in Plain English
Bryan A. Garner
What Editors Do
Peter Ginna, editor
Writing Science in Plain English
Anne E. Greene
Storycraft
Jack Hart
Economical Writing
Deirdre Nansen McCloskey
The Subversive Copy Editor
Carol Fisher Saller
The Writer's Diet
Helen Sword
A Manual for Writers of Research Papers, Theses, and Dissertations
Kate L. Turabian

Wordcraft

The Complete Guide to Clear, Powerful Writing

Jack Hart

THE UNIVERSITY OF CHICAGO PRESS CHICAGO AND LONDON

The University of Chicago Press, Chicago 60637
The University of Chicago Press, Ltd., London

Published 2021
Printed in the United States of America

30 29 28 27 26 25 24 23 22 21 1 2 3 4 5

ISBN-13: 978-0-226-74907-5 (paper)
ISBN-13: 978-0-226-74910-5 (e-book)
DOI: https://doi.org/10.7208/chicago/9780226749105.001.0001

This book was first published in 2006 by Pantheon Books, a division of Penguin Random House LLC, under the title *A Writer's Coach*.

Library of Congress Cataloging-in-Publication Data

Names: Hart, Jack, 1946– author.
Title: Wordcraft : the complete guide to clear, powerful writing / Jack Hart.
Other titles: Writer's coach | Chicago guides to writing, editing, and publishing.
Description: Chicago : The University of Chicago Press, 2021. | Series: Chicago guides to writing, editing, and publishing | Includes bibliographical references and index.
Identifiers: LCCN 2020032181 | ISBN 9780226749075 (paperback) | ISBN 9780226749105 (ebook)
Subjects: LCSH: Journalism—Authorship. | Creative nonfiction—Authorship. | Authorship.
Classification: LCC PN4775 .H324 2021 | DDC 808.02—dc23
LC record available at https://lccn.loc.gov/2020032181

♾ This paper meets the requirements of ANSI/NISO Z39.48-1992 (Permanence of Paper).

Contents

Preface

This book was first published by Random House in 2006 under the title *A Writer's Coach*.

I'd originally planned to title the book *Wordcraft* and conceived of it as book 1 in a two-book set. Book 2 would pass along what I'd learned in a long career of editing and coaching narrative nonfiction and would be called *Storycraft*.

But when Random House bought the rights to book 1, someone in the bowels of that giant company discovered a conflict with the title of another book on its list. My editor informed me that we'd have to change the title and came up with *A Writer's Coach*. Not a bad title, to be sure, but not what I'd intended. A few years later, I published book 2 as *Storycraft* with the University of Chicago Press.

Now that I have had the opportunity to bring the two books together at UCP as the package I'd originally envisioned, we've recovered the lost title. More important, I have revised the book to take note of the changes that have shaken the writing world since its original publication. While the original edition assumed an audience consisting primarily of newspaper and other print journalists, I learned over the lifespan of the original edition just how relevant the advice is to writers of all kinds. Some sections may still be especially useful to print journalists, but I now address most of my advice to anyone who wishes to understand and follow the principles of good writing. That means, of course, just about everybody. Professionals such as lawyers and advertising and public relations types have always had to reach out with the written word.

But these days we all have keyboards in our figurative hip pockets, and the amount of influence and connection we have in this world depends, to some degree, on how well we use them.

And so, as an outpouring of recent scientific research has demonstrated, does an ability to move audiences with effective stories. Those same lawyers and marketing types who depend on clear, effective writing to power their careers have discovered the value that good storytelling has in persuading juries or selling a brand. More than ever, the lessons I incorporated in both books 1 and 2 have proved useful far beyond print newsrooms.

So, while updating *Wordcraft* I simultaneously revised *Storycraft* so that the books function as the set I'd pictured at the very beginning. Taken together, the two volumes capture just about everything I learned about writing and storytelling over a long and very satisfying career. If I'd had them when I started out all those decades ago, they'd have speeded my education, eliminating years of trial and error and benefiting not only me but also all the fine writers and eager students I worked with over the years.

Now that you *do* have them, you have a leg—or two—up on me at your age. Which means you should be able to climb higher than I ever did. If you enjoy the fruits of fine writing half as much as I have, all of the effort—mine and yours—will have been more than worth it.

Introduction

You can't wait for inspiration; you have to go after it with a club.
—Jack London

Novices sometimes imagine writing as dark magic, something known only to some mystical inner circle. They pick up a professional's finished work, marvel at its seamless perfection, and think, *I could never do that.*

Nonsense. Take it from someone who's been scouting around inside the mystic circle for decades. I worked shoulder to shoulder with some of the best writers on the planet, and never once did we dance around a cauldron. Some hocus-pocus might have helped, but we didn't know any. So we just got down to work.

Great writing happens not through some dark art, but when method meets craft. The secret—if there is one—is to take one manageable step at a time. Superman may leap tall buildings in a single bound, but the best writers I know sit down at their keyboards and write one line. And then another. And another.

That's how it's done, in writing or anything else. Picasso crafted accomplished landscapes and portraits before he broke through into the terra incognita of cubism. Thomas Edison, the most prolific inventor of all time, broke innovation down into a step-by-step process for methodical efficiency. Genius, he famously said, "is 1 percent inspiration and 99 percent perspiration."

Writing poses challenges similar to any other creative process. A writer attending a narrative nonfiction conference once asked Morgan Entrekin, president and publisher of Grove/Atlantic Press, whether talent or hard work counted more among book authors. Talent matters, he said. But the writers who can manage their time and energy well show the best results in the long run. Then he pleaded with the writers in the room to do a better job of getting their manuscripts in on time.

Plenty of dull, disorganized writers meet their deadlines, of course, just as some of the most inspired live chaotic lives of confusion and angst. But the most successful writers I know have mastered a productive, efficient process that consistently turns out great work. They write without psychological meltdown, *and* they make deadline.

Yes, talent counts for something—superhuman performances in any field probably require hard wiring that sets the performers apart. Writing is no different. But for most of us, that's beside the point because we have no choice but to write. A certain skill with the written word is essential to almost anybody's success in the modern world: the cop filing a report, the foundation director pitching a grant, the moonstruck kid emailing flirtatious notes to that smokin' sophomore in third-period algebra. Whether we get what we want out of life depends, more or less, on how well we use writing to accomplish it.

Most of us don't do nearly as well as we might, largely because of that nonsensical notion that good writing is magic. Some schools add to the problem. They teach that other essential skill of the modern age—reading—as though it's a universal that every student must master. Most students do. But in far too many schools the invidious mystique of writing taints the curriculum. In literature classes, you read great works and marvel at the genius of the writers who produced them. In composition, you struggle to knock a few clumsy sentences together. Nobody expects you to see any connection between the diva's aria and your Neanderthal grunts.

In 2001 Tom Hallman, one of the writers I worked with regularly, won the Pulitzer Prize for newspaper feature writing. In journalism, Tom is widely recognized for his mastery of the newspaper narrative, true stories told using the techniques of literature. He'd been a Pulitzer finalist twice before, and over the years he won everything from the Ernie Pyle Award to top national awards from the American Society of Newspaper Editors and the Society of Professional Journalists.

So when Tom gave me permission to post multiple mark-ups of the rough drafts from his Pulitzer Prize–winning story on a website available to journalists across the country, interest was high, and the response was predictable. Tom's fellow journalists were astounded to see how far the story developed over the last three drafts he produced. They, too, had been victims of the writing mystique, assuming that someone of Tom's accomplishment would spin webs of gold the first time his fingers hit the keyboard. What they saw, instead, was a damned good writer hard at work, applying his method and honing his craft.

Tom's first draft was just that, an initial run at the story that mixed great promise with plenty of disappointments. The second draft tied up loose ends, tweaked the structure, and sharpened the character development. The third polished the language, refined the imagery, and pushed through to the final level of excellence. Seeing that progression, one editor told me, was the most instructive writing lesson he'd ever had.

I trust this book offers lessons of similar value.

My professional path informs those lessons. I started my career as a college professor with the requisite advanced degree and spent a dozen years teaching at big universities. That gave me a grounding in theory and plenty of practice communicating with novice writers. But I never really understood the importance of process and craft until I started meeting daily deadlines in the newsroom. I've tried to stress the real-world writing realities I learned there throughout *Wordcraft*.

You'll notice the newsroom influence as you read. Much of it will be from the *Oregonian* where I spent twenty-six years. If you're not a newspaper journalist—and fewer writers are every year—don't let that put you off. All writers face similar problems, regardless of their medium. The down-to-earth, practical advice I've gathered here should apply to almost any kind of writing, be it a novel, a memo, or a love letter.

The practical focus extends to the examples I've used. When I've written something to illustrate a point, my example is set off with quotation marks or in a block quote in roman type. But the vast majority of the examples I've included were actually published somewhere, and each of those is set in italic type. Because I took them from the reading I did every day, over many years, they represent a tolerably good sampling of the hazards and opportunities any writer is likely to encounter in the real world.

Bad examples are unattributed—the point is to learn from mistakes, not to shame anybody with them.

My experience in the newsroom was central to my growth as a writing coach. I was lucky to arrive at the *Oregonian* just before we began a long drive to improve its journalism. We succeeded gloriously. National recognition poured down on the paper. Pulitzer Prizes, Overseas Press Club awards, national business-writing and religion-writing awards. The *Oregonian* won major awards in everything from garden to food to television writing. The writing, reporting, and editing, not the subject matter, was the common denominator.

As the newspaper's writing coach, I was challenged to keep up with the staff's eagerness to improve. I scoured the literature on writing. I invited dozens of nationally known writing talents to our newsroom, where they shared their secrets and added to my store of teaching and editing strategies. For many years I produced a nationally distributed instructional newsletter on writing as well as a writing column for *Editor & Publisher* magazine. Both of those responsibilities forced me to think incessantly and analytically about the qualities of good writing.

I also spent a lot of time out and around the country and even abroad, talking to writers at other newspapers, at professional organizations, at colleges, and at private institutes. I spoke to organizations of food writers, wine writers, fiction writers, travel writers, advertising copywriters, medical writers, and investigative reporters—all sorts of writers facing every kind of writing challenge. They honed my sense of what works in writing, regardless of the topic. And they made me question assumptions I might have harbored if I'd been confined to the classrooms where I started my career.

When I conducted a writing workshop, whether it was in Augusta, Auckland, or Albuquerque, I almost always began by asking the participants to name the qualities that *they* associated with good writing. When a piece of writing grabbed them by the lapels, I asked, when it pulled them into the writer's world to the exclusion of everything else, what was it about the words themselves that attracted them?

Their terminology may have differed, but their answers invariably tapped the same half dozen or so attributes. Good writing, they said:

- radiates energy, crackling with a vigor that pulls readers along. It has internal strength, an inherent force that moves readers.
- gets to the point, regardless of what the point may be. Good writers don't waste their readers' time.
- transports them, putting them into a scene where they can see the autumn light and smell the fallen leaves crunching underfoot. It's rich, in other words, in what journalists call color.
- has a personality, a tone both appropriate to the subject and inviting for the reader. The words sound *right*. They fit with one another and the mood of the reading occasion.
- can dance. Good writing has a rhythm that pleases in its own right, creating cadences that give pleasure regardless of content.
- is clear. You never have to read a well-written sentence twice—unless it's for the sheer pleasure of the experience.

- is mechanically correct. Good writers know their tools, and they never trip readers up with lapses of grammar, usage, or style.

There's broad agreement on the goals. The trick is to achieve them in your own writing, regardless of your purpose. That means jumping from the abstractions—the broad goals such as clarity and color—to the actual hands-on-the-keyboard practices that work.

This book is intended to help you make that leap. Once you take it, the series of specific decisions that makes up any act of writing won't seem nearly so daunting. You'll have a method designed to make writing manageable and a craft guaranteed to make it clearer, more forceful, and more effective.

The inspiration is up to you.

1

Method

My father never had truck driver's block.
—Roger Simon

THE AGONY AND THE METHODOLOGY

The pain of writing is legend. And its intensity hardly varies between the student facing a research-paper deadline, the office worker thrashing out a report, and the seasoned professional writing for publication.

When I run a writing seminar, I often hand out a questionnaire that, among other things, quizzes the participants about the emotion they bring to their writing. Someone invariably quotes Dorothy Parker, the New York literary wit who said she hated writing, but loved having written. "It's agony and ecstasy," one writer said. "When I get the idea, and when I'm finished . . . it's joyful. Everything in between is agony."

Why should that be? Physically, writing's relatively easy work. Take it from a guy who's loaded log ships, pumped gas, and tarred roofs in the midsummer sun. Writers work on their butts and out of the weather. So what's with all this whining?

And why the avoidance, which one writer labeled "tap dancing"? "I'll dance around the story," he said, "putting it off because I think it's harder than it invariably is."

What's the first thing you do when facing a new writing assignment? I ask. "Get a cup of coffee," a journalist replied. "More difficult story, more coffee, more trips to the bathroom, more procrastination."

"But is it really procrastination," another writer asked, "when I'm walking around, getting another cup of coffee, and thinking about the story? More likely, it's a paralysis from possibilities: possible stories, possible leads, possible story flow."

Exactly! Paralysis from possibilities. The tendency to see the task ahead as overwhelming explains most keyboard anxiety. For a variety of reasons, we view writing from the back end. Day in and day out, we witness the finished work of accomplished writers. In our mind's eye we stroll down street after street of beautiful homes, ignorant of the piece-by-piece construction that created them, one two-by-four at a time. "Look at that gorgeous building," we think. "The craftsmanship. The detail work. The sheer size of the thing! I could never build something like that."

Time for another cup of coffee.

But there's another way to look at it. One year I watched four row houses rise on the lot next door. The work was noisy, messy, and distracting, but instructive, too. From the logging crew that brought in chain saws and cleared the lot to the roofers who nailed on the shingles, not one bit of work went into those houses that you or I couldn't do ourselves, given enough time and some research into the technical details. The secret is in the process, not the finished buildings.

The pain of writing stems from comparing your blank screen with the finished pages you see all around you. But beautiful writing is built one step at a time, just like a house. Take the steps slowly, break them down into pieces small enough to handle easily, and the agony will disappear.

Writing, it is often said, is thinking. And the most productive form of thinking, the method that built the modern world, is science. The discipline, the logic, and the procedural rules of science took us from oxcarts to interstellar probes. So it's not surprising that scientists place so much emphasis on process. Science, they will insist, *is* process. Articles in scientific journals invariably include detailed descriptions of how the authors conducted their research—the methodology. That mandatory section of the report sometimes takes more space than the section describing results.

Methodology is just as important for writers. "Genius," said F. Scott Fitzgerald, "is the ability to put into effect what is in your mind." In writing, that can involve a considerable journey. And, as every mother's cliché will have it, the longest journey begins with a single step.

THE BACK-END VIEW OF WRITING

For decades, I focused my writing-improvement efforts on the last stages of the writing process, the eleventh-hour nit-picking that burnishes words to a high gloss. That's what I spent my time doing in the newsroom. And those were the skills I taught in my magazine columns and workshops.

I wasn't alone. Most writing coaches, copy editors, workshop organizers, newspaper line editors, readers, and critics have focused on the polish stage of writing.

Harvard education professors V. A. Howard and J. H. Barton, authors of a wonderful summary of writing research called *Thinking on Paper*, note that a principal "obstacle to writing improvement is our tendency to dwell on either the final results or the mental origins of writing to the exclusion of the activity of writing, as if an empty gap separated writing from thinking."

As Bob Baker, the author of *Newsthinking* put it, "You have to stop concentrating on merely the *results* of good writing—the examples they show you in most textbooks. You have to begin thinking about the *causes*—the thought strategies that created those polished examples."

Baker, a former writer and editor at the *Los Angeles Times*, was one of the writing-process pioneers who helped me discover new dimensions to writing and editing. Don Murray, the Pulitzer Prize–winning University of New Hampshire professor, was another. Murray's seminal book, *Writing for Your Readers*, helped shift the focus of American writing instruction from results to causes.

I've seen the power of what Baker and Murray taught. Analyzing and improving process, making it less painful and more efficient, is the surest route to writing improvement. It's helped me with my own writing, and I'm confident it can help yours, too.

I. The Writing Process

Seize the subject, and the words will follow.
—Cato the Elder

WRITING ONE STEP AT A TIME

Most of us have had a classmate who could sit down the night before the due date for a big paper and bang it out in a couple of hours. He'd be heading out for a beer while we sat staring at our keyboards with—as journalist and screenwriter Gene Fowler described the predicament—little drops of blood forming on our foreheads.

Or maybe your experience was with a colleague who could knock out a big departmental report before lunch. Or a friend who dashed off long, beautifully organized letters in one continuous flow of words. Or a closet novelist who produced a book by turning out a few pages a day despite holding a full-time job and having two toddlers underfoot.

Maybe they're all writing gibberish. Or, like the reporters who shrug and say their stories just "write themselves," maybe they're mindlessly spewing out clichés according to a formula that requires no thought whatsoever.

Still, sometimes the two-hour research paper gets an A, the speedy report writer earns a promotion, and the relaxed reporter wins a Pulitzer.

That shouldn't be terribly surprising. Most accomplished writers follow an efficient road map that leads them through projects without a lot of angst. In the real world of experienced professionals, a published piece almost never originates at the keyboard.

Consider everything that typically leads to a final draft:

1. The idea that results in a piece of writing may take days, weeks, or months forming in the writer's mind. It probably will be shaped by discussion with others—editors, friends, sources. Eventually, the best ideas take the form of hypotheses that can be tested in the real world.
2. The information gathering can take anywhere from a few minutes to months. In the case of some Pulitzer Prize–winning feature stories, reporting lasted a year or more. Copywriters at ad agencies may spend months on research, interviewing, and brainstorming. Gathering string for a novel or a nonfiction book can take decades.
3. After the reporting, the writer has to ask, "So what?" What, in other words, is the focus of all the data pulled together during information gathering?
4. The raw material—notes, documents, database information—must be sorted and organized. That gives the report, essay, or story a shape, and it makes the raw material accessible during the writing.
5. The writer must work through the first draft.
6. The writer—and everybody else involved in producing the finished product—must dive into the final tweaking and polishing.

Of course, writing projects rarely conform perfectly to this idealized scheme. Ideas get refined as information gathering proceeds and the ultimate focus of the writing emerges. Drafting may suggest more meaningful approaches to organization. In the real world, writers jump around the process instead of moving smoothly from beginning to end.

Regardless of the writing project, however, one thing remains the same. Content problems are almost always process problems. And some writers

Idea
▼
Information gathering
▼
Focus
▼
Organizing
▼
Drafting
▼
Polishing

Figure 1. The writing process

struggle for their entire lives without tumbling to the First Law of Writing Improvement: A problem visible at any one stage of the writing process usually results from something that happened at the immediately preceding stage.

Why do some writers bog down in aimless morasses of information? Almost always it's because their original idea wasn't adequately developed. Why can't some writers find a focus? Probably because their undirected information gathering swamped them with irrelevant information. Why do some writers have a hard time finding a sensible organizational scheme? Maybe they have no focus. Poor organization, of course, will make it devilishly difficult to craft a decent draft. And if you have a lousy draft, you're bound to have problems polishing it.

II. Ideas

My working habits are simple: long periods of thinking, short periods of writing.
—Ernest Hemingway

MINING THE WORLD FOR IDEAS

The author wearily steps to the lectern, ten cities into a twelve-city book tour. She finishes her shtick, asks for questions, and scans the audience warily, leery of the hands thrusting toward the ceiling. She points at a smiling face in the back, grips the edge of the lectern, and tries to keep herself from glowering as the inevitable question floats toward her again.

"Where," says the adoring reader, "do you get your ideas?"

"You get a life," growls the author to herself before graciously answering the damnable question for the umpteenth time. And, despite the platitudes she dishes out for public consumption, "Get a life" is the right answer.

Experienced writers are swamped with ideas. The problem isn't getting ideas; it's getting around to the ones they already have. They have lives, in other words. And the lives they lead follow myriad paths to an unending supply of ideas.

For one thing, they're great readers. They read competitors, friends, enemies, and the best writers, living and dead. They read novels, memoirs, and billboards. Then they think about what they've read, exploring the possible application of new ideas to their own writing.

They don't get stuck in reading ruts, either. Lots of us wake up to the morning news feed and find time for a favorite magazine or two, whether online or in print. But inveterate readers sample the whole world of publishing. In my town, that's easy. Portland is home to one of the world's biggest bookstores, Powell's City of Books, and for years I made a habit of stopping into Rich's Cigar Store, which in addition to stogies carried somewhere between three thousand and four thousand magazine titles. On any given day I might have leafed through *Fine Woodworking*, *Wooden Boat*, or *Zyzzyva* (a literary journal).

I'm only following my own advice. I'm the guy who told folks in magazine-writing classes to read something unusual every week. You may not have a Powell's or a Rich's in your burg, but these days you can find just about anything online.

It helps to keep some crude files, too. They don't have to be fancy, just manila folders or computer files labeled with broad topics. Then, if you see something that grabs your fancy in one of those off-the-beaten-path publications you're reading, you can stuff it into a folder. Right now my idea file contains folders on "Overhead Wires," "Paisley Caves," and "Cutthroat Trout."

It doesn't hurt to get off the beaten path literally, too. Take a side road on impulse—that's how I ended up with a file labeled "Overhead Wires." Or turn your feet down a street that leads away from where you're headed, pop into a business you've never visited, and strike up a conversation with a stranger.

Then go write about your experience. Nothing generates ideas like getting your hands on the keyboard. The world is filled with writing wannabes who insist they'll write something wonderful as soon as they have a really good idea. But they'll spend a lifetime waiting for their muse to arrive because they have the process backward.

Writing generates ideas by encouraging the kind of sequential, cause-and-effect thinking that leads your mind into new territory. Howard and Barton, the authors of *Thinking on Paper*, scanned the scientific research on writing and concluded that writing is "the father to thought itself. . . . We do not so much send our thoughts in pursuit of words as use words to pursue our thoughts."

Roy Peter Clark of the Poynter Institute, a midcareer school for journalists, and Don Fry, a freelance writing coach, divide writers into "planners" and "plungers." Like Don, I'm a planner who likes to know the central point and general organization of what he's about to write before he types the first line. Roy's a plunger. So sometimes he just jumps into a topic and starts writing whatever comes to mind. After a while, a focus emerges. Then he backs out, throws away most of what he's written, and starts over. He calls that first round of writing a "vomit draft."

In more polite circles, that's called freewriting, and it's been a mainstay of writing-workshop exercises for decades. It's the keyboard equivalent of brainstorming, a chance to follow ideas wherever they lead. You muzzle your internal critic and start writing, as fast as you can, for a predetermined amount of time. Ten minutes, fifteen minutes, whatever. Only when time runs out do you start to think seriously about what you've done, sifting and evaluating and finding an idea that's worth developing in depth.

The important thing is that you spend a reasonable amount of time on the idea stage of the writing process. Resist the impulse to rush into the writing when all you have is a topic. I'd damn well better have something specific to say about overhead wires or cutthroat trout before I get too far into writing about those vague categories.

If I don't, I'm in trouble. The idea is the foundation for all that follows, and without a clear vision of your objective, you can't plan your information gathering or organize your material. Well-shaped ideas are one of the best antidotes to the pain so often associated with writing.

As a writer who attended one of my workshops put it: "The more I get a good solid story idea and get out of the office to talk to real people during the reporting of it, the easier the writing."

If the writing is hard for the writer, it's also likely to be hard for the reader. The most colorfully detailed, elaborately structured, and beautifully polished piece of writing will bore the hell out of the audience if the underlying idea doesn't take them somewhere they've never been before.

FINDING LESS-THAN-OBVIOUS IDEAS

When she was an award-winning feature writer for the *Washington Post*, Cynthia Gorney started writing even before she got to the keyboard. Gorney, who taught journalism at Cal Berkeley, freelanced for top national magazines, and recently dove into podcasting, made especially astute use of revealing detail. One of her secrets was to start jotting down lists of details when she was still in the field. That simple act of observation and rudimentary writing helped her focus, and the theme for her finished story began emerging as she worked her way through the process.

Dave Barry, the humorist, discovers his angle by thinking of a topic—not necessarily funny—and starting to write. The gags emerge as he works the keyboard. The novelist Cormac McCarthy recognized the same process when he wrote, "Where all is known, no narrative is possible."

Howard and Barton say the research on writing suggests that you begin writing "by thinking in writing in whatever way suits you: notes, list of crucial terms, questions, reminders, etc. Try to write in whole sentences. . . . This is one of the best ways not only to preserve but also to discover and to identify your thoughts."

Some writers keep a daily journal for precisely that reason. It forces them to write regularly, and it provides a risk-free arena where they can explore the contents of their own minds. The linear thinking that goes with actually writing down words often leads to interesting ideas that would otherwise go unremarked.

BILL'S BRAINSTORMS

Bill Blundell, the former *Wall Street Journal* writing coach, has one of the most systematic approaches to developing ideas. He lists four routes he considers when he's thinking about a writing project:

- **Extrapolation**: Bill asks himself if the cause of some phenomenon is likely to produce other effects. If a spike in gas prices increases the sale of small cars, maybe it also will boost the sale of bicycles. If you investigate and find out that's true, you may have something new worth writing about.
- **Synthesis**: Can you unify apparently unrelated developments to establish an interesting new pattern? Downhill skiers suddenly prefer wider, fatter skis. Water-skiers turn from slalom skis to wakeboards. Windsurfers adopt shorter boards and shift from sails to kites for propulsion, allowing them to leap and somersault. Has the influence of skateboarders shifted the emphasis in gliding sports from speed and grace to acrobatic tricks?

- **Localization**: Does some national or international development have local consequences that nobody's noticed? Maybe the ban on importing Iranian cashews has increased demand for locally grown filberts?
- **Projection**: How does some central development play out in terms of consequences? Bill looks for two types—impacts and countermoves. If interest rates fall, will home buyers buy the bigger houses they can suddenly afford? And if home buyers begin buying bigger houses, will home builders increase the average square footage of what they construct?

Bill has an especially effective method of projecting his ideas. He takes a blank sheet of paper and writes a causal statement in the middle. (In his book *The Art and Craft of Feature Writing*, he begins an example with "Shortage of Doctors Arises.") Then he draws an arrow to an implication ("Inferior Medical Care for Patients"). Then he heads off in another direction ("Fees Rise to What Traffic Will Bear"). Then another. Then he extends each of these logical progressions several more steps. Eventually, he gets to interesting implications ("More Doctors Quit or Limit Practices") that can be tested with reporting in the field.

I love these "Blundell chains," and I often use them when coaching writers to more fully develop their own ideas. Figure 2 gives an example using our falling interest rates idea.

The drill is to start with your initial premise dead center on a sheet of paper. (You can use one of the several mind-mapping programs available online, but I think a sheet of paper and a comfortable chair are much more conducive to the relaxed state that most encourages creativity.) In this case, that's "Interest rates fall." Then you start stringing together what logic professors call "hypothetical syllogisms." If X, then Y.

So: If interest rates fall, then what?

Well . . . if interest rates fall, then certificates of deposit will pay smaller yields and consumers will start looking around to find better uses for their money. If money flows out of CDs, then banks will have less cash on hand to meet their margin requirement, the minimum the government requires them to keep in their vaults. If they have less money on hand, they'll have less to lend. If they have less to lend, they may try to borrow more from the Federal Reserve. Or they may lend less, and their income on loans will fall.

Of course, once you get past the one assured fact in the center of your Blundell chain, you're speculating. I don't know enough about the banking business to predict, with any certainty, that a fall in interest rates will increase loan

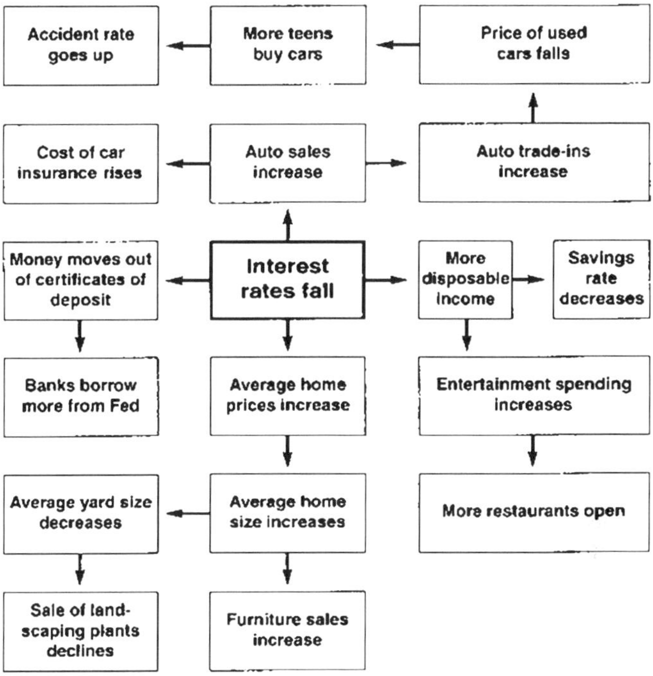

Figure 2. A Blundell chain

applications from local banks to the Federal Reserve. But hey! At least I have an interesting question. And if I get an interesting answer, I'll be ahead of the business writers who didn't ask the question.

Let's pursue this chain in one more direction before we leave it: If interest rates fall, then car sales should increase. And if car sales increase, then more buyers will trade in their jalopies. And if a flood of jalopies hits the market, the price of used cars will crash. Which means more teens will buy their own cars. Which means . . . Omigod!

Note that the longer you chase a chain of logic, the farther out on a limb you'll be. Each link in the chain is a leap of faith. Causality doesn't flow through reality in simple linear lines. The longer the chain, the more variables come into play and the less the likelihood that your logic will predict results accurately.

But that's OK. A Blundell chain is just a device to get you moving on a topic. It suggests questions to ask and sources to consult. The real payoff comes in the information gathering that your new questions provoke. The answers may surprise you. You may not end up where you thought you would, but your destination—wherever it is—will almost certainly be an interesting place.

LIBERATING YOURSELF FROM LOCKSTEP THINKING

Our information society operates as a series of concentric rings, with the original and outlandish ideas on the outside. By the time something works its way into the *Huffington Post* or onto CNN, it's moved to the center of the system, acquiring legitimacy and respectability as it goes.

But out on the edges are the small-scale information sources that operate as gateways to the larger system. Academic journals. Strange counterculture publications. Way-out-there online political sites. Hobby magazines, fanzines, blogs, oddball Twitter threads, and quirky websites. If it's truly different, it's by definition marginalized. You look for it in the back alleys, not on Main Street.

Anybody can cook up a list of tactics for breaking out of the daily routine, but here are some suggestions for getting started. Each activity is a good bet to shake the dust off your neurons.

- Allow a few extra minutes and take a different route home from work. Find as many alternative routes as you can.
- If you always drive, take a bus. If you always fly, take a train.
- Slide onto a stool at a bar you've never visited before. Strike up a conversation with the stranger next to you.
- Tune in to community-access television. Stifle your impulse to immediately tune out again.
- Instead of Googling once again, visit the nearest university research library and wander through the stacks. Pull a few books off the shelves at random and thumb through them.
- As long as you're at the library, hit the reference room and pillage ideas from *Famous First Facts*, now in its seventh edition. (Surely reading about the first balloon ascent or the first diving bell will lead your brain in some unexpected directions.) See how your city's spending in various categories compares with that of other towns by rummaging around in *Municipal Yearbook*. Look for local names in *Biography Index*, or check out the multitude of other biographical indexes, which catalog published references for everyone from folk artists, to scientists, to residents of New Jersey.
- Try freewriting. Sit down at a keyboard in front of a blank screen or get comfortable with a pen and an empty notebook. Start writing down anything that comes into your head, just as fast as you can. Exercise

absolutely no self-censorship. Don't worry about spelling, grammar, or accuracy. Once an interesting theme starts to emerge, go with it.
- Pick two words at random—off billboards, say, or out of headlines—join them with "and," and launch an internet search.
- Visit your local newsstand and buy some publication that's totally new to you.
- Drive to an unfamiliar part of town. Stop, get out, and walk.
- Drive out of town, pull off the road at the first major junction, and flip a coin to determine your direction. Keep it up with three or four subsequent junctions until you end up somewhere completely new. Talk to somebody.
- If you must, use a search engine such as Google to identify sources in a broad area of interest. Then randomly click through a few links in search of a new spin on the subject.

MISTAKING TOPICS FOR IDEAS

Early in my career as a journalist, the federal government rocked my part of the world by declaring the spotted owl a threatened species. On its surface, the act was a small thing. In its consequences, it was epic.

Spotted owls live only in old-growth forests, and for more than a century old growth had powered the Northwest economy. Saving the owl meant shutting down old-growth logging. That meant transforming the region.

Within a few years, the chain saws in old-growth forests had largely fallen silent, smothered by lawsuits, environmental-impact statements, and restraining orders. Logging towns withered. Angry loggers passed around tongue-in-cheek recipes for spotted-owl stew.

In those days my newspaper was as mossy as an old tree. Hardly anything received more than routine coverage, but we couldn't ignore the spotted-owl crisis. Two dozen editors filed into a meeting room to plan a project. The reporters must have been watching the closed door in terror as, inside, editors cooked up every logging topic they could conjure. I remember the conversation only dimly, but it no doubt went something like this:

"We'll have to take a look at the owl."

"And we'd better take a look at the Endangered Species Act."

"What about the lumber mills? We'd better see how many depend on old growth."

"Let's look at federal versus state timberlands."

When the storm of free association had finally sputtered out, the editors fanned out into the newsroom, inflicting their story topics on any reporters they found.

The result was an aimless, endless series of something like thirty-five stories. It ran on for days, page after page of boring gray type. I doubt that even the editors who created the monster actually read the entire thing. They just sat around waiting for the Pulitzer Prize that never came.

You could call them clueless, I suppose. But they actually had plenty of clues. What they lacked were real ideas. Nobody did the hard thinking needed to focus and refine that hodgepodge of topics so that we could actually say something meaningful.

We might have built a series around the hypothesis, for example, that the spotted-owl crisis was shifting the balance of political power from rural to urban Oregon. Or that it was creating a cultural divide between small-town loggers, farmers, and fishermen and a new high-tech workforce. Or that the use of "indicator species" such as the spotted owl was an effective new tool that would give environmentalists unprecedented clout.

The lack of real ideas plagues every corner of American writing. Government reports drone on and on, restating the obvious and cloaking the lack of substance in gobbledygook. Business marketing plans trot out page after page of meaningless statistics without ever offering an original insight about the unique benefits offered by a new product or service (a failing that once moved ace adman David Ogilvy to observe that "people don't want drills; they want holes"). Even online forums and chat rooms trot out the same tired concepts and observations.

The root problem in most aimless writing is the failure to recognize the difference between a topic and an idea. The tip-off is that dread phrase "a look at." Anytime a writer proposes "a look at" something, you can bet you're in for a boring account that rambles through a topic with no sense of direction, no momentum, and no surprises. To say something meaningful about the world, you have to make a causal statement. "A look at" is anything but.

The phrase also cripples the chances that you'll find anything revealing when you move on to information gathering. If you're merely pursuing "a look at" some topic, everything remotely related to it becomes relevant, and you'll scoop up everything you come across. In the end, you'll probably commit the sin that reporters call "notebook dump," dropping everything you have into a rambling, endless piece of writing that ultimately goes nowhere.

Strong initial brainstorming and constant tweaking as new information comes in is what guides the research in productive directions. The hope is to go beyond the obvious, to find patterns that make sense out of chaos, and to offer insights unavailable anywhere else.

And never, ever to assault readers with a thirty-five-part series that adds up to not much of anything.

A FAVORABLE WIND

My former colleagues no doubt grew tired of my favorite quotations, including one from Michel de Montaigne. "No wind favors him," wrote the sixteenth-century French essayist, "who has no destined port."

You may start your thinking about a subject with a question. ("What's over the western horizon?") But you're in for nothing but aimless wandering unless you convert your question into an assertion. ("If I sail southwest for forty days, I'll reach the Indies.") That gives you a course of action. And you're likely to have a purposeful, productive journey even if your assertion turns out to be wrong.

Good ideas, in navigation or in writing, take the form of hypotheses. Productive information gathering begins with a statement that helps focus study, limits the scope of the project, and separates the relevant from the irrelevant. The hypothesis creates a filter. It allows the writer to impose order on chaos. It may well be fine-tuned or completely overhauled as the reporting proceeds, but a hypothesis built on good preliminary information gathering will more often than not stand up to the research that follows.

Good ideas are organic. They don't materialize out of a vacuum. They originate in the real world and come to our attention through systematic investigation. That's why editors usually aren't the best sources of story ideas. While they're stuck in their offices, the writers are out in the world, moving around and encountering the kinds of things that can lead to great ideas.

Most of those ideas move through a circular process that begins when a writer spots something odd or curious or provocative. My former colleague, Amanda Bennett, who went on to become executive director of the Voice of America but who once served as a China correspondent for the *Wall Street Journal*, cites the example of the blue-collar Brit who learned Chinese, started singing in Mandarin, and became a pop icon for older Chinese women.

Interesting. Fascinating, even. But what's it mean? The *Journal* writer who tackled the story moved from the particular example—the Mandarin singer—to a much more general assertion about reality. As the writer himself put it:

> *Globalization has broken the barriers that used to restrain the flow of pop culture from one society to the next, reaching classes of people that were once untouched and busting boundaries that were once unbreakable.*

Then the writer went out and made a persuasive case to back up his broader hypothesis.

To the extent that the story began with a single case and led to a broad observation, it was inductive. But good writing ideas are both inductive and deductive. They are provoked by individual instances. But they also produce some kind of generalization, which is then tested by looking for additional evidence in the real world.

In science, that search for evidence helps to build theory. In writing, it helps build a theme. And a clear theme statement is one of the most powerful tools available for easing the writing process.

THE MYTH OF THE PERFECT FIRST LINE

It's a newsroom article of faith that you should begin by struggling for the perfect lead. Once that opening finally comes to you—according to the legend—the rest of the story will flow like lava.

Not likely. As Bob Baker, once a *Los Angeles Times* reporter, editor, and writing coach, put it, "We count on the lead to spark mysterious rhythms that will propel the rest of the story, bringing forth the paragraphs in the right order. And, like all long-shot bets, it sometimes works."

Starting with the lead is like starting medical school with brain surgery. We've all been taught that the first sentence is the most important; so it's also the scariest. Instead of writing it, we fuss and fume and procrastinate. Or we waste hours writing and rewriting the first few lines, rather than getting on with the body of the piece. By the time we do get moving with the rest of the writing, we're tense and tired. We've squandered the chance that something wonderfully creative might emerge from a relaxed, playful approach to the draft.

The chances are also high that we're headed in the wrong direction. The first sentence points the way for everything that follows. But writing it before you've sorted out your material, thought about your focus, or stimulated your thinking with some actual writing is a recipe for getting lost. When you're ready to write, what you need is not a finely polished opening sentence, but a clear statement of your theme.

The first line of Hemingway's *The Old Man and the Sea* did both. Challenged to write the perfect opening, he managed to get setting, protagonist, and complication—the basic elements of an entire story—into the first sentence:

> *He was an old man who fished alone in a skiff in the Gulf Stream and he had gone eighty-four days now without taking a fish.*

FINDING THE CENTER

Simplicity and clarity are important throughout the writing process, of course, but they're absolutely crucial when it's time to focus and organize your material. At that point you're probably too close to the subject, overwhelmed by the information you've gathered. You may have been seduced by a minor point. You may not see the pattern that ties disparate elements together. You may have forgotten the larger issues that led you to the subject in the first place.

Rather than trying to write an opening in the midst of all this confusion, you're better advised to step back and see the forest instead of the trees. You need a simple statement that cuts through the detail and exposes the heart of what you want to say. You need, in other words, a theme statement.

Good theme statements are short—most writing gurus advise one line—and simple. They aren't intended for publication, and so they lack the intimidation factor that makes writing the first line so daunting. In fact, a theme statement allows you to put off the first sentence until the very last thing, if that's what you want. You can simply start writing out of the theme statement. Somewhere along the way the perfect opener will occur to you, painlessly. Sub it in for the theme statement then.

In my experience, the best theme statements contain a transitive verb—an action word that raises the question "what?"—and a word or phrase that answers it with a direct object. "Jack hit *what?*" "Jack hit *the ball.*"

The beauty of a theme statement built around a transitive verb is that it contains an assertion about reality that can anchor your writing project. Transitive verbs require the "A causes B" brand of thinking that characterizes a true hypothesis. A theme statement for the preceding essay might be "The myth of the perfect first line (subject) obscures (transitive verb) *the importance of focus and organization* (object)."

Former AP feature writer Tad Bartimus once advised other writers to "tell your story in six words."

The form of your theme statement is less important than the fact that you write one, something I'm religious about in my own work. Once I even wrote a theme statement for a letter—a plea to the Planning Commission on an issue affecting my neighborhood. I wanted my argument to be short, persuasive, and on point. My theme was "New housing will overload an already crowded street."

I follow the same method regardless of the subject. The first thing that appears on my computer screen is the word "theme," followed by a colon. Then I sit and think for a while. What's this about? I ask myself. Then I write the subject of my theme statement. And what do I want to say about it? I ask. Then I write a transitive verb and its object.

The virtue of good theme statements is that they boil your material down to its essentials, and you shouldn't worry about the "isn't that obvious?" quality that often results. Subtlety, elegance, and sophistication emerge in the writing.

Here are a few examples of theme statements that worked as trusty guides for pieces I've written:

Theme: The Big Horn Mountains preserve the character of early fly-fishing in the West.

Theme: Journalism educators and professionals should quit bickering and start focusing on common ground.

Theme: Successful freelancers must master self-editing.

Theme: My father wanted me to understand the complexities and contradictions of war.

The theme stays at the top of the screen as I write. Occasionally, I refer back to it. If I've taken a break in the writing, it's the first thing I see when I return and boot up the computer again. So it helps keep me headed in the right direction.

When I'm finished with the draft, I erase the theme statement. Poof! It's gone. It was nothing I ever had to worry about another human being seeing and criticizing. That made it easy to write . . . and easy to discard.

That should be true in midcourse, as well as at the destination. On occasion, the writing reveals that my initial theme statement missed the mark. Maybe I find a better one. Or maybe I discover that my first take on a theme was just plain wrong. No big deal. I highlight the first theme statement and hit the delete key. Then I write a new one and adjust what I've already written accordingly. If one compass doesn't work, I get a new one. The important thing is to always have one in hand.

III. Finding a Focus

The most important thing in a work of art is that it should have a kind of focus. . . .
There should be some place where all the rays meet or from which they issue.
—Leo Tolstoy

ADJUSTING THE LENS

A running gag among writing coaches is that the three biggest writing problems are focus, focus, and focus. But what is this elusive virtue, and why do so many writers have such a hard time finding it?

The practical answer is that focus is the axis on which a piece of writing turns. Everything in any given composition revolves around it. Everything relates to it in some way. Focus emerges in the writing process, a product of the thinking you launch when you cook up your idea, take your hypothesis in hand, and set forth on your information gathering. It's a fully developed theme, the core idea that journalists often refer to as a nut.

The main thing any writer needs to find a focus is a constantly questioning attitude, a thinking process that incessantly reviews the original hypothesis as it bumps up against the real world. That's what keeps the hypothesis from turning into a bias that distorts the evidence. It's what leads to original insights and guides the search through a bewildering array of possibly related facts to find what truly matters.

The writer's thinking process is a kind of internal Q&A. You're assigned a topic or one grabs your interest. You start orbiting around it, asking yourself what you think about it. You challenge your own answers, sifting through the issues until you finally come up with a preliminary hypothesis.

The often-quoted Chief Seattle speech sent me down one such road. Seattle, or Sealth, the most prominent tribal leader during the early days of the city named for him, is well known in the Pacific Northwest. The speech attributed to him, a sentimental denunciation of the White man's disregard for the land, is often trotted out to promote environmental causes.

I sympathize with its sentiment, but the speech never smelled right to me. What's wrong with it? I asked myself. Then I gave it a close read.

The oration hardly sounds like something spoken by a Puget Sound Indian. It refers to piñon nuts, for example, which don't grow within a thousand miles of Chief Seattle's stomping grounds. It mentions vast plains covered with dead buffalo, which were almost as distant. It decries thickets of overhead wires, even though the speech was allegedly delivered before electricity or the telephone arrived in Seattle.

Surely it's a fraud.

Next question: "Why would well-meaning people perpetuate such an obvious flimflam?"

Maybe environmentalists are simply morons. Lots of folks in Chief Seattle country would make that argument; so it's hardly original. Besides, "Environmentalists are morons" didn't have the structure of a true hypothesis. It lacked a transitive verb and therefore failed to make a statement of causality. So it revealed nothing about the way the world worked.

Furthermore, I consider myself an environmentalist, and the only way to save my self-esteem was to extend the search for a more insightful focus. So I moved on, exploring a hypothesis stating that the Chief Seattle speech was a deliberate fraud, cynically calculated to serve a passionate cause. That angle would have allowed a good rant about the dangers of zealots who believe that the ends justify the means.

But that was also a timeworn theme, and it lacked a causal statement, too. Besides, the sheer ubiquity of the speech argued against deliberate fraud. All sorts of advocates were leaning on the old chief to make one point or another, and they couldn't all be linked in one vast conspiracy.

Hmmmm. Well-meaning, honest, intelligent people seemed to be perpetuating a fraud. Can it be that when we really want to believe something, we unconsciously overlook obvious evidence to the contrary, despite our intelligence and good intentions?

Now *that* was an interesting hypothesis. It wasn't completely original, of course, but it had never been applied to the Chief Seattle speech or, to my knowledge, American environmentalism. And it could serve as a workable focus: "Passionate belief leads good people down dangerous roads."

Once you have a hypothesis worth pursuing, it's time for some research. You review what others think about your topic, and you bounce your ideas off theirs. You check facts and figures to see how they fit. You toss some aspects of your original hypothesis and start to home in on an improved version that does a better job of pulling all the facts and opinions together.

In the case of Chief Seattle's bogus speech, my research encouraged an even stronger hypothesis. I quickly discovered that, yes, the speech was phony. An environmentalist in Texas (ah . . . piñon nuts!) had written it for an Earth Day radio program in the 1970s. He presented it as something Chief Seattle *might* have spoken, but others picked it up without citing the true author. Several later commentators had tracked down the facts and published their findings. But activists ignored them. I interviewed the publisher of a children's book based on the speech. So what if it never happened? she seemed to be saying. It's the thought that counts.

I was appalled. Not only were true believers ignoring evidence that was right in front of their noses, but they also were defending lies aimed at children! That smacked of the intellectual laziness and paternalistic we-know-what's-best-for-you attitudes that lie at the heart of totalitarianism. Which led me to the final hypothesis, the thought that became my focus: "The well-meaning thinking that nourished the Chief Seattle speech springs from the same psychology that enables vile dictatorships and ruthless ideologies."

That became the basis of an op-ed essay in my newspaper that a wire service picked up. It was then reprinted in major newspapers around the country. It's still used to spark discussion in some classrooms. Best of all, I'm seeing far fewer references to that damned speech.

JUST IN TIME

Just-in-time inventory control was a breakthrough for American business, a computer-age benefit that helped make US companies the world's most productive. The idea is that you coordinate a manufacturing and distribution system so that everything arrives "just in time." By tracking everything with sophisticated computer networks, you maintain an even flow of necessary supplies through the entire process. No expensive stockpiling of raw materials. No costly warehousing of finished products. No wasted time, energy, or money.

The same strategy pays off for writers, too. Starting with a firm hypothesis and refining your focus as you go allows you to keep things moving smoothly. You concentrate on important sources and ignore the irrelevant ones. You avoid the downtime that comes from failing to carry out your research efficiently. You simplify the organizational process, and you avoid gathering reams of information that you don't need.

It's your focus that tells you what to leave out. Eliminating the dross exposes the meaningful center of what you have to say, honing your clarity and impact. Truman Capote said, "I believe more in the scissors than I do the pencil." Elmore Leonard is even more to the point. He says he leaves out "the parts that people skip."

Of course, even the most efficient writers collect more information than they use in the actual writing. Some of that material helps orient you to your subject, providing the context that keeps key points in perspective. A successful writer who attended one of my workshops admitted that she "overreports." "But," she went on to say, "I think that's important as long as you don't dump your entire notebook into the story. Extra facts are useful for the feel and so on" of an article.

That's fine, so long as the "extra facts" supplement the focus rather than detract from it. Another writer at the same workshop admitted that overreporting was her main writing problem. "I tend to underreport the main stuff," she said, "and become ensnared in tangents." The tangents, she rationalized, might someday prove useful. But "someday" is the writer's enemy, the road to endless procrastination.

Inefficient writers who barely produce and never make deadline usually delude themselves with the notion that writing is a mystical process and can't be hurried. They aren't in charge—their muse is. And she's a fickle, sensitive creature.

That's just a comforting excuse for delay. You make inspired writing possible when you follow the natural progression of the writing process. If you're researching endlessly, then you don't have a well-defined, testable hypothesis. You're exploring answer after answer without knowing the question.

Productivity in writing, or anything else, flows from efficiency. If manufacturers can deliver more widgets at a lower cost with just-in-time systems, then writers can deliver more words. The point, after all, is not to agonize endlessly. It's knowing what you want to say and then developing a smooth, effective system for saying it. Just in time.

IV. Method and Process

The greatest masterpiece in literature is only a dictionary out of order.
—Jean Cocteau

FINDING COMFORT IN SMALL THINGS

OK. You have your idea. It's time to get to work.

Danger lurks ahead. The backward view of writing can assert itself at any stage in the process. You get a little tired, your spirits sag, and you start comparing your rough, preliminary work with the polished perfection you see in national magazines and acclaimed books.

Resist! Put your faith in the process, and take things one step at a time.

You move on from your idea by figuring out just what information you'll need to write the piece you have in mind. And collecting it. This is a step-by-step process that shouldn't cause an excess of anxiety. Once you've gathered it, you'll calmly sort through all that information, moving from information gathering to focus. Then you'll organize. Then you'll draft. Piece of cake.

Maybe you plan only a short article, a news brief, or a memo on the autumn sales goals. The information gathering will take a couple of hours, and the focus will be clear by the time you finish that. Then you can sort out your notes in twenty minutes and write a draft in another hour. You'll be home for supper by six. Then you can come back to polish the thing in the morning.

Or maybe you're planning a nonfiction book that will take five years. No matter. The principle remains the same. If you're writing a research-heavy book, the port's a lot farther away, but the journey still breaks down into the same stages. And the individual steps are exactly the same. Once you master the process, getting there can become the best part of the voyage. It's possible to be a relaxed, productive writer who enjoys the work and finds it an energizing challenge rather than a nightmare of frustration and burnout.

One of the writers who's figured out the system filled out my coaching questionnaire and reported that she found writing "joyful." She liked research, she said, "but the writing, that's what I disappear into."

Her other answers helped explain why. She described herself as "very fast," someone who overresearched a bit but found almost all of the information she gathered useful. Most of her writing was self-assigned. She wrote very short pieces to the specified length, but wrote longer assignments a little long "and then whittled back after a fast first draft." She talked regularly—but briefly—with her editor throughout the process.

Bear those hints in mind. As we move through the next chapter, you'll see how they explain much of what we know about the ingredients in a successful writing process.

The Chapter 1 Cheat Sheet

FIVE WAYS TO EASE THE PAIN

The secret to writing well is in the process, not the finished product. You get better not by sitting down at the keyboard and trying to match the finished work of good writers, but by changing the way you work. Here are some ways to get started:

1. **Think first; write later.** Why hurry to the keyboard if you're just going to sit there, stressing out and staring at a blank screen? Pave your way to a first draft with some sort of rough plan. Scan your notes. Jot down key points. Ask yourself some questions. If you have two hours to write, take an hour to prepare. If you're fifteen minutes from deadline, take five to think.
2. **Talk it out.** Nothing clarifies the mind like a little conversation. Prepare for your actual keyboard time by telling your story or explaining your subject. Corner a colleague. Entertain a buddy over a beer. Call Mom.
3. **Shrink your subject.** Most of us are way too ambitious when we set out to write. So we end up with a Missouri Basin phenomenon—a flood that's a mile wide and an inch deep. Give your readers some depth so that they can enjoy the water. Pick the most interesting, unusual, or surprising aspect of your subject and dive in.
4. **Doodle.** Take some time to visualize your writing idea. Grab a legal pad and curl up in a comfortable chair. Write down one thing you know about your subject. Draw a box around it and extend an arrow to another box. Write down something that follows from what you wrote in the first box. Draw another arrow.
5. **Write a theme statement.** Nothing intimidates like the feeling that you have to write the perfect first line. Forget it—you can always come back to your lead. What you need to get started is a short, clear statement that corrals your main idea. Don't worry about style. Just make sure you make a causal statement that's at the center of what you want to say. Use it for guidance, write what you have to write, and then zap it.

2

Process

Writing is an exploration. You start from nothing and learn as you go.
—*E. L. Doctorow*

GETTING STARTED

OK. You have your idea, which means you know where you're headed. So it's time to get moving. The main thing that distinguishes real writers from would-be writers is the gap between having the urge to write and actually writing. But that doesn't mean you should promptly plunk yourself down at a keyboard.

If you've taken time to fully flesh out your writing idea, you've crafted a tentative theme statement, which is, in effect, a hypothesis. To test a hypothesis you need to get into the lab or into the field. For a reporter, that means getting out of the office with a notebook. For a novelist, it may mean recording snatches of authentic conversation on a bus, collecting period detail from historical sources, or writing down character descriptions in a public square. For a business executive, it could involve checking the files for some statistics and calling the department heads for some facts. All worthwhile writing is built on information, and—somewhere and somehow—the writer has to collect it.

Then you can move on to the other steps that still separate you from a completed manuscript. You'll need to sort through the information you've collected to test your theme. You may choose to stick with your original hypothesis, as confirmed by what you discovered while gathering information, but chances are that you'll write a newer, richer statement of your core thesis, a good idea made better by the work you've done to make it fit the complexities of the real world.

Then comes the process of sorting through your notes, arranging information in categories, and outlining the possible routes through a maze of detail. Organizing can get tedious—on particularly tough projects. I've tackled it on the living-room floor, with dozens of three-by-five cards or little pieces of cut-up manuscript spread out in front of me. Commercial online writing programs include a segment that will walk you through the organizing process, but I've never found them necessary. Usually I just come up with a list of main topics or principal scenes in a computer file and block-move my notes into the appropriate headings. But however you do it, failing to spend the necessary time on organizing is one of the most common errors in the writing game. If you don't get your material into purposeful order, you face confusion, frustration, and angst when you take on what may be the most intimidating phase of the process—the first draft.

If you've done your prep work, the draft should flow fairly easily, especially if you draft the way the experts advise. Writer's block, the paralysis that seizes you when you finally do get your butt in the chair, is a failure to understand that the draft is just one more step in the process.

Eventually, you'll get to the polish stage, the final futzing that gets an inordinate amount of attention in the writing world. But by that time, you'll have your writing project virtually licked. Because you took the time to launch the process well and invested the necessary energy in the earlier phases, you'll have a richer, more insightful view of your subject than you ever expected. Process is a way of getting from here to there, but it almost always also leads you on a route of discovery. That produces the kind of writing that's especially rewarding for both you and your readers.

I. Information Gathering

You can't apply good writing after the fact, like some kind of lacquer. The reporting has to be there.
—James Gannon

EVERY WRITER A REPORTER

I remember hardly any of the reading assigned in my high school English classes, but one book that has stayed with me is Émile Zola's *Germinal*. I can't say that I recollect the story line, other than the fact that it was one of those French socialist odes to the working class. But I do remember the vivid details of life in the mines. The slow descent of a swaying elevator into the darkness, the dank heat and the stale air, the clang of metal on rock.

Zola, a pioneer of the realism that has been the focus of my writing and editing life, captured his details firsthand. He went to the mines, notebook in hand, rode the lift down the shaft, and watched the miners work the coal face. Then he brought the real world back to his desk, where he created the stories that gave it meaning. In the language of my world, Zola was a reporter.

So is every writer worth reading. Even the wildest fantasy must be anchored in a reality we can recognize. The details of a scene, the motives of a character, the mood of a place—all the elements that put us into the writer's world must in some part be drawn from our own.

A fiction writer or essayist may work with details gathered long before she actually puts hands to keyboard. But gathering those details is still reporting, and many a fiction writer draws on specifics recorded in a journal or a daybook at the time they were experienced.

In his groundbreaking essay "The Feature Game," Tom Wolfe said, "The crucial part that reporting plays in all storytelling, whether in novels, films, or nonfiction, is something that is not so much ignored as simply not comprehended." It follows that the better writers are also the better reporters.

Average writers complete their reporting and plunge into the rough draft. They call sources for more information only when they run into glaring loose ends. The small holes are easy enough to write around. If you're not sure about a date, you can always write "in early spring" or some such.

But Rich Read, a national correspondent for the *Los Angeles Times*, almost never writes around anything. As I discovered during several rewarding years of working with him, he invests prodigious amounts of reporting time before he even produces a rough draft. His drafts are nonetheless filled with blanks, notes, and question marks, all indicating some minor bit of information that he wants to find or confirm before submitting the final copy. He'll call a source in China to nail down some tiny detail that will help make a scene more authentic. The result is the kind of persuasive authenticity that won him a Pulitzer Prize in explanatory journalism and a piece of a Pulitzer Gold Medal for Public Service.

Writers who don't share Rich's commitment to rock-solid information gathering invite serious trouble. Remember: Any problem that occurs at one stage of the writing process shows up in the stage that immediately follows.

Poor information gathering shows up first during the organizational stage. If you're having a problem making sense out of the hodgepodge of notes, documents, and secondary sources heaped on your desk or littering your hard drive, then you probably didn't take good aim before you collected them. If you're going to gather the right information in a reasonable amount of time, you need to start with a testable hypothesis. The categories of evidence relevant to the hypothesis—be it the nature of a profile subject's character or the sales figures that cry out for a new marketing strategy—should be relatively clear from the beginning. The structure of what you're about to write emerges, organically, from your information gathering.

As Tom Tait, then editor of the *Desert Sun* in Palm Springs, once told me: "Our most common problem with poor writing is that it is usually a by-product of poor reporting. A story is difficult—sometimes impossible—to edit properly if it lacks essential facts. Details, which are the stuff of good writing, can't be edited in. I'd much rather edit a good reporter who struggles with how to say it than one who didn't say enough."

BUILDING MATERIALS

Every writer works with three forms of raw material:

- What people say happened (quotations from those who should know).
- Records of what happened (including statistics, databases, transcripts, videotapes, news story clips or computer files, still photographs, and so on).
- What we observed happening (what we have seen, heard, tasted, smelled, and felt happen with our own senses).

Journalists tend to rely on quotations, or—to a lesser extent—public records. They're weakest at observation, the descriptive detail that can bring writing to life. Other kinds of writers often rely almost exclusively on records or personal observation.

The most credible, engaging writing draws on all three sources of raw material, often buttressing each point with three kinds of evidence. Let's say that on a walk over to city hall to interview the police chief, a driver using a cell phone nearly runs you over. When you mention your close call to the chief, she says she's noticed a spike in car-pedestrian accidents. Later, you check the national statistics and discover a 22 percent year-over-year increase in pedestrian fatalities. Aha! You have the ingredients for an engaging personal essay.

NO INFORMATION BEFORE ITS TIME

A writer at one of my workshops once answered a question about her reporting by noting that "sometimes, the key person will appear right at the end of two weeks of interviewing, and I scrap all that work, with a feeling I've been stupid. Actually, I've probably only been unlucky."

She probably was right the first time. If it takes you two weeks to get to the first usable source, you haven't done much planning. Productive information-gathering strategies aren't a matter of luck. You create them, on the basis of your experience with the subject matter, your knowledge of the likely sources, and your understanding of some key principles.

Editors and writers are well advised to sit down for a session on information-gathering strategy before beginning the work. Writers working alone could benefit from some quiet time in a comfortable chair with a yellow legal pad. What are you hoping for in the finished piece of writing? What kinds of information will you need to get there? Where do you have to go? Whom do you have to call? What sit-down interviews do you need to schedule?

And what's the logical order for all this? Will one interview give you the baseline you need to conduct another interview? Then you'd better schedule them in that order. Good reporters often think in terms of early, middle-, and late-stage reporting, leaving the most sensitive, complicated, and close-to-the-ground sources for last. You don't want to accuse the corrupt politician of slipping her hand into the till until you have all your ducks in a row.

Seasoned writers often start with an expert who can give them a good overview of the topic. Such "rabbis," as they're known in newsrooms, usually aren't sources who will actually appear in whatever's written. But they know the whole congregation. They can suggest background reading, point you to sources, and tell you about the main issues among the congregants.

A rabbi can be useful to just about any kind of writing, not just journalism. If you're writing a novel about a Northwest timber town, better buy a few beers for the guy who used to own the local logging outfit. If you're hammering out a memo on next year's marketing potential, better buy a martini for the sales manager.

The rabbi tells you how to take the next step in your research. If you're writing a trade-magazine profile of the world's top civil engineer, you begin by visiting your rabbi—an old engineering professor, say—who knows all the leading figures in the field, including the engineering superstar you're writing about. You do some reading on the history of engineering. You talk with cultural experts about how major buildings, bridges, and dams shape civilization.

Then you get closer to your target. You talk with your celebrity engineer's colleagues and friends, you interview the spouse and kids, and finally you spend time with the man himself, collecting the observations that buttress everything you've learned as you worked your way toward him.

All the while, you look ahead to the writing, gauging how what you'll ultimately need will affect your information-gathering strategy. How much space do you have? Who are the members of your intended audience, and what questions are they likely to have? Does your publication's editor like anecdotal or summary leads?

Different kinds of writing may call for vastly different kinds of reporting. A business memo may require only abstract information—facts, figures, and quotations. A long magazine narrative will require much more specific material—sights, sounds, and smells gathered during hours and hours of hanging-around time.

One symptom is a sure sign of bad planning during the information-gathering stage: If you've finished your reporting and you find yourself constantly picking up your phone to call sources back, you did a lousy planning job. Yes, the best of reporters inevitably has to tie up an occasional loose end with a late phone call. But if you're abandoning your keyboard again and again to do more research, either you're disorganized or you're procrastinating.

Or you're a disorganized procrastinator. Remember the unlucky writer who stumbled across her key source two weeks into the reporting? Well, another writer at the same session had a different slant on information gathering. She, unlike her less organized counterpart, was a freelancer who figured efficiency was key to survival. "Time is money," she said, before noting that she always paused to spec out her reporting before she began. "Because I plan my interviews and research carefully," she said, "most of the information I gather is useful to the story."

Exactly! Reams and reams of unused information are not the sign of a conscientious writer. They're the core of what editors often refer to as a "productivity problem." In other words, it's a waste of time better spent writing. As a rather well-known shoe manufacturer from my neck of the woods once said, the best way to get something done is to "Just Do It!"

II. Organizing

The absolute first thing to do when you launch a writing project is to resist the impulse to start writing. You need to relax, to settle down, and above all YOU NEED TO THINK.
—Herbert and Jill Meyer

THE PAIN OF CHAOS

Failure to organize produces a long list of consequences: missed deadlines, excessively long manuscripts, formulaic writing, slow and unproductive writers. It may be the most dangerous failure you risk.

Organization should come dead center in the process, after idea development and reporting, but before drafting and polishing. In their work with writing coaches, Roy Peter Clark and Don Fry report that most writing problems occur in the organizing stage.

That's not so much because writers organize poorly; it's that they never organize. "Editors," Clark and Fry say, should ask their writers "to describe . . . everything they do from the time they finish reporting until they type the first sentence. Except for getting coffee and going to the restroom, the strugglers usually do nothing at all."

Editors can blame the journalism schools. For decades standard classroom practice has been to teach fledgling reporters that they should take their assignments, march into the field to gather facts, think of their opening lines on the way back to the office, walk directly to their chairs, place their hands on their keyboards, and begin writing.

For reporters or any other kind of writer, that's a recipe for trouble. Writers who skip over the organizational phase typically find that:

- writing is agony. If you have no guideposts to help you through confusing material, progress can be painfully slow. Every piece of writing degenerates into a stressful series of false starts, detours, and wasted effort.
- drafting goes slowly. Writers who don't organize well invariably push right up against—or past—deadlines. They're a terrible frustration to their editors.
- the writing is repetitious. Because no grand scheme guides the placement of material within some larger framework, the same

points show up in different places. Writers find it almost impossible to introduce topics, to dispense with them, and to move quickly into something new.
- quality declines after the opening. A newspaper editor once complained to me that "even our best writers tend to write a snappy lead and then the writing gradually trails off until it's merely pedestrian by the end." Of course. If you put all your effort into the opening and expect the rest of the story to write itself, the results are predictable.
- it's hard to settle on a single drafting strategy. Writers who write more than one opening for the same piece, or who do a lot of block-moving as they shift material around, have basic organizational problems. They're wasting time and mental resources. They'll end up driving themselves—and their editors—crazy.
- a lot of the information gathered never gets used.

Facing a large mass of unorganized material on a big project can be intimidating. But it's usually a lot easier than plunging into the actual writing. And organizing shorter pieces of writing can be a snap. Almost all the experts advise keeping your hands off the keyboard until you:

- take time to sift through notes and other background material. Mark key points and highlight especially valuable information. You can color-code or number-code the material, or you can use symbols such as stars, asterisks, and exclamation marks. If you're working with handwritten notebooks, you can stack the pages in labeled piles. In computer files, you can use boldface, italic, and all-caps to emphasize key points.
- list your main points. One objective of reviewing notes and marking them up is to make things easy to find when you write, but the critical mission is to figure out what the writing's about.
- refine the focus. A writer who has reviewed the notes and listed the key points is ready to confront the critical step in the organizational phase of the writing process—giving final form to the theme that holds the whole mess together.
- talk it out with somebody. Many writers have no contact with an editor between the assignment and a completed draft. Freelancers and book writers are especially isolated, and some even think they will destroy the magic if they talk about their current writing project before they've completed a draft. But talking over the material after information

gathering and before writing is always valuable. If you can't talk with an editor, talk with friends, family, or colleagues. An old newsroom expression is that, before writing, a reporter should "tell it to Mom," if only in an imaginary conversation if not in reality. Whatever your audience, a little conversation at the right point in a writing project helps sort things out in your own mind. That, in turn, can reveal worlds.

MAPPING YOUR STRATEGY

Some writers bristle at the very sound of the word "outlining." But please put aside all those negative connotations that linger from the outlines your grade school teachers forced you to do. Forget Roman numerals. Forget subheadings and sub-subheadings. All you need is a quick-and-dirty summary that cuts right to the key points.

Hence, the "jot outline"—a forty-five-second scouting trip that lets you see the overall shape of what you're about to write. Jot outlines go hand in hand with theme statements of the sort discussed in chapter 1. So if the theme statement for this essay looks like this . . .

Theme: Jot outlines simplify drafting.

. . . then the accompanying jot outline might look like this:

Resistance to outlining
Nature of jot outline
Benefits
Testimonials

That's it. You go through your notes and list the main topics you want to cover, jotting them down or typing them on the computer screen as you find them. If you're using a computer, you then block-move those broad topics into logical order.

The act of writing down your few main topics, in order, gives you a step-by-step approach to the chaos of detail you often face when information gathering ends. It relieves panic because it allows you to ease into the writing incrementally. It creates some distance between you and the story. And it's a relaxing ritual.

If you're facing a deadline, you may think you don't have the time to outline. But you probably don't have time not to.

For one thing, the failure to take time for organizing ends up wasting huge amounts of time in the writing. All those false starts, dead ends, and what-not . . . For another, organizing isn't as complicated or time-consuming as it seems. For most routine writing assignments, the organizational phase consists of about five minutes or less to review notes and ninety seconds or so to produce a jot outline.

One of my workshop participants, a fine feature writer at a large eastern newspaper, said that her first priority when she got back to the office was to "do a rough outline, including points I want to cover." A food writer said her strategy was to "make a very sketchy outline: a list of points to cover and the rough sequence in which to cover them."

Most good writers, I've discovered, do something similar, even for short pieces. They may not call their short guides to structure jot outlines, but they serve the same function. The result is the same, too. Short outlines save time, reduce anxiety, and result in better writing. So why would anybody launch a first draft without one?

PROFESSIONAL-GRADE JOTS

Typical theme statements and jot outlines are no big deal. Here's one for a newspaper feature story on a high school engineering project, conducted in cooperation with a university engineering school:

> Theme: Local schools encourage cooperative learning.
> The project
> Who's involved
> Background
> Future

And here's a slightly more complicated one:

> Theme: After a year community policing shows some signs of progress but some officers are still skeptics.
> Intro—example
> How it works/How it's different
> Why?/history/flaws of old system
> Cons
> Apartment managers

District Attorney's comment
One cop's experience/drug awareness
Future

Like me, some writers prefer creating their jot outlines on their screens. They leave them at the top as they proceed with the stories. Once they finish, they erase the outlines and file the stories. The obsessively neat sometimes erase each of the main points as they finish writing those sections of their stories. That's a way of marking progress and creating a sense of accomplishment. It also helps writers focus on what's left to be done.

You may prefer to sketch the outline on a sheet of paper and then post it where you can see it from your keyboard. Leaning back, putting your feet on the desk, and doodling on a legal pad may release your creative juices while letting you avoid the anxiety a computer screen can create.

Whatever the approach, simplicity is a key. A jot outline that grows excessively detailed is no longer a jot outline. And a writer who creates really detailed outlines is back in the same morass encountered by the reporter who jumps into the story cold.

The other key is actually doing it. Lots of writers dismiss the need for an outline with the argument that they do the same thing in their heads. So why bother to write it down? But those of us who do this for a living know that magic doesn't happen until we actually force fingers onto keys and make words appear on a screen. New ideas flood our brains, and points we never considered suddenly appear to us. The discipline of writing itself imposes order and sense in a way that never happens so long as we review the material in our heads. Writing, ultimately, is the highest form of thinking. And that's what organization is all about.

III. Drafting

Write freely and as rapidly as possible and throw the whole thing on paper. Never correct or rewrite until the whole thing is down. Rewrite in process is usually found to be an excuse for not going on.
—John Steinbeck

DRAFTING WITHOUT PAIN

Race-car drivers figured out the strategy decades ago. Slip in behind the car directly ahead and relax while the other driver sucks you along in a bubble of low pressure. When the time is right, break out of your pocket and push on through to the finish. The drivers call it "drafting."

Productive writers follow similar tactics, thereby avoiding the ordeal many of us face every time we agonize our way through a first draft. Instead of writhing in pain, they charge through big projects with scarcely a wrinkle in their foreheads. They're amazingly productive. They turn in drafts fairly close to the target length. And their copy flows with a pleasing, conversational rhythm.

Somehow they've learned what appears to be the secret to successful drafting—operating with a split personality. They have one mind-set when they're getting through a first draft. But they adopt a completely different approach when they go back to polish the copy into finished form.

The happiest, most productive writers approach their rough drafts as a literary version of Mr. Hyde. They cast civilized restraint aside, letting an uninhibited process of creation carry them quickly through the first version of the story. They don't stop. They don't revise. They don't look back. They push relentlessly forward, guided by their theme statements and jot outlines.

Only when they're finished with the draft do they slip back into a Dr. Jekyll persona. Then they sweat each detail, checking facts for accuracy, revising sentences for rhythm, and scrutinizing words for precise meaning. They're more like meticulous race mechanics than go-for-broke drivers.

Oliver Sacks, the neurologist who wrote *Awakenings* and *The Man Who Mistook His Wife for a Hat*, found evidence for the two-sided nature of writing and editing in the experiences of Ivan Vaughan, a psychologist. Vaughan had Parkinson's disease, which can slow the mind's sense of time to a near standstill. The treatment—L-dopa—speeds things up. "He sought to do all his writing," Sacks reported in the *New Yorker* "while he was under the influence of L-DOPA, for at such times his imagination and his mental processes seemed to flow more freely and rapidly, and he had rich, unexpected associations of every sort. But, when the effects of L-DOPA wore off, he turned to editing, and would find himself in a perfect state to prune the sometimes too exuberant prose he had written while he was 'on.'"

The research supports the Hyde/Jekyll, fast/slow approach to drafting and editing. Howard and Barton, the Harvard psychologists, summarize existing studies of writing with the observation that drafting involves "intuition, imagination, risk-taking, a headlong plunge down new corridors of thought and experience." Only after the draft is done, they conclude, does the writer give way to "cool detachment, doubt, skepticism, testing, rigorous assessments of logic and evidence."

Nearly all observers say that we should place fewer demands on ourselves when we're drafting. If we let harping little voices pick, pick, pick as we write, they will sap our confidence, tense us up, and paralyze our creative subconscious. At their worst, these hobgoblins of the keyboard can freeze us entirely, creating the dreaded writer's block; that is why poet William Stafford said, "The cure to writer's block is to lower your standards."

Trying to get every sentence perfect during drafting is a fool's errand. Wait until you're ready to put the polish on a piece of writing before sweating the small stuff. The important thing at the drafting stage is roughing out what will later become a great piece of work.

A writer who attended one of my workshops passed along this beautiful metaphor: "Years ago I used to futz with every sentence, but then an editor told me something that really made sense. He said that when a carpenter builds a piece of furniture he doesn't first make one side, perfect that, and then construct another side and perfect that. He must build the entire frame and then go back and put the finishing touches on each section. Even when I am on deadline, I think of what I write first as an imperfect frame that will be improved later."

Unfortunately, lots of pressures encourage the one-side-at-a-time approach. We journalists are urged to watch ourselves at every step of the draft, guarding against factual errors, misquotes, and libel. A Wall Street analyst will be mindful of SEC regulations. A cookbook author will worry about poisoning his readers.

But some writers manage to push all these gremlins to the side. They draft easily, naturally, armored against anxiety-producing distractions with tactics that keep them moving ahead along the paths they have set for themselves. If they have doubts about a fact, they flag it for checking later. If they need a quotation or some other tidbit from their notes, they mark the spot and move along. They stroll through the story at a steady, even pace.

When she drafts, one of them told me, "words just flow easily out of my brain like a bubbling brook—with effervescence, energy, enthusiasm, and giddiness."

REMEDIAL DRAFTING

When it comes to producing a first draft quickly and easily, I confess that I'm my own worst example. My tendency is to fine-tune as I go, repeatedly looping back to the beginning, rewriting everything from the first line on down, plodding ahead on the leading edge of the piece. The advantage is that when you're finished, you're finished. As a like-minded reporter once told me, "By the time I get to the end of a draft, it's a polished story."

The disadvantages loom larger. You've taken much longer to get to your destination. You've sweated the journey far more than necessary. And your writing is far less likely to have the appealing voice that emerges only when you're relaxed enough to let your true self shine through.

One way to conquer an uptight approach to drafting is to practice freewriting. Simply launch into the subject, writing as fast as your fingers can move. Don't worry about typos, misspellings, or loose ends. Plunge ahead fearlessly, knowing that you can go back and sort things out later, or that you can start over once you've discovered the nuggets that emerge when you're completely uninhibited at your keyboard. You want to outrun the nagging voice in your head that tells you you're no good, that each word misses the mark, that everything you've written sounds awkward and amateurish.

Writing coach Don Fry suggested a drafting exercise that really helped suppress my own inclination to futz. Do your jot outline, he said, print it out, and hang it on your computer monitor. Then darken the screen completely and start typing, ignorant of what's actually appearing on the monitor.

The trick is that with the screen completely black you can't go back or you'll lose your place. You must forge implacably ahead to the end. Then you can turn your screen back on and see what you have wrought.

IV. Polishing

I can't write five words but that I change seven.
—Dorothy Parker

PUTTING A SHINE ON IT

In one sense, the polishing is the least important phase of any writing project. The important decisions, the commitments that will have the most impact on readers, take place when you find and focus the idea, sort the material, and settle on a deep structure for the writing. Some popular novelists with minimal polish skills sell millions of books to mass audiences because strong characters and classic plot complications propel their story lines. For their audiences, clunky sentences and laughable language don't dim the attraction one watt.

Abundant brain research on storytelling explains why. Good writing has its highest impact when it takes the form of narrative, telling an engaging story that rivets reader interest while teaching timeless lessons. (For more on the relevant brain research, see my book *Storycraft*, which takes the lessons in this book to the next level.)

But it's the polish that more discriminating readers see when they first encounter your writing. Weak verbs, clichés, and redundant modifiers will brand you as an incompetent, regardless of brilliant ideas or masterly narrative. The more educated your audience, the more your ham-handed handling of individual sentences will offend. The critics savage popular novelists who neglect basic word craft.

Even unsophisticated readers no doubt feel the effects of sloppy polishing. They may not think consciously about a writer's deadly rhythms or lifeless verbs, but they'll sense that something's amiss. Instead of losing themselves in a good yarn, they'll struggle to stay involved, constantly slipping out of the story with every little distraction.

Stephen King, a popular storyteller who's also in complete charge of his sentences, demonstrates the power you can generate when you understand both word craft *and* story craft.

On a work of any length, polishing involves hundreds of minor decisions and calls on a vast range of skills that are acquired slowly, if at all. I've spent a lifetime acquiring the tricks and tactics useful when polishing a finished draft. I'm still learning.

That's why many of the remaining chapters in this book explore the principal polishing strategies in detail. It's during the polish stage of the writing process that you refine your work to make it more focused, forceful, rhythmic, clear, and colorful. In and of themselves, such qualities have little to do with content or structure. All together, they have a huge amount to do with how readers will receive your writing. They're the clothes you wear in public, the style and panache that others will know you by. They're the personality you project through the written word.

Because polishing creates the public face a writer presents to the world, it can loom excessively large in the writer's mind. I came into this business thinking it was everything, and for years it monopolized my attention as a teacher and editor. I learned a lot about polishing, but I was far less effective at helping writers than I might have been.

By all means make your writing graceful, colorful, punchy, and evocative, but never forget that the purpose of writing on topics big and small goes beyond the appearance you make. The way you frame your subject, gather information to make your case, and organize your material creates the bone and muscle of what you write. The polish stage adds the indispensable skin, but with writing, as with people, it's what's under the skin that really counts.

The Chapter 2 Cheat Sheet

FIVE WAYS TO PERFECT YOUR WRITING PROCESS

Most writing problems originate at the immediately preceding stage of the writing process. If you're having trouble with your draft, look back to see how you organized your material. If the material just won't assume a shape you can work with, rethink the way you gathered your information. If the information gathering is going poorly, look to your original idea.

Try these techniques for avoiding problems at each stage of the process:

1. **Prove it.** Start with a hypothesis, not just an interesting topic. Then ask yourself what further evidence you'll need to make this theme credible. Use your answers to guide the rest of your information gathering. Whom should you consult? What books and records do you have to read? Where do you have to go? What do you have to see?
2. **Plan it.** Take at least a few minutes to organize your information gathering into a logical order. Divide your to-do list into "early," "middle," and "late" on the basis of your assessment of how one kind of information may lead to others.
3. **Structure it.** Pause during the critical period between the end of your information gathering and the beginning of your writing. Review your notes, and think about the key points you want to make or scenes you'll want to include. Jot those down as key words or short phrases and sort them into logical order. Use the resulting jot outline as a guide to your draft, knowing that you may change course once you dig deeply into the material.
4. **Write it.** Stay loose through your first draft and write fast. You may want to put your notes aside while you write, leaving blanks where you need specific information that you'll retrieve later. In any event, don't futz. Keep moving steadily from beginning to end regardless of how rough, awkward, or incomplete the writing may seem.

5. **Change hats.** Once you've finished a draft, find your dark side. Comb through the text with the no-nonsense attitude of a drill sergeant. Root out clichés and replace them with fresh figures of speech. Question every fact. Check every doubtful spelling. Make vague, weak, or unimaginative word choices more precise and vigorous. Then relax.

3
Structure

Structure is everything. When authors come to me complaining of writer's block, it means they are too lazy to work out a structure, either in their lives or their work.
—Paul Johnson

THINKING AND WRITING

Writing is, in one sense, simply organized thinking. Left to its own devices, the mind runs off in random directions as synapses connect to others that happen to be in the neighborhood. ("I remember that song. I used to play it in the Chevy. Geez, that's the car I had when I dated Julie. Ouch! That sure bombed. Wonder why I'm so afraid of commitment?")

Organizing your material is the first step toward imposing order on the process, thereby disciplining the mind. A theme statement and a jot outline provide a map, a simplified representation of the territory you hope to cover in a writing project. But as the linguist S. I. Hayakawa pointed out, the map is not the territory.

When it comes to writing, the structure you create to hold your words *is* the territory. It takes shape as you generate the words that serve as its building blocks, and its form emerges bit by bit as the most basic units combine to create the most complex. Verbs follow subjects, leading to objects. Sentences build to paragraphs. Paragraphs collect to form reports and stories, with beginnings, middles, and ends.

Because structure influences everything else that goes into a piece of writing, it's hard to overstate its importance. In the forward to *The Hot Zone*, his book on the Ebola virus, Richard Preston described a disagreement with his editor. Preston tried to bolster his case with the argument that "God is in the details."

That's a natural-enough perspective for a writer. Writing requires intense concentration on the minute matters at hand—word choices, sentence flow, transitions, and the like. A nonfiction science writer like Preston spends much of his time chasing after the details that help him make a case and tell his story. But it's easy to lose sight of the forest while pursuing those trees.

Preston's editor took a broader view. "No, Richard," she told him. "God is in the structure."

I. The Shapes of Things to Come

The White Rabbit put on his spectacles. "Where should I begin, please, your majesty?" he asked.

"Begin at the beginning," the King said, very gravely, "and go on till you come to the end; then stop."

—Lewis Carroll

WRITING REPORTS AND TELLING STORIES

Novels, grocery lists, encyclopedia entries, research papers, love letters, podcasts, documentary scripts. . . . Writing takes infinite forms. Even the most formulaic news-report structures—accounts, say, of fires or traffic accidents—vary in some measure from the shapes of their predecessors.

Despite that complexity, it's useful to think of writing as falling into two categories. In terms of both form and function, every piece of writing is, at the most basic level, either a report or a story.

If your primary goal is to convey information, you'll probably choose to write a report of some kind. In the broadest sense of the word, a report simply records somebody's research findings. The definition may be simplistic, but it has profound structural implications. For one thing, reports are usually organized by topic. They begin with some kind of overview and then proceed, methodically, through Topic A, Topic B, and so on. Hence, the Roman-numeral outline form that Ms. Grundy taught you in fourth grade.

Journalists refer to almost everything they write as a "story." They mostly produce—as the name "reporter" suggests—topically organized reports. They begin with statements that summarize their findings. They almost immediately move from such "summary leads" to a succession of topical subdivisions.

They apply traditional journalistic values such as timeliness, proximity, prominence, human interest, and consequence to determine the relative newsworthiness of the topics, and then arrange them in descending order of importance.

That structure has obvious advantages. Editors can cut from the bottom, thereby eliminating the least important information first, and readers can move on to something else as soon as they've descended far enough into the structure to satisfy their curiosity. Because the broadest and most important information goes at the top and the narrowest and least important goes at the bottom of such reports, journalists call this structure an "inverted pyramid." The form is usually the first thing students learn in journalism school.

It's not the only form a report can take, of course. A blogger might summarize a recent trip by briefly describing the itinerary. A business executive might report on manufacturing efficiency by tracking each step of the production process. A military after-action report might describe a battle chronologically. But, in each case, form tends to follow function.

Essays of various kinds are basically reports. The Latin root for the term "essay" means "to venture forth," and the sense survives in the modern meaning of "to attempt." Essay writers set out to explore ideas by forging connections between points, moving from topic to topic until they reach new insights that they then report to readers.

Essays and other reports will often share characteristics other than their topically based structure. They may include direct quotations from commentators whose observations seem valuable to the writer. Because they summarize the reporter's findings, they are often written in summary narrative, in abstract observations that collapse time and space: "Six days of rain bogged down the advance, and the division moved only twenty miles instead of the 120 the plan called for."

If reports are structured primarily to convey *information*, then stories are structured primarily to reproduce *experience*. For that reason, their basic structural element is not the topic, but the scene. You'll find the purest scenic construction in a movie script, which explicitly organizes the writing into descriptions of actions that take place in a series of locations. But novelists do much the same thing, as do writers of literary nonfiction and narrative journalism.

The point of scenic construction is to drop readers into a story so that they can experience it themselves. In a simple yarn, the audience reads its way through a series of scenes for nothing more than their entertainment value. In a work with more literary substance, readers also discover some larger truth about the human experience. Because the process is experiential rather than merely informational, storytelling can have a powerful emotional impact on readers.

In a story narrative, scenes unfold along a narrative arc. Roughly speaking, they provide locations where we can meet the protagonist and learn something about her, followed by scenes in which she encounters a series of challenges before facing the ultimate complication and, finally, a scene or two that tie up any loose ends. This exposition–rising action–climax–denouement story form is the basis of most storytelling.

Like reports, stories typically share elements other than structure. Rather than direct quotations, for example, they may include dialogue. In the context of reporting, sources generally utter pronouncements. In stories, characters usually talk among themselves.

Instead of the summary narrative common to reports, writers tell stories largely in dramatic narrative, which is much more specific to one time and place. To readers, events appear to unfold in real time, and they're described so concretely that they form images in the reader's imagination. "He paused on the end of the board, arms raised. Then he flexed his knees and dropped his arms. The board bent and sprang upward as he straightened his knees and reached for the sky. He rose, body rigid, and began a graceful arc outward."

Brain science reveals that the powers of dramatic narrative originate in our *mirror neurons*, a part of every human brain that allows us to empathize with story characters in the deepest sense. When we read about that diver springing upward off the board, the same areas of our brain light up as they would if we were diving ourselves. When we feel emotion in a movie theater, it can be as deeply felt as any "real" emotion. Because of our mirror neurons, it is, in fact, real.

Emotional reactions to writing aren't, of course, restricted to pure narrative. For one thing, the forms that underlie most writing are seldom so clear-cut as the simple division into reports and stories suggests. In the complicated landscape of story structures, the pure report and the pure story occupy two opposite horizons. Dozens of hybrid forms fill the space in between.

A blog entry may borrow from both informational and experiential structures. A writer might, for example, summarize something she's done recently ("We spent most of the two weeks on Maui") before zeroing in on a specific scene ("One day we were sitting on the beach when I looked up and saw the lifeguard scrambling down from his tower").

Journalists sometimes build explanatory narratives with a structure that shifts back and forth between scenes and topically organized segments. *New*

Yorker writers such as John McPhee and Susan Orlean favor this "layer cake" form, which delivers the best of two worlds. The scenes draw readers into the material with action and vivid detail. The topically organized segments, which McPhee calls "digressions," convey information that makes the scenic material more meaningful.

The thousand-word personal essay, long a staple of the magazine world, may also blend scenes and topics. It often begins with a scenically constructed, first-person account of some experience. ("Down the hill from my grandparents' place, a stone bridge leads into a neighbor's meadow. Last month, on our annual summer visit, I took an early morning walk and crossed it.") After 650 or so words of narrative, the writer negotiates a "turn," which takes the essay out of specific dramatic narrative and up into the more abstract writing typical of reports. ("The tracks the deer had left in the soft earth made me think about the signs we leave behind us as we pass through life.") Then the essay ends with an abstract conclusion that offers some insight about the human experience. ("Like the tracks, the visible evidence of our passing fades quickly, but . . .")

Other purposes call for different combinations of informational and experiential material. Personality profiles might include scenes drawn from the lives of their subjects as well as more abstract information about their backgrounds and accomplishments. A review might mix scenically constructed narrative with reports and evaluations.

The basic forms, in other words, may be relatively limited, but imaginative writers can explore virtually endless permutations. Whole libraries exist on some of the forms, such as the news report, and specific directions for structuring a scientific paper or a news feature are beyond the scope of this discussion. The point here is that effective writers take time to think about what they want to accomplish, and then choose a form suited to the task.

II. Getting Started

A bad beginning makes a bad ending.
—Euripides

TAKING THAT LONG FIRST STEP

Writers live or die on their leads, the opening lines that set the stage for all that follows. Good leads hook readers immediately, drawing them into their stories with a crafty succession of enticements. A lead that lags for an instant risks losing a reader forever.

A good lead must also offer some substance. Readers see right through literary hot air. Fancy verbal footwork can't substitute for solid information that engages the reader's interest. So savvy writers know they have to produce, right away.

What readers—and some writers—often don't realize is that good leads tap into a central theme and thereby provide an organizing principle for everything that follows. John McPhee, the dean of America's narrative journalists, once described a lead as a "flashlight shining down into the story." To give that flashlight the proper aim involves sorting through the facts you've gathered, considering organizational schemes that might fit the material, and assessing the themes that might unify all those disparate story elements.

That process can be intimidating, which is one reason you're usually better off writing a theme statement before you try crafting an actual lead. Find the thread that holds everything together. It will give you a clear idea of your target as you work at writing a lead to match.

FISHING FOR READERS

More than one writer has argued that the only real standard for measuring a lead is whether or not it lures readers into the next paragraph. But the "whatever-works" school of lead writing doesn't stand up to close scrutiny. Lots of tricks will get readers into the second paragraph, and quite a few of them will disappoint or anger readers. Think of the high school journalist who launches a column with "Sex" and then continues with "Now that I have your attention . . ."

To entice readers into the body of a piece, a writer must promise some reward for continuing. The most direct approach for a report is a summary of the content that follows. Readers scan the summary and decide whether the content has relevance to their lives. In journalism, such a beginning takes the form of a straight-news or "summary" lead. Outside of journalism, the approach can work for everything from a marketing plan ("This year our strategy is to bypass consumers in favor of a campaign designed to get retailers excited about our new product line") to directions for assembling a bicycle ("Follow these step-by-step directions and it should take you about ten minutes to attach the wheels, seat, and handlebars").

Summary leads succeed or fail to the extent that they clearly and accurately describe the essence of what follows. But writers can stray from that goal in several ways. They can focus on something other than the report's central point, which is what journalists mean when they talk about "missing the lead."

They can express the central idea in a way that fails to make the connection with the lives of readers apparent. They can be so vague that they give readers no clear idea about what is to follow. Or they can fill their leads with detail that obscures the overview readers need before they can make up their minds about reading the report.

If we set out to tell a story, we can stimulate a reader's curiosity with literary devices such as foreshadowing, which creates dramatic tension by suggesting that something significant is about to happen: "The wheels lifted from the ground, and the plane banked to the north. Gibson scarcely noticed the barely audible whine in Engine No. 2."

Or we might do what filmmakers sometimes do with music that creates a sense of foreboding, an ominous sense of imminent action: "The door opened with a creak. In the darkness outside, she could make out the dim outline of a human figure. It moved slowly forward."

Or we could seize on an interesting dramatic detail ("She saw the knife first . . ."), or sketch an involving scene ("The river curved past the front of the shack, eating away at the crumbling bank"), or launch a sequence of events readers will want to see through to some kind of conclusion ("He threw open the door and jumped from the plane"), or tease with a pronoun that lacks an antecedent (Joan Didion's "Imagine Banyan Street first, because Banyan is where it happened").

Whatever approach they choose, writers must never lose sight of the fact that they have only a few seconds to capture and hold readers who have plenty of choices about how they'll spend their time. And whatever form their writing takes, they should never neglect the three essential questions that Steven Pinker, the Harvard linguist, said—after reviewing the brain research on storytelling—you must answer right away in the first few opening lines:

1. *Whose story is it?*
2. *What's happening here?*
3. *What's at stake?*

A LEXICON OF LEADS

A lexicon is a collection of terms that apply to a particular skill or field of study. Auto mechanics have a lexicon. So do fly fishermen. Writers have their own set of terms, although they often must rely on more vague, incomplete, and inconsistent labels for the tools they use. That limited lexicon can restrict their choices.

It's tough to think about alternative approaches to writing challenges if you don't have a menu of words that can summon up the appropriate possibilities.

An inadequate writing vocabulary also makes it hard to talk turkey with editors and fellow writers. Vague analysis and confusing advice are epidemic in the writing world.

A comprehensive writing lexicon may not exist, but journalists have developed terms that help them talk about lead possibilities before writing begins. These terms are widely shared in the world of nonfiction, and they're useful for thinking about beginnings for lots of different kinds of writing.

Report Leads

1. SUMMARY LEADS

The university must move more women into higher-level faculty jobs or face federal sanctions.

Summary leads present the most important idea in the story, and they often top inverted-pyramid news stories. Because a good summary lead makes meaning clear at once, it's often the preferred form for breaking-news and issue stories. It's the logical choice in many other fields, as well. A lawyer might begin a brief with a summary lead, and a marketing executive might do the same with her annual report.

2. BLIND LEADS

The state's land-use planning agency on Friday chose a former city planner to be its new director.

A blind lead is a summary lead that leaves out potentially confusing detail. The lead cited here omits the name of the planning agency (the Department of Land Conservation and Development) and the city planner, who was relatively unknown.

A "catch-all graf" immediately follows a blind lead. The catch-all paragraph includes the specific detail omitted from the lead.

3. WRAPS

Thursday's storm caused the deaths of a Madison woman who broke her neck in a fall, a Milwaukee man who had a heart attack while shoveling snow, and a Green Bay teenager struck by a skidding car.

An editor's order to "wrap it" means to combine several items. The reporter usually goes into detail on each of the items under a lead that refers to them all.

4. SHIRTTAIL LEADS

A man taking photographs from a scenic overlook at 2:15 p.m. Sunday apparently was struck by a car and knocked into the Missouri River. . . .

Another Sunday accident, this one involving a hit-and-run driver in St. Louis, left a Chicago man in serious condition. . . .

The shirttail is the alternative to the wrap lead, and a reporter may choose the shirttail approach if one incident is significantly more important or dramatic than the others she has to cover. She produces a summary lead focusing on the most newsworthy or important element and follows that with a more detailed explanation, exactly as if she were writing a complete report on just that one action. Then she writes a transition—"Another Sunday accident" in the example above—and proceeds with another report. Any number of reports can follow, each with its own lead. The form takes its name from the way the subsidiary reports hang like "shirttails" from the reports that come before.

Shirttail leads are traditional for stories about meetings. The first lead targets the most important item on the agenda. The remaining items are introduced with an "in other business" transition.

Feature and Story Leads

1. ANECDOTAL LEADS

Richard Leakey likes to tell about the day in 1950 when he was a six-year-old whining for his parents' attention. Louis and Mary Leakey were digging for ancient bones on the shores of Lake Victoria, but their little boy wanted to play. He wanted lunch. He wanted his mother to cuddle him. He wanted something to do.

"Go find your own bone," said his exasperated father, waving Richard off toward scraps of fossils lying around the site.

What the little boy found was the jawbone—the best ever unearthed—of an extinct giant pig. As he worked away at it with the dental picks and brushes that served for toys in the paleontologists' camp, he experienced for the first time the passion of discovery. (Kathleen Merryman, *Tacoma News Tribune*)

An anecdotal lead is a short narrative with a beginning, middle, and end. Although the writer will elaborate in the rest of the story, the end of the opening anecdote is particularly important. It's analogous to the punch line in a joke—it wraps up the story with a flourish that makes a key point.

An anecdotal lead illustrates the story's central theme. Kathleen Merryman's anecdote, for example, explains something central about her subject, Richard Leakey.

2. NARRATIVE LEADS

Timmaira Wilson tossed her serving tray in the bin and leaned one hand against the stainless-steel countertop, the other hand defiantly on her hip. She brought her face close to mine as if to share a secret or a juicy bit of gossip. Instead, her eyes narrowed and she pursed her lips. (Leila Atassi, *Cleveland Plain Dealer*)

A narrative lead launches a sequence of actions. It puts central characters into a scene and begins telling the story that pits those characters against some kind of complication. Narrative leads are—surprise!—most appropriate to narrative stories. But they work on other kinds of stories, too. A news feature with a bookend narrative structure, for example, begins with a short narrative line, turns to standard news-feature style for the middle of the story, and returns to the narrative for the story ending. A bookend narrative might begin by describing a test pilot taxiing a newly designed airplane into position for its first takeoff. The plane arrives at the head of the runway, the engine roars, and the pilot prepares to release the brakes. Then the opening narrative pauses, and the writer launches a more abstract report that reviews the airplane's design history, the potential market for the new design, and the timetable for bringing it into full production. The closing narrative begins as the pilot releases the brakes. The plane rushes down the runway and soars into the blue sky. End of story.

3. SCENE-SETTER LEADS

A woman with tormented eyes talks to herself as she plays a battered piano in Ward D's dayroom. Other psychiatric patients shuffle on the beige linoleum or stare from red-and-green vinyl chairs.

A bank of windows opens to a fenced courtyard. Outside . . . (Brian Meehan, *Oregonian*)

Scene-setters open with description. They may contain some action, as is the case here. But the primary objective is to create a stage on which action can unfold or to give a sense of place important to the focus of the story. Brian

Meehan's story concerned conditions at a state mental hospital. So a description of those conditions was an appropriate way to begin.

4. SCENE-WRAPS OR GALLERY LEADS

> *A man claiming to be a Catholic priest sits in a Santa Claus suit in a wheelchair outside a supermarket collecting money for the "Holy Order of Mary Inc."*
>
> *Across town, a supposed South African visitor asks a holiday-spirited shopper for directions to a local church. The South African then launches into a complicated tale that soon has the victim withdrawing $2,000 from the bank. . . .*
>
> *Elsewhere, a boiler-room telephone-sales company . . .* (Jim Long, *Oregonian*)

Scene-wraps show that the same thing is happening in a variety of places, and they're commonly used to begin news or magazine trend stories. Because they consist of a series of pictures, they're also called "galleries."

5. SIGNIFICANT-DETAIL LEADS

> *Hidden beneath a heap of inner tubes in a tiny storeroom on an island in the middle of the Vistula River is the statue of Lenin that stood for decades inside the Gdansk shipyard.* (Joseph A. Reaves, *Chicago Tribune*)

As you might expect, this report explored the continuing influence of Communism and central planning on the operation of the shipyard and the economy of Poland. The detail about Lenin's statue—hidden, but still in the neighborhood—symbolized the story's central theme.

6. SINGLE-INSTANCE LEADS

> *For five days, Alice's husband, high on drugs, threatened to kill her. He hit her and abused her.*
>
> *Terrified, Alice fled the house when she finally got the chance and ran to a local business to call the police. "He would kill me. He's very scary," Alice said. "He would walk through walls if he had to."*
>
> *The police advised her to contact the Domestic Violence Resource Center in Hillsboro, and Alice found her way there.* (Nancy McCarthy, *Oregonian*)

The single-instance lead uses one example to illustrate a larger topic. For that reason, single-instance leads are also called "microcosm leads." In this case, Alice's story was a gateway to a larger story on the Domestic Violence Resource Center.

7. WORDPLAY LEADS

In Michael Crichton's previous novel, Jurassic Park, *a tropical island has been transformed into a zoo whose denizens are dinosaurs brought to life by a group of greedy, irresponsible scientists who have been cloning around.* (Paul Pintarich, *Oregonian*)

Wordplay is essentially lighthearted. Wordplay leads therefore work best on less-than-serious stories. They're popular in sports and entertainment, but they can delight readers in other forms as well.

Dangerous Leads

1. QUESTION LEADS

What's black and orange and the worst nightmare for teams headed to the state football playoffs?

Some editors ban question leads, reasoning that readers want answers, not questions. Questions seldom perform the basic function of a lead—stating the central theme that organizes and explains the entire story. And readers probably do resent frivolous questions when what they want is information.

Still, some stories deal with fundamental questions, and a question lead can be appropriate. If you're writing about the search for water on Mars, you might begin by asking where it could possibly be hidden. But question leads seldom represent the best solution. Be especially cautious when using them.

2. QUOTE LEADS

Quotation leads have been banned in some newsrooms, too. The rationale is similar to the justification used for banning question leads: The chances that a quote is the best way to express the story's theme are slim.

But quote leads can work well, too, especially when they take the form of an engaging snippet of dialogue. Consider the Saul Pett lead for a profile of Dorothy Parker, the noted author and wit:

"Are you married, my dear?"

"Yes, I am."

"Then you won't mind zipping me up."

Zipped up, Dorothy Parker turned to face her interviewer, and the world.

3. TOPIC LEADS

> BOARDMAN—*The prospect of tripling this town's population with a 3,000-inmate prison was the subject of a hot debate Tuesday.*

Topic leads simply tell readers what a piece of writing is about. They do nothing to explain what of consequence happened or why readers should care. In the case of a meeting report, what's important is not that the meeting took place, but the result of the meeting. What was the key decision? Why is that important? Where do things go from here?

4. TEASER LEADS

> LONDON—*The fabled Lloyd's of London has insured just about everything: Elizabeth Taylor's eyes, Bruce Springsteen's voice, Marlene Dietrich's legs, even a prize for the capture of the Loch Ness monster.*
>
> *But now the 308-year-old insurance market is trying to write a policy for a shakier proposition: its own survival.* (Lawrence Ingrassia and Dana Milbank, *Wall Street Journal*)

Teaser leads run against conventional journalistic wisdom. The standard the inverted pyramid's who, what, where, why, when, and how does anything but tease. The journalist spills everything with the speed of a cat burglar rummaging through a bedroom.

And so it should be . . . at least when the reader's hunger for news matches the second-story man's lust for loot. Tease 'em in the lead of a hot breaking-news story and they most certainly *will* mind. If it's news they want, they want it fast. Imagine a teaser lead on the story announcing that the Japanese have bombed Pearl Harbor or that three poor souls were killed in a head-on car crash.

But the truth is that in an era when most news breaks online or via broadcast few newspaper reports qualify as breaking news. And little other writing produced these days deals with urgent information. Teaser leads are appropriate when:

- the news or information value of the writing is low. Yes, Lloyd's of London is a household name. And *Journal* readers would no doubt be interested in its financial collapse. But will the *Journal* report break news that directly affects readers? Or is it just the basis of an interesting yarn?
- the writer doesn't fool around too long. Every word in the setup should lead to the main point. And the main point—the punch line for the

setup lead—should come quickly. At the least, the writer should launch an engaging narrative that leads out of the setup and to some appropriate conclusion.

- the piece has high entertainment value, whether it's a letter or a *Wall Street Journal* feature story. That doesn't mean it must be fluff. But if you use a long setup for a boring read, you build nothing but resentment. The writing must have a payoff. The bigger the payoff, the more you can tease before getting to it.

Loser Leads

You can invite readers into a story in multiple ways, and you also can find multiple ways to chase them away. Knowing the lexicon of tried-and-true leads helps alert you to possibilities for success. By the same token, knowing the lexicon of common pitfalls helps you avoid failure. Journalists have developed one of those, too:

1. SUITCASE LEADS

The City Council tagged a last-minute amendment Wednesday onto an ordinance approving the transfer of control over the Rogers Cable–systems franchise to Kblcom. The addition gives the city the right to lay a future claim to some of the $4.55 million the Regulatory Commission will receive from the franchise transfer.

Imagine yourself back in your hotel room, at the end of a trip, trying to force everything you've collected into a too-small suitcase. You sit on the lid, but everything from underwear to tacky souvenirs still squeezes out the sides. You didn't make the tough choices that would have left you with a reasonable load.

The same thing can happen with a lead. You collect facts and don't winnow them adequately when deciding what's appropriate for the lead. You need to sort through them so that you can discover what's important. Then you discard the less important material, relegating it to some less exalted position in the report or throwing it out altogether.

Our example boils down to the fact that City Council members want to make sure the city profits from a cable-TV deal. Why not just say so? The writer can fill in the details later.

Newsroom old-timers called suitcase leads "clothesline leads." A writer created one by stringing all of the five W's—who, what, when, where, and why—together like freshly washed items hanging on a line.

Whatever you call them, they're a disservice to readers. Good summary leads offer quick, simple overviews of the reports that follow and suggest a core theme. If a summary lead runs more than twenty- to twenty-five words, the suitcase is probably too full.

2. GENERIC LEADS

It is true what they say. History repeats itself.

You win some you lose some. And sometimes you win again.

Mother knows best.

None of those leads does any real work. Each is a truism, the sort of obvious observation likely to produce a "so what else is new?" response.

When it comes to leads, one size doesn't fit all. Each should be tailor-made for the story at hand. The test of whether a lead meets the standard is simple enough: Ask yourself if you can imagine the lead heading a significantly different story. If the answer is yes, it's time to start customizing.

3. CLICHÉ LEADS

In the face of fear, we often retreat into the familiar, and that's a powerful temptation when you have to come up with the first line of a challenging piece of writing. Other writers have tackled comparable projects, and they have left behind workable ways to get started. The temptation is to follow their paths.

Resist! If you grab some hackneyed opening in desperation, you'll avoid the work of designing a lead that expresses the core theme of what you're about to write. That skipped step will, in turn, leave you unsure of where you're headed. You risk turning the entire enterprise into a cliché.

Some cliché leads are so timeworn that editors joke about them. The short story or day-in-the-life profile that begins with the sound of an alarm clock's buzzer. The essay that begins with a dictionary definition. The "what do *x* and *y* have in common?" lead.

Dick Thien, a legendary copy editor who helped invent USA *Today*, once compiled a lengthy list of threadbare leads. Here are nine of his worst offenders:

- The "good news, bad news" lead:

The good news is that online classes have begun. The bad news is that most students don't have computers.

- The "that's what" lead:

Some leads are easier to write than others. That's what fifteen reporters participating in an online seminar said Monday.

- The "thanks-to" lead:

Thanks to Bud Pagel, the supermarket chain considers customer convenience first and sales second.

- The one-word lead (variation of "that's what"):

Cynical.
That's what most people think journalists are.

- The "I fooled you" lead:

Sex, drugs, and booze. That's not what you'll find in newsrooms today, Kent Clark, *managing editor of the* Metropolis Daily Planet, *said.*

- The "now look at" lead:

When your parents bought their first home, mortgage interest rates were only 2 percent. Now look at what they are.

- The "welcome-to" lead:

Computer keyboards are clicking away, telephones are ringing, and people are shouting across the room to one another. Welcome to the Daily Nebraskan, *the student newspaper at the University of* Nebraska *in Lincoln.*

- The "meet John/Jane Doe" lead:

Few have ever held jobs in the private sector. Many have worked for government for decades. Too many have gold-plated medical insurance, but have no idea of what the average taxpayer has to pay for similar coverage. Meet the bureaucrats who rallied to demand cost-of-living raises in Courthouse Square Saturday.

- The "Museum of the Hard to Believe" lead:

When Bill Gates was playing in his sandbox at age three, he never realized that he'd grow up to become the world's most powerful businessman.

Forty years later, he did just that.

III. Building Blocks

I'm a great believer in the power of the paragraph. I think paragraphs should have a little plot, should lead you into something strange and different, tie the knot in the middle, and at the end do a little surprise, and then prepare you for the next paragraph.
—Norman Maclean

PLUNGING INTO THE MIDDLE

If you're writing a report, you'll move from the lead into the series of topics you listed in your jot outline. Some writing coaches call that basic report arrangement a "boxcar" structure because the blocks of writing devoted to each subtopic are lined up like boxcars in a freight train.

If you're writing a story, you'll arrange scenes along a narrative arc. And if you're tackling any of the myriad hybrid forms, you may mix scenic construction with a topical structure. An "hourglass" news report, for example, opens with a summary lead but quickly moves into a chronological narrative that is essentially scenic in design. A "bookend" narrative has a scenic opening followed by a topically organized section followed by a scenic ending.

One of the basic building blocks shared by virtually all writing structures is the paragraph, a key ingredient in anything more complicated than a grocery list. Once upon a time, every good grammar school curriculum included a unit on writing effective paragraphs. Miss Messler, my third-grade teacher, drummed a formula for writing paragraphs into our hard little heads until we dreamed in it. The formula was unrealistically simple, but the focus on paragraphs with a logical internal structure made perfect sense. In writing, much of the meaning emerges from the relationships between phrases, clauses, and sentences. Paragraphs are the principal structural method of showing the relationships between the ideas expressed in sentences. They deserve serious attention regardless of the larger structures that contain them.

PARAGRAPH CONNECTIONS

One of the important ways paragraphs help us communicate is by showing the relationships between ideas. We group certain ideas to show that they're drawn from the same general categories, or that they follow logically from one another.

That's the point of the classic paragraph Miss Messler taught her third graders. It begins with an assertion of some kind—the topic sentence. That's followed by two or three sentences containing evidence backing up the assertion. Those, in turn, are followed by a conclusion that wraps up the argument. Not many real-world paragraphs follow that exact form, of course, but it still makes sense to show the relationships between ideas through paragraph structure. It's another way of helping readers understand complicated material.

Note this example from an essay on writer Henry Roth:

> *The next turning point in Roth's creative and emotional life . . . was the Six-Day War. Suddenly, Roth saw Jews as fighters who were as tough as the Irish kids he had known in Harlem. And he saw the Soviet Union, which he had once idealized, allied with Arabs bent on annihilating the Jewish state. Roth, who was starting to come to terms with his painful personal history, also began to embrace Jewish history and his own place in it, and to feel that the two were intertwined.* (Jonathan Rosen, *New Yorker*)

That's a fair approximation of Miss Messler's ideal paragraph. The first sentence introduces the topic—the impact of the 1967 war between Israel and its Arab neighbors on Roth's self-concept. The next two sentences give specific examples of how Roth changed. And the final sentence reaches a conclusion about how Roth's work changed as a result. The paragraph's structure clearly displays the relationships between the ideas it contains.

Many journalists fail to tap the extra layer of meaning that paragraph structure provides. In some news stories, 90 percent or more of the paragraphs consist of only one or two sentences.

Note this example:

> *Halibut propel the Homer sportfishing fleet.*
>
> *Salmon are of secondary interest to this recreational fleet.*
>
> *Peter Udelhoven, who owns Silver Fox Charters, presides at the filleting table when his boats return.*

> *Boat boys hose and scrub the halibut hung all in a row, their gleaming white undersides facing outward for the ritual catch photos.*

The second sentence follows logically from the first. Or, you might argue, the first sentence follows logically from the second. The two could be combined, which also might encourage writer and editor to eliminate the awkward repetition of "fleet." The fourth sentence is a nice bit of imagery that's logically set up by the third. Why not combine those two in one paragraph as well?

> Homer sports fishermen catch some salmon, but their main quarry are halibut. Peter Udelhoven, who owns Silver Fox Charters, presides at the filleting table when his boats return. Boat boys hose and scrub the halibut hung all in a row, their gleaming white undersides facing outward for the ritual catch photos.

Just as you can confuse the issue by separating ideas that should be together, you can bring readers up short by combining ideas that should be separated. Note this example:

> *Olum was asked by the board to retire, angering students, faculty, and other supporters of the popular president. The current salary for the president's job is $95,760.*

But salary didn't relate to the issue of this college president's forced retirement. Suggesting that there is a connection, as this paragraph structure does, can't help but confuse readers.

PARAGRAPH PUNCH

In addition to showing relationships, paragraph structure can add emphasis. When a short, punchy graf suddenly appears after a long, languid one, it helps hammer home a point.

For example:

> *Jean didn't miss Kansas a lick. She almost pitched a fit when her husband suggested they move again and readily admits, "I was a very poor sport about it." But her husband was already practicing his full-court press. So she grudgingly pulled her winter coat out of mothballs, and Miller took the job on Feb. 2, 1948.*
>
> *Three years later he won a state championship.*

Because short paragraphs imply emphasis, good summary leads often consist of a single, short paragraph. The technique helps underscore the story's most important point. Note how an editor could have strengthened the following lead by breaking the second sentence off into a separate paragraph:

A countywide library serial levy proposal of more than $5.3 million heads up the ballot in Clackamas County's March 28 mail election. Municipal spending proposals and other measures, plus school board, fire district and water district director races, also are before the people.

You also can add emphasis by breaking off an idea that contrasts sharply with what has come before. The last line in the following lead would have carried a lot more punch had it been set up as a separate paragraph:

Paper is as necessary as water in our day-to-day lives. Whether it's white, 8½-by-11, or legal-sized and attached to a lawyer, paper for the most part plays an uninteresting yet major role. But not for Marel Kalyn.

NUT GRAFS

A nut graf is an explanatory paragraph that appears near the beginning of a news or feature story. It answers questions such as "What's it mean?" "So what?" and "Who cares?" It tells readers why they should bother investing their time and effort in reading the story. Here, for example, is how one *Wall Street Journal* story began:

Staten Island N.Y.—Old Fort Tompkins, tufts of grass peeking through cracks in its granite walls, looks down on a new concrete pier that juts 1,410 feet into the entryway to New York Harbor. The fort is abandoned now, a museum piece, but the pier below buzzes with activity. Soon it will be home to the battleship Iowa. . . .

And here's the nut graf that quickly followed:

There are really two issues here. The first involves the usefulness of the battleship itself in the late 20th century. The second involves building costly new ports when others are already functioning.

"Nut graf" is jargon particular to journalists. But the same idea pops up among nonjournalists as well. Similar terms include notions of "establishing" or "rationale" paragraphs. And many forms of writing would benefit from a nut paragraph or its equivalent. Even a teacher's research-paper assignment could use a quick accounting of the assignment's purpose, its intended effect, and the reasons students should take it seriously.

Effective nut paragraphs serve an impressive variety of purposes. They answer questions raised in leads, explain why a piece of writing is significant, and place the piece in a meaningful context. By explicitly stating what's important and why, nut grafs establish priorities, which in turn help writers organize their material. They also provide cues for headline writers, copy editors, and designers, and tighten writing by creating an organizational focus. Most important, they provide a rationale for reading by suggesting the benefits to come.

NUTS ON WALL STREET

The *Wall Street Journal* gets credit for developing the nut graf as a standard journalistic technique in the 1960s. The paper still includes one almost every time a feature begins with an anecdotal lead.

After beginning a story with an anecdote—and an additional one or two paragraphs that expand and explain the anecdote—the nut graf appears, explicitly stating the larger point suggested by the anecdote. It also explains why that larger point is important and how it is likely to affect us.

Here are two *Journal* opening grafs, followed by the nut graf that came along four or five paragraphs later:

> TOKYO—*Before Japan's Recruit scandal, Kayoko Ishizuka might never have given a second thought to Takao Fujinami's house. Now, it's outrageous, the moral equivalent of Imelda Marcos's 2,000 pairs of shoes.*
>
> . . .
>
> *Class-consciousness is rising. More than 90 percent of Japanese who responded in an opinion poll last year still considered themselves middle class. But 29.2 percent, the highest percentage in twenty years, called themselves lower middle class. "A wealth gap has been opening," says Hiroyuki Hisamizu, a private economist: "Consciousness of it is just beginning, but in five to ten years, this could be a big social issue."*

> PERKASIE, Pa.—*As millions of Americans still do, Meredith Campbell used to throw things away without giving it much thought. But now that she has to pay $1.50 for each forty-pound bag of trash she sets out at the curb, Mrs. Campbell . . . has a new attitude.*
>
> . . .

Since 1978, more than 70 percent of U.S. landfills—14,000 facilities—have closed primarily because of Americans' growing fear of landfill-contaminated drinking water. . . . The cumulative effect of all this . . . is that much of the U.S. will be mired in garbage. . . .

PARAGRAPHS AND QUOTATIONS

One of the strangest myths floating around the writing world calls for an automatic paragraph break before each direct quotation.

True, paragraph breaks separate utterances by the participants in a dialogue. When Jane says, "I love you," you must start a new paragraph before Jim can say, "I love you, too." But that doesn't mean every direct quotation has to stand alone. If you fall into that habit, you sacrifice a good deal of your power to convey meaning through paragraph breaks.

For one thing, good quotes make excellent graf kickers—the punchy endings that signal an end to one paragraph and prime readers to make a leap to the next. Many quotes read out of the preceding material quite naturally. Introducing an artificial paragraph break between the quote and its setup disrupts the logic of the sequence.

That's the case with this example:

Rather than rushing flames and an ominous column of blue-black smoke, the fire's presence was marked only by lines of wispy white smoke rising from the fire.

"It looks like an entirely different fire than it was yesterday," said Warren Olney, a Forest Service information officer. . . .

IV. Connections

If the reader is lost, it is usually because the writer has not been careful enough to keep him on the path.
—William Zinsser

TYING THE PARTS TOGETHER

Virtually every authority on modern English touts the value of unity, the quality that readers recognize in writing with a clear overall structure and closely related parts.

Transitions are one means to that end. By their nature, transitions build unity with connections that link paragraphs to what comes before and after. Here are five common transition devices:

1. Paragraph Hooks

Hooks are among the most obvious—and effective—forms of transition. They make a clear link between one paragraph and another by duplicating a key word from the last sentence of one paragraph in the first sentence of the next:

> *"For food and water, we depend on* ***heaven****," said Li, who has lived for 60 years in a dugout carved from a barren hillside high on China's vast loess plateau.*
>
> *Last year,* ***heaven*** *proved unkind. Drought seared farmland throughout the desolate region, destroying the wheat crop. . . .*

> *A couple of years of counseling at the VA hospital left his vocabulary salted with the* ***syntax*** *of self-help.*
>
> *But* ***syntax*** *doesn't settle bills.*

2. Signal Words

Readers automatically link certain words with transition. The classic is "meanwhile," as in "meanwhile, back at the ranch . . ." Other adverbs—including "however," "therefore," and "thus"—work almost as well. So do the six coordinating conjunctions—"and," "but," "or," "yet," "for," "nor."

> *The owners' association met and decided to go ahead with the landscaping.*
>
> *But the Bradshaws, who didn't attend the meeting, were already moving ahead with their own plans for the yard.*

3. Pronouns

Wherever they appear, pronouns create a natural connection to their antecedents—the nouns or pronouns to which they refer. When that connection stretches across a break between paragraphs, the result is a natural transition. Here's an example in which a pronoun—"that"—in the second paragraph refers back to the noun that concludes the first:

> *What's it like to have a wife and mother gone for six months and maybe longer? Ask Rick Devilbiss and ten-year-old Patty, seven-year-old Jennifer, and five-year-old Danielle Lonely. Scary. An act of faith.*
>
> *The family has that. Devilbiss says, "We turned everything over to the Lord when we started."*

4. Twists and Associations

A paragraph hook drives straight ahead, moving forward with the kind of logic that connects points in a straight line. Another kind of transition suddenly turns to the side by twisting the meaning of a word or striking off in a new direction in pursuit of some related meaning. Note this example:

> *. . . but with seven seconds left in the game a well-dressed fan in the fifth row let him have it.*
>
> *"Russo, why don't you resign?" he shouted.*
>
> *Russo didn't quit. But his players did—with almost fourteen minutes left in the second half.*

5. The March of Logic

Explicit transitions are often unnecessary if a writer's material has been carefully organized. The inexorable flow from one point to the next creates a sense of overall structure.

The most clear-cut example is a simple yarn organized chronologically.

Each action leads logically to the following action, even without obvious signal words such as "then" and "next."

Less obvious, but equally effective, is a structure built on paragraphs that represent clearly defined steps in a logical sequence:

> *Mr. and Mrs. B., before their fertilized embryos were frozen, signed a contract stipulating that should they die or divorce, the embryos would become property of the university, for donation to another couple.*
>
> *"They could have chosen to have them destroyed, but they checked 'Donated,'" explains Jean Craemer.*
>
> *Even so, had Mr. and Mrs. B. and their lawyers come to a different agreement . . .*

V. Endings

Great is the art of beginning, but greater is the art of ending.
—Henry Wadsworth Longfellow

THE NEVER-ENDING TALE

One of the worst problems afflicting newswriting is the lack of attention to endings. It's the curse responsible for all those reports that cook along nicely and then just stop. No bang. No whimper. Only a jarring halt that leaves readers wondering what happened.

The problem lingers from the days when printers used hot lead to craft metal type. Once a news report was set in type, the only practical way to cut it was to remove individual lines from the bottom. Writers didn't bother to create true endings because they were so likely to be lost in the production process.

The advent of the computer made it just as easy to cut from the middle as from the end, but old habits die hard. Journalists still have a tendency to truncate their endings. They may spend weeks on research, pour sweat and tears into leads, struggle through complex story structures, and fine-tune transitions. Then they let their stories fade out like an overgrown path disappearing into the woods.

Worse yet is when a writer creates an ending appropriate to the story, but the editor follows blind habit and blithely cuts from the bottom.

No matter who's responsible, letting a story that deserves a strong ending appear without one is a serious mistake—in journalism or any other kind of writing. The ending is a crowning touch. A well-crafted finish gives any piece of writing a sense of completion, a wrapping up that leaves readers feeling satisfied.

And the ending is, after all, the reader's last taste of the story. It's the bit he remembers best because it's freshest in mind, and it colors his perception of everything that came before. What's the point of all the hard work on the beginning and middle of a draft if it's ruined by a few careless words tacked on at the end?

FULL CIRCLES

Good endings take an infinite number of forms, and no formula guarantees a satisfying conclusion. But most strong finales do fall into a few broad categories.

Some of the best loop back to the beginning, closing a circle, tying the whole story together and creating a sense of completion.

David Sarasohn, one of the *Oregonian*'s cleverest opinion writers, demonstrated the effect in a column on railroad travel. He began by observing that some parts of the country deserve to be flown over, but that others should be seen from the ground. Trains are a grand way to do that, he added, before observing, in the sixth paragraph, that the Pacific Northwest is train country. And, he continued:

> *The only reason nobody ever wrote a song about riding a train here—something like "the Chehalis Choo Choo" or "Midnight Train to Gresham"—was that everybody was too busy looking out the window.*

A dozen paragraphs followed. David wrote about all the different forms of rail travel that had taken hold over the past few years. Then he wrapped it up by referring back to that sixth paragraph:

> *Somewhere around here, somebody might even be writing a song.*

In addition to a strong sense of completion, a good ending delivers a punch that signals the story's conclusion. That's one reason journalists call an ending a "kicker."

Part of that punch comes from the rhythm of the final sentence. Like any paragraph kicker, the story kicker should snap to a close. If the last word has only a single syllable and ends with a hard consonant, so much the better. Note that David Sarasohn ended with the word "song."

There's also something to be said for the ending that contains the story's most memorable line or image. Henry Morton Stanley saved his most famous line—"Dr. Livingstone, I presume"—for the end of his *New York Herald* story on his quest for the lost Scottish physician and missionary. In addition to providing emphasis for important points, good endings often have a startling quality. Endings that loop back to the beginning or to some seminal point early in the story startle by reminding readers of what they read earlier and confronting them with the sudden realization that the story has come full circle. David Sarasohn made his conclusion especially sharp and surprising by saving "song" for the end of his piece.

Other writers startle by coming out of left field with a clever—but totally unexpected—line. Dave Barry is a master of the technique, as illustrated by this classic column kicker:

> *. . . the younger generations today are already so conservative they make William F. Buckley Jr. look like Ho Chi Minh. What I'm wondering is, what will they be like when they're our age? Will they, too, change their political philosophy? Will millions of young urban professionals turn fifty and all of a sudden start turning into left-wing antiestablishment hippies, smoking pot on the racquetball court and putting Che Guevara posters up in the conference room and pasting flower decals all over their cellular telephones? It will be an exciting time to look forward to. I plan to be dead.*

The *Oregonian*'s Steve Duin, who in 2003 was named the best columnist in the country by the National Association of Newspaper Columnists, ended one of his pieces on an equally surprising note. He explained an off-the-wall bit of proposed legislation by tracing it to the connection between a school-board president and her husband, a state representative. "Bedfellows," Steve wrote, "make strange politicians."

A New York Times News Service profile of an eighty-six-year-old millionaire ended with surprise, quite literally. The thrust of the story was that the millionaire often gave money to deserving little people, and that he almost always demanded anonymity. The writer, Douglas Martin, wrapped things up by actually including the word "surprise" as a parenthetical wink to his readers:

> *Time to leave. Petrie summoned his chauffeur to take the columnist home in a Rolls Royce, the columnist's accustomed style when out of tokens.*
>
> *"This guy's in my will for $1 million and he doesn't know it," Petrie said of the driver. (Surprise!)*

Puns and wordplay can introduce the element of surprise, too. A story on new types of disposable diapers concluded that the diapers don't really signal any great gain for the environment. "A new diaper, it turns out, doesn't always mean a change."

CLOSED CYCLES

The most natural endings may be those that simply complete the arc that formed the basis for the story's underlying structure. The story of a life ends with a death. The story that details a visit with an interesting character ends with the visit's conclusion. The story of a day-in-the-life ends with the close of day.

A day-in-the-life story on a fitness resort ended this way:

> *As darkness closes in around the picturesque villas tucked among the hills, the mood is tranquil, the air cool. A few figures walk briskly around the track that circles a grove of fruit trees. The only sound is the thump of a tennis ball in the distance.*
>
> *For the moment, routine concerns have been forgotten. The mind seems clear. The body feels restored.*

Sleep almost always announces a conclusion. A story on biologists collecting cougar data described a chase that ended with one specimen in a tree:

The cougar watched disdainfully for a few minutes, then stretched out between the limbs. Biology and the chase, she obviously figured, could wait. And soon she was asleep.

LAME LAST LINES

One of the keys to crafting a good ending is knowing when to quit. Remember the maxim that describes one of writing's principal pitfalls: The typical writer creates the perfect ending . . . and then writes one more line.

Indeed, lots of endings could be improved by cutting the last line. Many of us are still heeding the bad advice we heard in grammar school, where we were told that essays should end with a summary or a restatement of the main point. But such summaries usually tip readers off to the ending, bore them by telling them what's already been said, and dilute the punch that characterizes a more natural ending.

So double-check your endings by dropping the last line to see if that improves things. That simple procedure sure would have done wonders for the ending to this story about a girl who was named queen of Portland's Rose Festival, which that year carried the theme "As If by Magic":

> *For some princesses, the most magical moment will be boarding the float at the Grand Floral Parade. . . . "I've watched the parade since I was six," said Shannon Stice, eighteen, of Wilson High School. "I remember watching the floats go by and wishing I could be on one some day. As if by magic, I will. Things happen as if by magic when you put a lot of work into them."*

FINAL WORDS

For several reasons, quotations often make ideal endings. The best ones are dramatic. They restate a story's central theme, and they can be manipulated to take the rhythmic form of a good ending. Placing the attribution after an opening clause sets up a closing clause that finishes things with a flourish. Note these two examples.

> *"You know," said Bradley, bending close as if sharing a big secret, "I think I love this job."*

> *"It was the biggest frog I ever saw in my life," says Henry. "He wanted me to see it."*

Note how this ending would have been improved if the writer had followed the same pattern:

One Doolittle raider told Drew recently, "One thing I learned from that mission, and I have practiced ever since: Never volunteer."

Whatever you do, don't end with the attribution, which will just trail off instead of wrapping things up with a bang. Witness this poorly placed attribution at the end of a page-one news feature:

Bostrom didn't need special equipment, either. "I just wore my Nikes," she said.

That ending fizzled not only because of the poor attribution placement, but also because it just popped up, rather than following an appropriate buildup. Even the best quote endings can't hold up the finale of a story if writers don't set them up properly.

That's largely because the setup gives the ending the heft it needs to assume its proper significance. Good endings must have a certain amount of substance that brings them into proportion with the rest of the story. Carol McCabe, a prizewinning *Providence Journal-Bulletin* feature writer, says a piece of writing with a strong lead and a strong conclusion is "like some kind of basket where you've got to have a handle at both ends." She adds that she wants "the finish of the story to hold up the weight of the beginning. I want the whole thing balanced."

And that, in the end, may be the most critical element in a satisfying conclusion. It is balance, after all, that creates the harmony in most art. When everything clicks into place, a story assumes a kind of pleasing symmetry. It just feels right.

The Chapter 3 Cheat Sheet

FIVE TIPS ON WRITING BEGINNINGS, MIDDLES, AND ENDINGS

1. **Don't stall on the first line.** The important thing is to get moving, not to write the perfect opening before you write anything else. If an acceptable lead doesn't pop into mind, simply jot down your core idea and keep writing. Chances are good that a decent lead will appear before you get through your first draft.
2. **Make paragraphs work for you.** Scan a page of your manuscript. Is it a solid block of type? Or, at the other extreme, is it filled with staccato bursts of one- and two-line paragraphs? In the first case, look for opportunities to arrange the material in shorter blocks of related

material. In the second, look for opportunities to combine. And mix it up, producing a pleasing mix of short, medium, and long paragraphs. Use short paragraphs to emphasize key points.

3. **Find the nut.** Once you're well into your draft, step back to ask basic questions. What's this piece of writing about? Where am I going with it? What does it mean? Why does it matter to my readers? Then fold your answers into a single paragraph. Insert that a couple of dozen lines below your opening.
4. **Circle around.** Some of the best endings create a sense of closure by somehow returning to the beginning. If you've almost finished your first draft and you can't find an ending, read your lead once again. Look for a word or an idea that you can return to in the last paragraph.
5. **Avoid that lame last line.** Don't fall prey to one of the oldest temptations in writing—to ruin the perfect ending by writing one line too many. Once you've finished your rough draft, mentally remove the last sentence. Is the ending better without it?

4

Force

How forcible are right words!
—Job 6:25

DEMANDING ATTENTION

Want the world to turn its head and take notice? Take your cue from physics. The bigger and faster a moving object, the harder it hits.

Same thing with words. The more energy they carry, the more response they get. Military types think in terms of projecting force, and so should you.

For one thing, your forcefulness affects your credibility. The research says three things make a source believable: (1) its perceived mastery of the subject, (2) its perceived similarity to the audience, and (3) its sheer energy—the enthusiasm and vitality it displays.

So speak forcefully. The energy your writing radiates—regardless of its content—changes the odds that you'll be believed. And you won't have much impact (intended impact, anyway) on somebody who doesn't believe you.

Whether we give it much thought or not, we all sense the energy level in any piece of writing. When a criminal piloted a helicopter into a prison to rescue his former partner in crime, the newspaper reporter who covered the event captured the James Bond–style drama with description that radiated energy:

> *Finally, as Stevens swooped into the prison exercise yard and Kramer grabbed onto the landing skid, the struggling whirlybird lurched into a chain-link fence and slammed to the ground.*

But another reporter completely missed the intensity and energy of his subject in this passage from a feature on glassblowing:

> *Bowl or balloon shapes can be blown with the use of a blowpipe. Variously shaped pieces of hot glass can be fused together. In its molten state, glass can be twisted or "slumped." Color can be added in powdered form. Since abrupt cooling can result in breakage, each piece must endure the slow cooling of the annealing ovens where the glass is gradually reduced to air temperature. . . .*

The prison-break sequence employs specific techniques to grab your attention. The glassblowing sequence neglects them. The trick is knowing what they are and how you can put them to work.

You can start by thinking of writing in terms of personality. How we say something reflects, to some degree, who we are. So it's no great surprise that forceful writing displays the characteristics of a strong, vibrant human being. Powerful people, most of us would agree, are:

- **active**—When you think about force in the natural world, you naturally think about action. Motion is an elemental part of force as it plays out in the visible world. Forceful human beings keep on the move, and your writing should, too. That means you need to master verbs, understanding which carry the most power and why. You want to package verbs in sentences that showcase their natural energy.
- **confident**—Movers and shakers don't pussyfoot around, and your writing shouldn't either. Chances are, you'll be facing busy, easily distracted readers. You don't want to frustrate them with long introductory phrases, meandering sentences, and convoluted syntax.
- **hardworking**—Once you learn to recognize the lazy elements in your writing, you can bypass them in favor of words and phrases that get real work done.
- **lean**—Nero Wolfe almost never left his New York brownstone. The fat detective did some powerful thinking, but he sent knife-edged Archie Goodwin out to get things done. That's a decent metaphor for the writing process. Your ideas can be self-indulgent in the comfort of your own mind. But they'd better be lean and ready for action once they reach the hostile world outside your front door.

One caution before we look at how those general goals translate into writing specifics: Forceful writers aren't necessarily loud writers. If you walk past the same noisy street preacher enough times, you'll learn to ignore him. Readers will ignore you, too, if you pitch everything at the same high-decibel volume. Insistently quiet writing also exerts impact. The secret's not in the volume, but in the delivery.

I. Potent Syntax

A sentence should read as if its author, had he held a plow instead of a pen, could have drawn a furrow deep and straight to the end.
—Henry David Thoreau

All it takes to make a sentence is what's called a "basic statement," a subject-verb combination that describes someone—or something—performing an action. It tells, in its briefest form, a story. "Horse rears." "Car crashes." "Politician talks."

Sometimes you don't even need two words. When you give a one-word command—"Run!"—the subject is understood, and the basic statement is complete.

The linguist Noam Chomsky argues that the basic statement is the core unit of human thought. Every language builds on this deep foundation, he says, and even the most complex linguistic structures stem from it. Given the fact that the sentence is also the key tool of the writer's trade, it makes sense to occasionally ponder sentences at their most primitive levels.

Roy Peter Clark's essay "The American Conversation and the Language of Journalism" tracks the way American newswriting moved away from complicated sentence structures. From Tocqueville to Orwell to E. B. White and Red Smith, Clark traces the rise of simple sentence forms that served democratic purposes by making public affairs accessible to all.

The key modern American language structure, Clark says, is the "right-branching sentence." It begins with the basic statement ("A horse reared . . ."). Then it adds meaning with a series of language units that branch off to the right. These may include prepositional phrases (". . . in front of Henderson's Saloon . . ."), individual modifiers such as adjectives and adverbs (". . . yesterday . . ."), participial phrases (". . . knocking Parson Pugh to the ground . . ."), subordinate clauses (". . . because the parson failed to notice that . . ."), and even whole clauses (". . . and the sheriff came running when . . .").

Diagram something like that and you get a tree lying on its side, with the trunk to the left and the branches to the right. It's a form that promotes clarity because, as Clark puts it, a sentence beginning with subject and verb "makes meaning known early."

That's an admirable goal for any writer. It certainly makes sense for a news report. And the best way to begin a narrative in either fiction or nonfiction is often with the name of the protagonist and a transitive verb.

The lesson's most practical application may be to the long, convoluted sentences that typify the bastard form of English we call journalese. Look at any day's *New York Times* or *Washington Post* and you'll see a primary symptom of the disease—opening sentences that back into the main thought with a long prepositional phrase, a subordinate clause, or a participial phrase. One day I picked up the *Times* and found this:

> *After a long campaign of ideological clashes, policy debates, and talk of a grand reckoning on the direction of the Democratic Party, the presidential primaries starting on Monday will be shaped by a less lofty but increasingly urgent matter: determining the best incumbent who has already proved to be a political survivor.*

That fifty-two-word lead sentence is convoluted past the point of understanding. The basic statement—"the presidential primaries . . . will shaped by" is in passive voice and begins after a twenty-two-word windup that contains four prepositional phrases. To clean up the mess, find the central thought and lead with that in a right-branching sentence. Then deal with those distracting subordinate thoughts.

> The Democratic primary campaign now boils down to a key question. For months the campaign swirled around lofty issues of ideology, policy, and party philosophy. But on Monday Iowa chooses, and from here on the outcome hinges on who voters think can beat Donald Trump.

II. Exploiting Action Words

To produce something of real merit, the author must inject enthusiasm proper to the occasion.
—Zane Grey

VERB HUNTING

Action defines our reality. Time passes because things *happen*. And in writing, the verbs carry the action. One of the keys to writing more forcefully, then, is seeking out the most potent verbs available.

Those of us lucky enough to write in English have no excuse for using anything less than the strongest verbs. For one thing, we can pluck our choices from a huge array of possibilities. Our mongrel mix of Germanic and Romance languages dishes up verbs for every occasion. You can run, dash, dart, sprint, jog, canter, or lope. You can walk, saunter, amble, or stroll.

Finding just the right verb takes commitment. With such an array of choices available, merely sifting through the possibilities takes time. Wise writers may settle for so-so verbs in a first draft, but they'll focus their rewrite efforts on refining them.

William Zinsser, author of *On Writing Well*, advises that we target verbs with inherent qualities that evoke action. He noted that "many verbs also carry in their imagery or in their sound a suggestion of what they mean: flail, poke, dazzle, squash, beguile, pamper, swagger, wheedle, vex."

Strive for specificity, too. The more concrete the verb, the more likely it is to evoke the real world. "Dashed" is more specific than "ran." "Strode" is more specific than "walked."

Master verb hunters base their keyboard tactics on specific knowledge of their prey. They learn the varieties of verbs and the forms most likely to suit the need of the moment. That means knowing how to distinguish the three main types—transitive, intransitive, and linking—and how to sort out their strengths and weaknesses.

TRANSITIVE VERBS

Transitive verbs create the most ruckus. And when you think of action words, that's probably what you're thinking of.

Transitive verbs carry action from a source and inflict it on some receiver. "Its claws *raked* her back." "He *drove* two runners home." "The fire *swallowed* the first floor." Such verbs, in other words, take a direct object.

Consider this lively sentence, built entirely on transitive verbs:

> *The explosion that* ***ripped*** *Mount St. Helens this week* ***gouged*** *a 600 foot-long gash in the crater's lava dome,* ***slammed*** *six-foot rocks into crater walls, and* ***unleashed*** *an avalanche and a mudflow.*

Not only do transitive verbs pack power, but they also trace causality by revealing who did what to whom. Or what action sparked what reaction. Identify them by asking "what?" If the sentence tells you what the verb affected, you're working with a transitive verb.

A boiling pot of glue ***ignited*** *an ocean of flame.*

Anderson ***grabbed*** *a pail of water and* ***threw*** *it on the fire.*

The glue ignited what? (The ocean of flame.) Anderson grabbed what? (The pail.) And threw what? (It.)

Transitive verbs generally drive a sentence with more power than any other kind. But not always. Some of the more abstract and bureaucratic transitive verbs can drain life from a sentence:

We can ***purchase*** *supplies from sources outside the company and* ***effect*** *considerable savings as a result.*

After a visit to the food court, we ***completed*** *our shopping in the two department stores.*

Fortunately, zippy substitutes exist for most flabby transitive verbs: "We can *buy* supplies." "We *ate* at the food court and *shopped* our way through the two department stores."

INTRANSITIVE VERBS

Intransitive verbs make up the second major class of action words. The action ends with the intransitive verb, rather than carrying over to some person or object. For that reason, intransitive verbs reveal less causality than their transitive cousins. The action happens, but no consequence follows:

Christmas music ***played*** *faintly as carts* ***rolled*** *over clean linoleum. . . .*

But then the overburdened water flow ***dwindled*** *to a trickle. . . .*

Despite their lack of objects, intransitive verbs don't always lack power. Vivid, concrete intransitive verbs can pack as much punch as the action they describe.

Thousands of ground squirrels ***erupt*** *from their burrows.*

The room ***jerked*** *violently. An overpass outside* ***swayed*** *and* ***split*** *with a loud stereophonic rumble.*

LINKING VERBS

Linking verbs defy the whole idea of a verb. At their roots, they're mere definitions. They can convey opinion. But they can't portray action. All they tell you is that some things are (or are not) in some way the same as other things. "The moon *is* blue." "The contract talks *are* tedious exercises in futility." "The ground *felt* spongy."

Linking verbs simply join categories of things; they tell you that A is in some way equivalent to B. That the universe of things that are A, in other words, overlaps the universe of things that are B. For example:

> *The sound and lights* ***were*** *excellent. Levels* ***were*** *comfortable and the definition of the keyboard-dominated band* ***was*** *fine.*

The thing we call "sound," in other words, partially overlapped the thing we call "excellence." At this time and in this place, the two were equivalent.

Because they lack action, linking verbs work like a sea anchor on a sailboat, crippling something that should be sleek and speedy. Various forms of "to be" dominate the linking verbs:

> *The dawn* ***was*** *beautiful.*

> *As the men, work Kim's embarrassment* ***is*** *apparent in her flushed cheeks.*

Linking verbs often conceal the lively action that actually unfolded in the real world. Consider possible alternatives to our examples: "The sun *crested* the hills, and rosy beams of light *flooded* the valleys." "As the men worked, the flush on her cheeks *betrayed* her embarrassment."

Sense verbs such as "smell," "feel," and "sound" can work as linking verbs, too. Note these examples:

> *. . . he* ***appeared*** *stunned and saddened.*

> *Your home can* ***smell*** *as good as it looks.*

> *"It* ***feels*** *great to be a part of it," he says.*

You can avoid linking verbs by thinking about causality. What made the poor guy stunned and saddened? Bring the causal agent into the sentence ("The *news* stunned and saddened him") and you automatically introduce force.

TWO-WAY VERBS

English, ever-flexible language that it is, often swings more than one way. Lots of verbs operate in two modes, sometimes serving as a transitive verb and sometimes as its intransitive counterpart, or vice versa.

So a car might simply slow on the freeway, but . . .

*Lisa McConnell **slowed** her shopping cart.*

A politician might blast his opponent in a debate, but . . .

*The players **blasted** onto the field.*

And while you might flee a fire, it's also possible that . . .

*Fallen women, pimps, and white-aproned bartenders **fled** before the flames.*

Note, however, that some verbs never oscillate between transitive and intransitive forms, and assuming that they do can lead you astray. A simple dictionary check will reveal the secrets of a verb's status as transitive or intransitive. The abbreviation "tr." follows the one, and "intr." follows the other. *Merriam-Webster's Collegiate Dictionary*, 11th edition, uses "vt" and "vi." If you look up "pervade" in most dictionaries, you discover that the word experts have laid down the law—the verb is transitive and only transitive. It must take a direct object. Which means a reporter clearly erred when he wrote:

*A guarded optimism about election outcomes **pervades**.*

Many writers also struggle to untangle "lie" and "lay," which are two different verbs, one intransitive and one transitive. The intransitive "lie" takes the forms *lie-lay-lain-lying*. "I *lie* on the bed." "I *lay* on the bed." "I *had lain* on the bed." "I *was lying* on the bed."

The transitive "lay" takes the forms *lay-laid-laid-laying*. "I *lay* the book on the table." "I *laid* the book on the table." "I *had laid* the book on the table." "She *was laying* the book on the table."

Here's an all-too-typical example of the failure to make the distinction:

> *Once-stately live oaks have been ripped out of the ground and strewn carelessly across paths and parking lots—including a 100-year-old oak tree that is now* ***laying*** *across the picturesque reflecting pool.*

VERBICIDE

You can destroy the life in any piece of writing by gutting its verbs. Some crooks break into a building? Hey! You can write that "the suspects gained entry by damaging the facility."

Sooner or later dull writers stumble across an efficient way of murdering verbs, discovering that they can turn just about any sparkling snippet of action into a ponderous noun by adding a leaden ending. Take "use," a plain, honest verb that does plenty of work with only three letters. Give it a suffix and it becomes "usage." Add "-ive" to "support" and—voilà!—you have "supportive." If those suffixes don't offer enough options, you can try "-able" or "-tion." Sometimes "-ure" will work. So will "-ance," "-ent," or "-ment."

You can totally transform some verbs. A little thought ages a bouncy, teenage action word to near senility. Instead of writing that your action hero flies, you can say she "engages in flight." When she hits another plane, you can say she is "in a collision." And you don't have to say her plane falls. You can write that she's "beginning her descent."

Once unleashed, that kind of verbicide drains the life from the most vibrant writing, leaving behind verb corpses such as "closure," "dependent," "acceptance," "intrusive," and "replacement."

Such violence against verbs ought to carry a criminal penalty. Unfortunately, however, you won't serve time for turning "pass" into "passage" or "seize" into "seizure." But you will lose readers. And, in the writing game, that's penalty enough.

Note these mortal remains of what once were living verbs:

> *The biggest short-term winners in a breakup may be the computer makers and customers who have been* ***dependent*** *on the software giant.*

(". . . who have *depended* on the software giant.")

Built in 1951, the mill will begin an indefinite ***closure*** *Thursday.*

("... will *close* indefinitely Thursday")

The company planned the remodeling before the ***passage*** *of Measure 5.*

("... planned to *remodel* before Measure 5 *passed*.")

Gary Schrader ... is ***supportive*** *of the plan.*

("Gary Schrader *supports* the plan")

HALF VERBS

Half a verb often is better than none. Fortunately, English offers an array of half verbs. We call them verbals, and they preserve much of the vigor carried in the original verb while serving as another part of speech.

An "-ing" ending, for example, can turn a verb into a gerund, which serves as a noun. "I *run* around the block," but "*running* around the block helps pass the time." An "-ing" ending can also create a participle, which serves as an adjective. "The *running* dogs of imperialism." You create an infinitive by putting "to" before a verb. "To *run* is to live."

This sentence builds on the lively verb "whacked" with four strong participles:

> *Hurricane Frances' wind and water* ***whacked*** *swaths of Florida with fire-hose force Sunday,* ***submerging*** *entire roadways and* ***tearing*** *off rooftops before* ***weakening*** *to a tropical storm and* ***crawling*** *inland with heavy rain.*

Of course, weak verbs beget weak verbals.

We hope ***to be*** *in Kansas City by Dec. 3.*

Verbals often do their best work when they substitute for nouns created by adding suffixes to verbs. Such nouns are the dead remains of what were once lively action words. Converting them to verbals regains at least some of the energy they once had. Like this:

> *The **decipherment** of Mayan writing indisputably demonstrates that the Western Hemisphere had a rich and complex human history before 1492.*

("*Deciphering* Mayan writing . . .")

> *Most of her business colleagues express **bafflement**.*

("Most of her business colleagues are *baffled*." Or, better yet in this case, "Her actions *baffled* most of her colleagues.")

> *About the same time Jerry was preparing for **graduation** and **marriage**.*

(". . . was preparing *to graduate* and *to marry*.")

III. Mastering Active Voice

Reduced to its essence, a good English sentence is a statement that an agent (the subject of the sentence) performed an action (the verb) upon something (the object).
—John Ciardi

THE VOICE OF AUTHORITY

A century ago, William Strunk, writing in *The Elements of Style*, recommended "the habitual use of the active voice," observing that an active style "makes for forcible writing." Just about every writing authority since has agreed.

But the reality is that writing generates anxiety. Anxiety in turn produces timidity, which often expresses itself in the passive voice. You sit down at the keyboard, your shoulders tighten up, and you write that "the airliner was struck by lightning" rather than "lightning struck the airliner." That "more votes were cast for Murphy" instead of "voters elected Murphy." Or that "we were delayed by a huge snowstorm" rather than "a huge snowstorm delayed us."

Verbs degenerate into passive voice when we twist sentence syntax so that the original object of the verb becomes the subject of the sentence. A stressed-out sports reporter may write that "the ball was clobbered by the cleanup batter." But the truth is that the cleanup batter clobbered the ball.

Any self-respecting writer will leave it that way, with the action rushing through the batter to the bat and into the ball.

The key to recognizing the passive voice lies in the preposition "by." In a passive construction, "by" either follows the verb or could follow the verb. "The ball was clobbered" remains passive, even when we drop the prepositional phrase that would ordinarily follow.

Passive sentences that omit the actor cause the most confusion. If you run into "The ball was clobbered," you can easily confuse it with a sentence built around a linking verb, such as "The ball is red." That's a weak sentence, but it's not passive.

Here's a rule of thumb for recognizing passive sentences that omit the person or thing performing the action: Try adding a prepositional phrase beginning with "by" and ending with the name of the actor. If the result makes sense, the sentence is passive.

So . . . "The ball was clobbered *by the cleanup batter*." "It is expected *by the delegates* that the session will end early." "Hanging plants could be seen *by any observer* in the entry."

Note these published examples:

Within a matter of days, his paperwork is ready to be submitted to the doctors.

You can add "by him." The sentence is passive.

To many, the West was seen as a utopia.

The West was seen as a utopia "by many." The sentence is passive.

DODGING RESPONSIBILITY

This Big Ten Conference grudge match is considered too close to call by many. . . .

Who considers it too close to call? The Vegas oddsmakers? Other sports pundits? The writer? Somebody the writer talked to on the bus?

One of the principal problems with passive sentences is that they hide the true causes of things. Adding nonsubjects such as the mysterious "many" doesn't help a bit.

The president is not expected to make a final decision on a national missile defense before next summer at the earliest.

Who expects the president to delay his decision? Why did the writer lack the confidence to assert that "the president probably won't make a final decision before next summer"?

Passive sentences also can stymie readers who'd like to do something about what they've read. Let's say you're an environmental activist who reads this announcement:

> *The draft copy of the environmental-impact statement on a request to expand the twenty-year-old ski area will be released about Feb. 20 according to a U.S. Forest Service official.*

Who's releasing the statement? If you want to weigh in on this issue, do you call the Forest Service or the ski resort, or somebody else entirely?

The real crime is committed when a writer uses the passive voice to conceal the fact that no actor exists. You have to wonder about all those news reports carrying phrases such as "it is expected that." How often are those merely code words for what the writer expects to happen?

IV. Empty Words

The obligation of the writer is to maintain the vigor of the language and the vigor of the imagination.
—Carlos Fuentes

EXPLETIVES DELETED, PLEASE

Those of us old enough to remember the "expletive deleted" notations on transcriptions of Richard Nixon's Watergate tapes may think of expletives strictly as profanities. In fact, the word "expletive" also has a broader sense. One dictionary definition of "expletive" is "a word, phrase, etc. not needed for the sense but used merely to fill out a sentence. . . ." Consider this example:

> *There is a serene peacefulness about the newly renovated sanctuary of Congregation Neveh Shalom. . . .*

Your first thought may be that peacefulness is invariably serene and that we probably don't need that adjective. But you might also note that "there is" refers to nothing in reality. The phrase merely fills out the sentence. That makes it an expletive. Other common expletives are "it is," "it was," "there were," and "there are."

Grammatically speaking, "there" as it's used in "there is a serene peacefulness" is an adverb. But it modifies nothing. And the true subject of the sentence—in this case, "peacefulness"—follows the verb.

But that's just grammar-babble. What matters is that expletives usually weaken sentences. Because they refer to nothing in particular, they convey no concrete meaning and can't create an image in the reader's mind. More important, expletives drain vitality from sentences. Many expletives contain some form of the verb "to be," the weakest of the weak verbs. So eliminating the expletive opens the possibility of a sentence built on a strong, transitive verb. Mull this example:

There were so many visitors at the zoo Monday morning that machines to tabulate attendance were overwhelmed.

Eliminate the expletive "there were," and the true subject jumps to the head of the sentence. The writer then faces the question, The visitors did what? And that, in turn, opens the opportunity for a strong verb. "So many visitors flooded the zoo Monday morning that they overwhelmed the machines used to tabulate attendance."

The new syntax eliminates the second "were," too. But the energetic writer won't stop there. A little more fiddling will strengthen the sentence even more by eliminating the subordinate clause. That produces this construction: "A flood of Monday morning visitors overwhelmed the machines used to tabulate zoo attendance."

Not every sentence should be streamlined, of course. Certain contexts call for the discursive style that expletives encourage. We'll all use an occasional expletive, and some publications are full of them. The *New Yorker*, with its unhurried pace, is a prime example. But you'll usually want to craft writing that's strong, active, and vital. So you'll want to minimize the use of expletives.

Note the possibilities for strengthening the following examples:

There's not one family car into which she can squeeze herself anymore.

("She can't squeeze herself into . . .")

There aren't too many people who even come around to take her places anymore.

("Hardly anybody even comes around to take her places anymore.")

It must have been difficult for California coach Lou Campanelli to prepare his players for Friday's Pacific 10 Conference tournament game.

("California coach Lou Campanelli must have had a tough time preparing his players . . .")

It is hardly a secret that there is a flourishing drug trade inside all the state prisons.

("The flourishing drug trade inside all the state prisons is no secret.")

V. Little Timidities

The writer follows after the spoken language, usually timidly.
—John Updike

THE PARASITES IN THE POND OF PROSE

They are, said E. B. White, "the leeches that infest the pond of prose, sucking the blood of words." He had in mind needless qualifiers, petty modifiers such as "rather," "somewhat," "generally," "virtually," "pretty" (as in "pretty much"), "slightly," "a bit," and "little."

White's image of small creatures draining the life from large ones is especially apt. A single unnecessary qualifier does little damage, but a few thousand carpenter ants can bring down a house. Qualifiers that creep into sentence after sentence can nibble the foundations right out from under your writing.

Almost all of us can find opportunities to eliminate timidities that sap the strength of our writing. Consider the use of "rather," one of the wimp words White specifically cited:

. . . somehow the festival's summer opening seemed ***rather*** *remote and static by comparison.*

. . . enduring her much younger and ***rather*** *madcap mother. . . .*

> *. . . tanning salons, tattoo parlors, used clothing stores, and a* ***rather*** *wild leather store that caters to sexual fantasies.*

Like most petty qualifiers, "rather" seldom adds anything essential. Pull the modifier out of each example and ask yourself what's been lost.

An American press critic recently referred to British newspapers as "indeed rather partisan." If the finger-pointing, name-calling, slash-and-burn style of British political reporters isn't partisan, you have to wonder what is.

"Rather" may be a bad habit, but "somewhat" can become an obsession. It constantly shows up with nouns that hardly need qualifying. My files show references to study findings that are not merely contradictory, but "somewhat contradictory." A bad day of fishing wasn't plain disappointing, it was "somewhat disappointing." And police backed off a bad decision "somewhat sheepishly."

Once timid writers start spitting out "somewhat," they usually make it a habit. These three examples are from the same short travel story on a hotel carved from blocks of ice:

> *Hallways in Finland's Snow Castle hotel are wide and tall,* ***somewhat*** *dim and definitely chilly.*

> *. . . in a refined, civilized, technically efficient if* ***somewhat*** *frostbitten way.*

> *Instead, the* ***somewhat*** *dark rooms are suffused with a cool glow from embedded lights.*

Qualifiers seem to beget qualifiers. One writer concluded that a government investigator was not only "somewhat harried" but also "a bit bewildered."

And "a bit" isn't just somewhat common. It's all over the place:

> *The National Academy of Recording Arts and Sciences always has been viewed as stodgy and* ***a bit*** *behind the times when it comes to keeping up with all that is hip in popular music.*

> ***A bit*** *hesitant to face the world without drugs but buoyed by completing the four-week treatment program, Mickie asked his counselor for a hug.*

You can get carried away with the drive to banish qualifiers from your writing, of course. Some assertions need qualification, and sometimes good writers use qualifiers to add ironic understatement. E. B. White, a puckish sort who never took himself too seriously, recognized that when he made "Avoid the Use of Qualifiers" number eight in his influential list of writing rules. "We all should be very watchful of this rule," he added, "for it is a rather important one and we are pretty sure to violate it now and then."

VI. Positive Thinking

One can cure oneself of the "not-un" formation by memorizing this sentence: "A not unblack dog was chasing a not unsmall rabbit across a not ungreen field."
—George Orwell

ON THE PLUS SIDE

One of the basic strategies for forceful writing is to tell 'em what is, rather than what isn't. Choose positive phrasings, in other words, rather than negative constructions. The result is usually crisper, more direct, and easier to understand.

Stand back and listen to this negative construction from a reader's perspective:

> *Conversely, it is not difficult to spot young people who lack self-confidence. . . .*

Then try the positive version: "It's easy to spot insecure young people."

Positive phrasings also have more punch. Here's the negative version:

> *The unidentified woman was added to the list because her body was found near Liles, making it unlikely that the two deaths were unrelated.*

Here's the alternative:

> *Police added the unidentified woman to the list because the killer left her body near Liles, making it likely the two deaths were linked.*

Note that we're not talking about positive versus negative phrasing in the good news/bad news sense of the terms. You don't have to be a sales rep who sees the sunny side of everything. But you want to maximize your impact with clear, direct writing. For all our sakes, please avoid constructions like this:

> *Had they done what we asked, we would not be in the position of not having the information we don't have.*

Now *that's* confusing. How about this paraphrase: "If they'd followed directions, we'd have the information."

The Chapter 4 Cheat Sheet

FIVE WAYS TO ADD OOMPH TO YOUR WRITING

1. **Find action verbs.** Don't define the world; describe it in motion. Verbs such as "to be," "looked," "appeared," and "felt" simply classify things according to other things. ("The sky is blue. The sky looked blue.") Action verbs capture movement and causality. ("The lightning bolt splintered the oak, toppling it into the pond.") Prefer transitive verbs, which transfer action from a subject ("bolt") to an object ("oak"), often with some explicitly stated effect ("toppling it").
2. **Avoid flabby suffixes.** Word endings such as "-able," "-tion," and "-ance" turn lively action words into immovable objects. Why write "He gained entrance into the residence" when you could write "He broke into the house"?
3. **Prefer the active voice.** The voice of the verb determines the way action flows in a sentence, and in the strongest sentences action flows from the subject through the verb to the object. If Jack has a baseball and he hammers it into deep left field, then the active way of describing that act is "Jack hit the ball." The passive voice, on the other hand, begins with the object of the action, follows with the verb, and tacks the actor onto the end of the sentence, if the actor appears at all. "The ball was hit by Jack."
4. **Minimize expletives.** An expletive is not just a curse word, but any term that merely fills a hole in a sentence without carrying any meaning. Common expletives include "there are," "there were," and "it is." Expletives waste space and drain energy; eliminate them when you can. "There were six ducks on the pond" becomes "Six ducks paddled across the pond." "It was dawn" becomes "Dawn broke," or—better yet—"The sun rose."

5. **Be bold**. Wimps spend their lives apologizing. Confident, in-charge types don't equivocate. So avoid little qualifiers such as "somewhat," "rather," and "a little bit." If the boor in the theater seat next to you talked through the entire performance, he was rude. Not *somewhat* rude. Not *rather* rude. Not *a little bit* rude. Just plain rude.

5
Brevity

Let the speech be short, comprehending much in few words.
—*Ecclesiasticus 32:8*

GETTING TO THE SUPERMARKET

Brevity is the handmaiden of force. Long, flabby digressions weaken impact by blurring focus and diverting attention from the core message. So high-impact writers make every word count, shedding verbiage until their central point stands in high relief.

Consider the Gettysburg Address. Or the Twenty-Third Psalm. As Lincoln and the psalmist so beautifully demonstrated, brevity is a means of making words memorable. But determining focus and trimming excess demands hard thinking and sustained effort. Mark Twain once apologized for writing a long letter because he didn't have time to craft a short one.

Writing is a journey. As in other forms of travel, the length of the trip depends on the destination and the route. My parents spent forty years arguing about the best way to reach their favorite supermarket. The store never moved, and they could easily have figured out the shortest route. Only the joy of combat kept them from settling the argument.

Writing is more complicated. The destination shifts from one outing to the next, and you have to build a new route every time. But writing also has its constants. When you set out to write, your destination is always the overall point you want to make. If you're a literary type, that's your theme. If you're in the boardroom or the newsroom, you may call it your focus. In either case, finding it maximizes your impact.

Once you know your destination, you have to figure out your route—the sequence of subtopics or scenes you must pass through to take your reader along with you. Good routes move inexorably closer to the goal, never retracing steps or circling around to visit the same place twice. They avoid traffic, and they seek out shortcuts known only to those familiar with the territory.

In writing, that translates into a mind-set that alerts you when you're tempted to stray from the most direct route. As you learn certain danger signs, you acquire your own mental road crew, helpful guides who pop up and wave red flags when you turn into unnecessary detours.

In my mind, the red flags wave whenever I use an adverb or adjective. They pop up again when I connect two nouns with a conjunction or stack nouns up against each other. Long sentences get me thinking about using a few more periods. Perfect tenses make me wonder if life has to be so complicated.

Brevity, in other words, results from a series of small decisions that follow familiar patterns. They're tricks of the trade, and anybody can learn them.

I. Without One Wasted Word

If you would be pungent, be brief; for it is with words as with sunbeams—the more they are condensed, the deeper they burn.
—Robert Southey

STICKING TO THE POINT

The power of the written word derives largely from the focus it demands of writers. Speech wanders, but the contemplative nature of writing gives time to pare away the irrelevant, leaving a laser-sharp point that penetrates and illuminates. That leads the reader's mind to the same crisp conclusion.

At least that's the hope. Realizing that potential takes steely discipline and intense mental work. What is your point, anyway? How does *this* word or phrase advance your story or your central thesis? Steely discipline and intense mental work are demanding colleagues, and some writers brush them aside in a slapdash rush to meet a deadline or push a piece of writing out of the printer. Consider this lead for a news report:

> *While investigators 500 miles away in Arkansas sought the cause of a casino tour bus crash that killed fourteen Chicago-area travelers and injured sixteen others, grief*

overwhelmed Sunday services at a church on Chicago's South Side yesterday as a community in mourning prayed for victims who had been loved ones and neighbors.

That fifty-three-word beginning overwhelms readers with an excess of detail. What's the heart of what happened? How about this twenty-one-word version?

Grief overwhelmed mourners at a Chicago church yesterday after a casino tour bus crash killed fourteen of their friends and relatives.

Some of the other information included in the original lead is important, too. But it would fit nicely into a second paragraph like this one:

The crash twenty miles north of Memphis also injured another sixteen of the mostly elderly passengers, some critically.

One additional point: Cluttered sentences don't have to be exceptionally long or packed with disparate elements. A living room can be cluttered. So can an alcove. Consider this example:

Bold red and yellow lava layers jut out here and there from the dry, rolling hills, like toys peeking out of piles in a child's sandbox.

The sentence is fairly clean. But does it need "child's"? After all, sandboxes generally serve children. And does "here and there" add all that much? How about "rolling"? Don't most hills roll? Drop those unnecessary elements and you're left with:

Bold red and yellow lava layers jut from the dry hills like toys peeking out of piles in a sandbox.

Of course, it's easy to spot the flab in someone else's work. It's considerably harder to assess the words you've produced yourself and assassinate all the little darlings that stray from your central point. But if you're dispassionate about the process, you're bound to find plenty to cut. Lack of focus plagues all of us, the tight writers along with the loose, the careless along with the vigilant. It creeps into rambling sentences. And it turns up in punchy little packages of wit.

But we owe readers an unceasing effort to eradicate it. When they pick up a piece of writing, be it a memo or a news story or a novel, they generally expect a flow of words that's easy to absorb. One of the writer's first obligations is to deliver just that.

LOST IN A THICKET

Drifting off point not only makes your writing longer than it needs to be, it also can turn your work into a thick, forbidding bramble. *Density* affects the way readers react to your writing, too. Cram too much into your sentences and paragraphs, and you increase density beyond the level that readers can easily comprehend.

The basic tactic for avoiding that pitfall is to limit each sentence to one main idea. No experienced writer will be absolutely bound by that old grammar school maxim, of course. Sentences containing lists, interjections, and subordinate clauses are essential tools of communication. But no accomplished writer will clog a sentence with a lot of underbrush, either.

Unfortunately, we're sometimes caught between a natural desire to avoid excess density and a powerful drive to unload everything as soon as we begin writing. But when we dump everything in the road all at once, we create a barrier that blocks the reader's progress into the body of whatever we've written.

Journalists are frequent offenders. Note this paragraph from a football game story:

> *Musgrave threw for 443 yards and three touchdowns and scored once himself on a third-period keeper as the Ducks launched what they hope will be another bowl season with a forty-two to twenty-one victory over the Aztecs before 35,118 noisy fans in Autzen stadium.*

All the information contained in the sentence belongs *somewhere* in the story. But does it all belong in a single sentence? The fact that the University of Oregon Ducks were hoping for another bowl invitation, for example, has little to do with the fact that the fans at this game were noisy.

The sentence contains at least ten separate ideas, some of them only marginally related. That's a long way from the one main concept that's supposed to underlie each sentence, and it's not a tactic that's likely to attract many readers.

II. Cutting the Flab

I believe more in the scissors than I do the pencil.
—Truman Capote

SHARPENING YOUR AX

Most old-timers in my part of the country—the Pacific Northwest—have seen a skilled logger fell a tree the old way. The axman takes one smooth, flat stroke. Then another elegant, economical arc on the down cut, and a wedge the size of a logger's lunch pail falls from the trunk. A few more efficient strokes and the tree topples exactly where the logger wants it.

Contrast the city slicker who thrashes the tree with a dull blade, scattering tiny chips. If the tree gives up before the exhausted fool hacking at it, it falls randomly, threatening any bystanders still in the vicinity.

Skilled writers cut through their material with the easy athleticism of an experienced logger. But writers who clog their prose with redundancy thrash around like an amateur with an ax. They may batter their way to their destination eventually. But by then nobody cares.

Such redundancy falls into several predictable forms, and writers with pride in their craft will be on the alert for them. Half the battle is staying relaxed, alert, and focused.

Surely no one who was concentrating could have written the published reference to "a rap singer who performed a sexually explicit song about sex." And surely a copy editor was dozing when Knight Ridder's wire service released a story that mentioned a "random lottery" and the "random chance discovery of a shipwreck."

Some redundancies are so well known that they've become code phrases readers recognize as a sign of carelessness or amateurism. I've seen letters of condescending complaint from readers, and if you want to avoid the same contempt, you'll steer clear of "reason why," "final destination," "final resolution," and "final results."

You'll avoid less common but equally obvious redundancies, too, unlike the editors who allowed the reference to "150-room palaces gilded with golden walls" to find its way into print. You'll be particularly careful with adjectives, which all too often duplicate meaning already in their antecedent noun. You won't write of a "broad array" because you'll recognize that arrays are broad by nature. And surely you won't write about "ski runs that share a common denominator" or ethnic groups that don't even "share a common alphabet" as though sharing could involve something other than common experience. Nor will you commit abominations such as "mutually agreed upon" as though mutuality and agreement were different qualities.

Not all redundancies are so obvious. But a moment's thought should unravel the claim that "more and more incest survivors are defying the taboo as never before," or discourage mention of "the first visual sighting" of a volcanic eruption on a remote Alaska island.

With the same ineptitude, many writers add automatic adverbs, which they use to prop up verbs perfectly capable of standing on their own. "Off," "up," and "out" are frequent offenders. They write of "freeing up" space, when they could simply free it. They report that a fire "swallowed up" expensive homes. They describe an elephant tusk capped with teakwood as "capped off" with teakwood. The tide "ebbs out" as they "plan out" the schedule for the coming fall.

Some of the most common excess adverbs deal with time. Tense tells the whole story. But something compels careless writers to add an unnecessary "formerly" or "currently," as in the description of a businessman who "formerly used his helicopter to help police fight crime," or the man who "formerly was president and chief executive officer of Graphics Arts Center." Simply noting that the businessman used his helicopter or that the man was president does the trick, with no "formerly" required.

Of course, the title "president and chief executive officer" suggests that the business world builds redundancy into much of its basic vocabulary. That's part of a larger pattern. Consider this description of a young man with a genetic disease: "Day by day, Brossard's muscles continue to weaken." Or a new breed of food-bank client: "Mill workers who have never before sought a dime's worth of public assistance in their lives."

Watch out for "in the past," too. Like one-word adverbs, it seldom adds anything not contained in the tense of the verb. What does it contribute in these sentences? "The station has often exaggerated casualty figures in the past." "The twenty-third tourney isn't as exciting as some have been in the past."

ONCE IS ENOUGH

When they polish their drafts, experienced writers pay attention to certain warning signs. They're particularly alert to coordinating conjunctions, which often connect redundancies. "And," "or," "for," "nor," and "but" are special offenders, with "and" the worst of the lot.

Frankel hopes the public dialogue will move beyond outrage **and** *anger.*

The marketing department has submitted several interesting ideas **and** *concepts.*

Proceeds will go to mass transit, intercollegiate athletics, and to keep **and** *retain university faculty.*

Anger encompasses outrage, and outrage is built on anger. An idea is a concept and vice versa. You keep that which you retain. So what does a writer gain by mentioning both elements?

BORING BEGINNINGS

Beginnings matter, and human beings naturally pay special attention to them. Great ceremony attends births, marriages, and the opening pitch of baseball season. But some writers carry their interest in beginnings way past any point of reader interest. They dwell on the beginning to the exclusion of the action that follows.

Let's say you write "He began to run toward the bow of the ship," rather than "He ran toward the bow." "Began to" is a useless bit of information that adds nothing to the main verb. "Ran," on the other hand, represents lively action much more likely to capture the attention of your readers.

Note how much stronger each of these examples would have been had the writer put the beginning aside and moved right into the business at hand:

Suddenly, the room began to shake.

("Suddenly, the room shook.")

He was flying from Minneapolis to Detroit when the plane began to have engine problems and crash-landed on the highway.

(". . . when the plane had engine problems and crash-landed . . .")

We're beginning to wrestle with the new emission regulations.

("We're wrestling with the new emission regulations.")

THINK ABOUT IT

*The city **currently licenses** 261 taxicabs. . . .*

We often hang adverbs relating to time on verbs that already say it all because of their tense. If the city licenses 261 cabs, then it currently licenses 261 cabs.

*"Research on obesity is at an exciting **point in time**," said Henry Lardy of the University of Wisconsin in Madison.*

"Point in time" dates back to the Richard Nixon crooks club and has typified bureaucratese ever since. Sure, the offending phrase appears in a quotation here. But what's so great about the quote? Why not paraphrase?

*Too bad because what running really offers is the **single most** immediate and beneficial fitness paycheck on the market.*

If it's the biggest, it's the single biggest. Or the biggest single. Or the single most. You avoid a whole class of redundancies if you avoid modifying superlatives.

*A string quartet played **various** selections of classical music.*

"Various" seldom serves any useful purpose. If the quartet played selections, it played various selections. And don't string quartets usually play classical music?

*. . . leaving many survivors living in **virtual** squalor.*

What's the difference between virtual squalor and squalor?

*Given the fact that there have been **death threats on his life**. . . .*

Aren't most death threats on lives?

*. . . Sanchez was shot in the chest, then **ran away on foot**.*

As opposed to running away on what? Roller skates?

. . . detective Philip Marlowe becomes involved with a ***rich heiress. . . .***

And he'd be well advised to avoid poor heiresses.

. . . this ***rugged, isolated mountainous region . . .***

Mountainous regions are by definition rugged, and most are isolated.

But only a ***pale shadow*** *of that bill . . . ever made it to the floor.*

Isn't it safe to assume that a shadow is paler than the original?

. . . grass-seed farmers argued that more limits would ***economically damage*** *their industry.*

Well, maybe the farmers are worried about damage to their reputations. But it's probably safe to conclude that the damage they're really worried about is economic.

Things quickly ***mushroomed.***

Yes, and they probably sprinted rapidly after cowering fearfully. Don't insult a perfectly good verb by making it carry a modifier that duplicates the meaning it conveys.

Longtime retailer Tom Peterson, whose crewcut and smiling face is a ***familiar fixture****, became the new owner of Stereo Super Stores on Thursday.*

If you're longtime, you're a fixture. If you're a fixture, you're familiar.

. . . even if he and his four-legged chicken never make the big time, the ***future looks bright ahead****.*

The future usually is ahead somewhere. Futures usually seem to be bright, too. This is another way of saying that "bright future" is a cliché.

. . . that the ***main thrust*** *of the program was offensive.*

A thrust is main. So is a focus. Or a consensus. Or a theme. None needs modification.

> *From his* **small cubbyhole** *office, he oversaw operations. . . .*

A large cubbyhole would be worth remark. Let's also keep that in mind when we write about small villages and tiny hamlets.

> *A fiber-optic switching device* **interconnects** *huge computers at the Supercomputing '93 conference. . . .*

If something interconnects, it connects. So "connects" is all that's necessary. Ditto with words such as "interlinked" and "intermix."

> *Mount Rainier the largest volcano in the Cascade Range, last* **experienced an eruption** *about 150 years ago.*

So why does the pilot say, "We may experience slight turbulence," instead of just saying that "it's going to get rough"? And why does the warranty for your toaster say, "Should you experience difficulty with this appliance, please return it to one of the dealers listed below"? Surely there's a more direct way of telling you what to do if the damned thing breaks. Couldn't we just write that "Mount Rainier last erupted 150 years ago"? "Erupt" is a beautiful verb, oozing with the power of the process it describes. Why downgrade it to a noun—"eruption"—that the reader merely "experiences"?

III. Modifiers under the Microscope

It took me my whole life to learn what not to play.
—Dizzy Gillespie

BETTER LEFT UNSAID

As a young reporter I covered a drowning in a rural swimming hole. A swift-flowing creek formed the pool, I wrote, when it plunged into a rocky pit "surrounded by steep, vertical cliffs." That line haunts me to this day. What is a cliff if not steep? And isn't vertical about as steep as you can get? For a professional writer, repeating yourself so baldly is a sign of inattention, inexperience, or incompetence—or perhaps all three.

Most experienced writers know that a carefully chosen noun beats a careless adjective-noun combo any day. As E. B. White said, "The adjective hasn't been born yet that can pull a noun out of a tight spot." So the careful writer describes a "saunter," rather than a "slow, casual walk." She chooses "abyss" instead of "bottomless pit." She opts for "rage" over "out-of-control anger." And if she writes "cliffs," she's satisfied with that.

Not that a well-chosen adjective can't sometimes enhance a bare-bones noun. Bill Blundell is a master of the well-chosen modifier. He once described a row of cowboys sitting along an old bunkhouse porch in "rump-sprung chairs." He portrayed a hefty Havasupai Indian standing in the wind as "a great billowing woman in a print dress."

The writers who produced these examples aren't in Blundell's league:

The butterfly looks lost in this ***dry desert****.*

What's a desert if not dry? Would we write of wet oceans or damp mud?

The ***end result*** *is pain without resolution. . . .*

There was no similarity in the finishes, but the ***end result*** *was the same Wednesday as Atlanta and Toronto won berths in the World Series.*

A result is—by definition—an end.

The state's persistent drought has turned grass and forest land into ***parched tinderboxes****.*

My dictionary defines "tinder" as "dry, easily flammable material." Such material is also, presumably, "parched."

When their ***former construction business failed*** *six years ago . . .*

Was it a former business when it failed?

Angela decided her house's birthday party would be open to everyone in the neighborhood as well as her ***personal friends****.*

Heaven protect us from impersonal friends.

> *Sternberg . . . is not the first to challenge the* **standard orthodoxy** *regarding intelligence. . . .*

Back to the dictionary, which defines "orthodox" as "conforming to the usual beliefs or established doctrines . . . approved or conventional." All of which sounds fairly standard.

> *The extreme dry air of Mongolia's Gobi desert preserves* **ancient fossils** *extraordinarily well.*

The recent fossils, on the other hand, don't fare so well.

> *The vouchers entitle panhandlers to* **basic necessities**.

Hmmmm. These vouchers must be different from the ones that entitle panhandlers to less basic necessities, such as brie and chardonnay.

> *Russians saw the election as a* **key milestone**.

Which is a good thing. We often let the insignificant milestones slip right by.

> *. . . others* **lingered behind**. . . .

As opposed to lingering ahead?

> *To NASA's surprise, the critical wiring job took less time* **than expected**.

An expected surprise would, of course, be no surprise at all.

Such screwups appear often enough in print to suggest that most writers could do a better job of questioning every word and eliminating a healthy percentage of them. You might try thinking of your rough draft as a pack you're about to carry on a fifty-mile hike. Some items are essential. But everything you can leave behind will make the trip a lot easier.

Barely Visible

If the best modifiers create specific images, it follows that the worst fade into meaningless abstraction. Instead of lighting up their nouns and adverbs, they drag them into the shadows. That's the problem with higher-order abstractions such as "patriotic," "beautiful," "generous," or "caring." And that's why writing teachers tell their students to "show, don't tell."

When it comes to abstract modifiers, one of the worst is "very." It has some value in rare instances, but most of us would be better off never using the word again. If it shows up on your screen, make a fast move to the delete key.

It all came down to some ***very*** *soggy dirt.*

I'm ***very*** *anxious to hear your reply.*

EMBARRASSING ADVERBS

Stephen King, who writes some of the leanest, hardest-working sentences around, reveals the secrets of his style in *On Writing*, his autobiographical guide to the craft. In it, he expresses a particular horror of unnecessary adverbs. As he rewrites, he scrutinizes every adverb, discarding all but the essential.

So you'll never find his work marred by any of these constructions:

The arrow entered his eye and ***penetrated through*** *the back of his skull.*

If it penetrates, it's through.

Today the town is ***filled to capacity****. . . .*

. . . who sat in the courtroom, which was ***packed to capacity*** *with her supporters.*

If it's filled, it's filled. Could it be filled—or packed—to less than capacity?

He ***linked them together*** *in a nine-room Victorian mansion as the perennial murder suspects in the classic game "Clue."*

The two are ***bound together*** *by a common thought. . . .*

A new coach and new players are ***blending together*** *. . .*

If you're linked, bound, or blended, you're about as together as you can get, short of sex. Less extreme examples of the same principle include "gather together" and "join together."

. . . and that would ***free up*** *more federal old-growth timber sales for log-hungry mills. . . .*

. . . which he already has ***filled up*** *for this season.*

We attach "up" to all kinds of verbs that need no help. "Free up." "Climb up." "Divvy up." "Divide up."

If these candidates persist in ***dodging around*** *this issue . . .*

"Around" wastes almost as much total space as "up." If you dodge something, you're moving around it—by definition.

David Tuckness, a technician with Morrison First Alert Professional Security Systems, ***tests out*** *the burglar alarm. . . .*

And he probably climbed up a ladder to do it.

IV. Creeping Nouns

A sentence should contain no unnecessary words, a paragraph no unnecessary sentences, for the same reason that a drawing should have no unnecessary lines and a machine no unnecessary parts.
—William Strunk

ON LITTLE CAT FEET

Military strategists raise red flags about "mission creep," a phrase that refers to a gradual expansion of goals that turns a simple expedition into an unmanageable mess. William Zinsser condemns "creeping nouns," referring to the way new nouns keep attaching themselves to perfectly good nouns that were doing fine on their own. "Situation" attaches itself to "crisis," yielding "crisis situation." "Conditions" joins "weather," producing "weather conditions." "Event" gloms onto "sales," resulting in a "sales event." But the phrases that replace the original nouns add nothing but dead weight. Like a Boy Scout who offers to help Usain Bolt across the street, they serve only to slow things down.

If we could eliminate unnecessary use of "situation," "field," and "condition," we would probably eliminate half the creeping nouns published. But not all. This particular redundancy is sneaky. We write, for example, about a basketball player "battling the effects of a cold," rather than simply "battling a cold." We report "a nationwide roundup of Bloods and Crips members," rather than a "roundup of Bloods and Crips." We pass along a bureaucrat's remark that an investigation was "nearing the completion phase," rather than paraphrasing to report that it was "about finished." We note that "private forests have been closed in dry summer and fall periods," rather than simply saying that the woods were closed when dry.

Note how removing the creeping noun from each of the following examples strengthens it:

activity

. . . and one source said the Cincinnati Reds manager faces a possible suspension for gambling ***activities****.*

concerns

. . . "retirement resorts" where the emphasis is on active lifestyles but provisions are made for residents' eventual health-care ***concerns****.*

conditions

Officials are saying the combination of millions of dying trees, the seventh year of drought ***conditions*** *and . . .*

We hiked out safely, but the second party became lost in the whiteout ***conditions****.*

event

Nuclear engineers fear the possibility of a meltdown event at the nuclear power plant.

Announcing our autumn sales ***event****.*

experience

. . . a relaxed holiday shopping ***experience****.*

facilities

A canoeist gave Butler a ride to the search area from shore because there were no dock ***facilities*** *nearby.*

field/industry/profession

Most American companies are paying on the average of 12 percent of their annual payroll to finance programs in the ***fields*** *of health care, education, housing, and youth development. . . .*

I entered the teaching ***field*** *four years ago at the age of 35.*

Note: Watch out for "field" when it is attached to the name of any occupation or profession. "Journalism field." "Legal field." "Plumbing field." And beware of "industry" or "profession" or any other term used in the same sense:

He's sixty years old and spent a long and productive career in the banking ***industry****.*

Bozzelli, a former Washington attorney, left the legal ***profession*** *to become a Catholic priest.*

situation

. . . but apparently Carlesimo isn't sure he can be trusted in a pressure packed playoff ***situation****.*

Small children can often acquire hepatitis A in day-care ***situations****.*

status

A soft-spoken man who achieved national celebrity ***status*** *. . .*

PERFECT SENSE

Effective writers stick to the most direct verb tenses possible, using simple past or present whenever they can and reserving perfect tenses for situations that demand them. They'll recast sentences to avoid blitzing readers with auxiliary verbs.

Note the suggested revisions for each of the following published sentences:

Goryachova has survived a criminal libel suit brought by the mayor of Berdyansk for her reporting on the firing of a hospital administrator who ***had backed*** *one of the mayor's political rivals.*

(". . . who *backed* one of the mayor's political rivals.")

> *Tom Imeson . . . said* **it has been difficult** *to get a solid vote count.*

("Tom Imeson said it *was difficult* . . .")

> *They* **were bouncing** *around on the deck behind the house, singing and dancing as if it was a stage.*

("They *bounced* around . . . as if it were a stage.")

The Chapter 5 Cheat Sheet

FIVE WAYS TO TIGHTEN YOUR WRITING

Anything that doesn't contribute to a piece of writing detracts from it. So create the strongest possible prose by eliminating everything that isn't essential.

1. **Question everything.** Read slowly through your draft, mentally dropping every word, phrase, and clause. If cutting a word sacrifices no meaning, cut it. If cutting a word sacrifices only a tad of meaning unessential to your main point, cut that, too. Pay particular attention to the words or phrases on either side of conjunctions such as "and," "or," and "but." Do you really need "color" *and* "tint"?
2. **Make each modifier work.** Make your modifiers specific. Instead of writing that the chair was "worn," say it was "rump-sprung." Drop modifiers that repeat meaning already conveyed by their nouns or verbs. Do you need to write that your character "slowly ambled" down the aisle, or does "ambled" do the job?
3. **Don't overfill.** Limit most of your sentences to one or two main ideas. Excessively dense writing intimidates readers and adds unnecessary length.
4. **Kill creeping nouns.** Never use two nouns when one will do. It's not a "sales event," it's a "sale." And a "crisis" is much more urgent than a "crisis situation."
5. **Avoid complicated tenses.** Simple past and present tenses can drive most writing. Elaborate perfect tenses bog the action down. Why write "he was skiing down the hill" when "he skied down the hill" does the job without the auxiliary verb?

6
Clarity

Good prose is like a window pane.
—George Orwell

A CLEAR VIEW

Like a clean window, the best writing disappears into the foreground, calling no attention to itself and offering an unobstructed view of what lies beyond. No sentence should ever force a second reading, unless captivating writing demands another pass for the sheer joy of it.

Even Einstein's explanations of special relativity—the ordinary English versions rather than the mathematical—are accessible to any educated reader. And Lincoln Barnett's wonderful book on Einstein (*The Universe and Doctor Einstein*) is simplicity itself.

Writers who confuse their readers haven't yet mastered their material. They need to do more hard thinking, more sorting and rearranging and refining before daring to appear before readers with the written word.

I. Empathy

If any man were to ask me what I would suppose to be a perfect style of language, I would answer, that in which a man speaking to five hundred people, of all common and various capacities, idiots or lunatics excepted, should be understood by them all, and in the same sense which the speaker intended to be understood.
—Daniel Defoe

IN THE READER'S SHOES

Clear writing requires empathy. The ability to see things from the reader's viewpoint determines whether a message gets through or not.

At a fundamental level, all writers are merely in the business of moving symbols. Every day millions of them fill computer screens with zillions of squiggles and dots. Then they punch "send" and those symbols zip across the planet at the speed of light.

But meaning is in people, not in symbols. By themselves, all those arbitrary squiggles and dots mean nothing. They acquire meaning only through the individual lives of the receivers into whose awareness they ultimately pass.

Think about the way a child acquires language. "Ball," says her mother, holding up a rubber sphere. "Ball, ball, ball." She links the object with the sound, over and over. Gradually, the child learns that the sound—the symbol—signifies the object. The sound has acquired meaning, and the meaning is in the child's head. It's the accumulated memory of all the times the symbol has been associated with the object.

Then the child's father presents her with a football. "Ball," he says, despite the different shape, texture, and color. The meaning attached to the symbol broadens as the child's life experience broadens. She learns about tennis balls, golf balls, wrecking balls, and military balls. She learns to substitute the written symbol for the spoken one. Eventually, she's equipped with the basics she needs to read a sports story.

But the boy next door will have a slightly different experience. His life will inevitably link the same symbol with another collection of objects, some the same and some different. When he encounters the same symbol, his internal reaction will vary just a little from his neighbor's.

The more alike two people are, the more their experiences will overlap, and the more similar their associations with any given symbol. For common symbols, which may be linked to familiar objects many times every day, the meaning is, for all practical purposes, the same. Longtime married couples share meanings so rich and so parallel that just a few symbols can convey worlds. The two might make plans for an entire evening with little more than grunts.

Figure 3 depicts such a pair. The circles represent the total of their experiences, the entire range of remembered associations available to them. The Xs represent symbols. Assume that A sends a message to B. If he crafts his message from the symbols that occur in the area of overlap between the circles, he'll communicate effectively. The symbol will produce the same reaction in

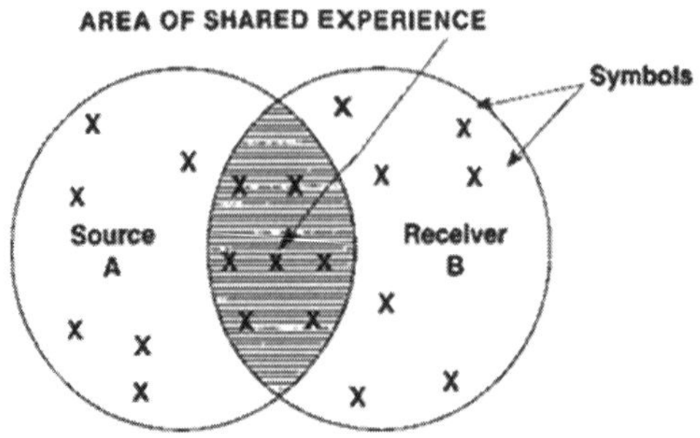

Figure 3. Communication between a source and a receiver with similar backgrounds

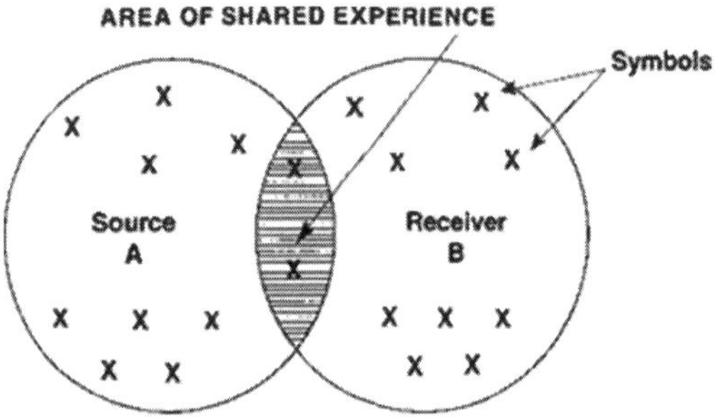

Figure 4. Communication between a source and a receiver with extremely different backgrounds

the receiver as the one intended by the sender. But if he picks a symbol that exists in his realm of experience and not in B's, he's in trouble. A skier won't get far talking to a flatlander about stem christies and moguls.

Anybody trying to communicate with someone from a less similar background faces more of a challenge. Figure 4 illustrates the basic problem. Fewer Xs fall in the area of overlap. So the sender has less chance of picking a symbol with a meaning similar to the one intended. A stockbroker and a rancher may get the same general idea when they hear the word "ball." But their reactions to "bull" may be completely different. And a science-fiction writer will think one thing on hearing "alien," while an immigration agent thinks quite another.

The chances that a message will go awry soar when you start factoring more receivers into the equation. Figure 5 illustrates this principle. Every time you add a circle, you reduce the area of overlap. Mass communication reduces the overlap to a minimum—thousands of circles overlapping in just one tiny area. That's one of the reasons communication researchers have found the mass media so feeble when it comes to changing audience attitudes.

Almost all news writers have had personal experience with the problem. A reader calls to complain about a story, and the writer is flabbergasted by

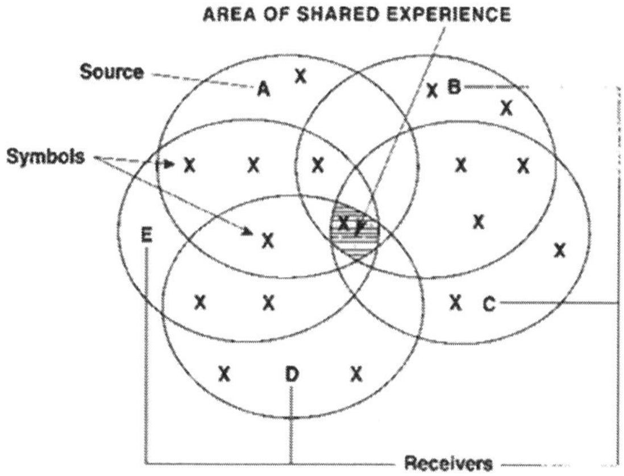

Figure 5. Mass communication between a single source and many receivers

the way that reader has interpreted the copy. The two might as well be talking about completely different stories.

Less thoughtful writers blame readers for such misinterpretations. "That's not what the story means," they say. "How could anybody be so stupid?" A natural-enough reaction. But it overlooks the principle that meaning is in people, not in symbols. The writer carries full responsibility for picking symbols that will elicit similar meanings among all—or at least most—of her readers. Pick an X, in other words, that falls in that overlapping area of experience.

You develop the ability to do the job by getting out in the world and learning how others live. You can't communicate in a vacuum. If you aren't familiar with the environment in which your readers will receive a message, you can't be sure how they'll interpret the symbols you send.

You should always be able to manage some communication, no matter how different the receiver. All human beings share some overlapping experience. A smile or a clenched fist means much the same everywhere, and most audiences will have reasonably similar responses to a large number of signs and symbols. The key is using empathy to find the common ground.

MISSING THE MARK

One of the quickest ways a writer can confuse and alienate an audience is with a vocabulary that falls outside the readers' ken. Word choice is a test of the writer's empathy.

It's easy to go wrong. We develop an old-shoe familiarity with our individual worlds, taking our surroundings—and the language we use to describe them—entirely for granted. When we're talking with someone face-to-face, a blank stare alerts us when we stray into confusing language that describes unshared experience. But the written word seldom offers such feedback. All too often, we toss out references likely to go right over the heads of the readers we'd most like to reach:

> *Dave O'Roke smoked his first joint when he was twelve. By the time he was sixteen, he was selling marijuana and crank.*

Most readers probably know that a marijuana cigarette is called a joint. But crank? The world of methamphetamine addiction—and the lingo that goes with it—is alien to much of the population. Words such as "crank" can add color and authenticity to stories. And you wouldn't want to insult readers who know what they mean by defining them directly. Use the true name and then slip 'em the slang: "He was selling marijuana and methamphetamine. But weed and crank . . ."

> *The recommended daily allowance of protein is .8 grams of protein per kilogram (2.2 pounds) of body weight.*

Yeah? So how much should I eat? Most Americans know their weight in pounds, not kilos. For that matter, few Americans would be able to visualize a gram of protein. How about telling readers how much steak or lean hamburger or peanut butter a 130-pound woman would need to meet the daily allowance? Most readers could extrapolate from that.

> *Moscow Goes on 5 Billion Ruble Spending Spree*

How much is 5 billion rubles? That's not within the ken of most American readers. What's it worth in dollars? How many mobile phones or SUVs or whatever we're familiar with will it buy?

Loose Ends

Writers who communicate effectively make sure they express themselves in terms familiar to readers. The same kind of empathy leads them to anticipate a typical reader's questions. They know where readers are coming from. They know where readers are going. They sense what readers must know to get from one place to the other.

But all of us sometimes get too wrapped up in our subject or our own point of view. That's when obvious loose ends break free from the fabric of what we've written, frustrating readers who find that they've finished a passage with more questions than answers. For example:

> *Stored in the cavernous belly of the world's second-largest cargo plane was . . .*

Whenever you refer to the second-largest anything, you can be confident readers will want to know what's largest.

> *When a new WTD Industries Inc. mill opens in Tillamook next May each worker will make 1 million board feet of lumber studs. That's equal to the amount of lumber used in building 100 single-family houses. . . .*

The reference to one hundred houses was a nice touch. But was the writer talking one million board feet in a day, week, month, year, or lifetime?

> *Kramer, then 26, took eight months of lessons from Volodya, as his friends called him (out of earshot).*

What's "Volodya" mean? Why would Vladimir Horowitz, the musician in question, object to the term?

> *"This site merits high consideration because of the many factors of location and topographic features."*

Just because the speaker spouted some planner jargon doesn't mean he said anything. What's so great about the location? And what's this business about topographic features? Does that mean the site is flat?

> *Veterans Affairs Secretary Edward Derwinski apologized for using a derogatory reference to Hispanics during a campaign stop for a Republican congressional candidate.*

Shades of Earl Butz, the secretary of agriculture who resigned in 1976 after telling a racially charged joke. Hardly anybody would publish the joke, and Butz left Gerald Ford's cabinet under a mysterious cloud.

So what did Derwinski say? When a member of the cabinet—on a campaign trip, no less—says something that demands an apology, readers should know what it was. If editors determine that it's too profane to print in a newspaper, then the reporter can paraphrase.

II. Context

An ounce of example is worth a pound of generalities.
—Henry James

COMPARED WITH WHAT?

Once upon a time, the vast majority of news reports consisted of bare facts listed in descending order of importance. But as the world grew more complicated reporters came to realize that what the daily blizzard of facts *meant* was even more important than the fact that they existed.

Now first-rate reporting often contains substantial context. A good news story, according to this approach, draws connections in a way that helps explain the world. Understanding flows from seeing how what happens in one time or place is related to what happens in other times and places.

That kind of context helps keep the news from overwhelming readers, and it's just as important in reports produced outside of journalism. Jumbles of unconnected facts can make someone feel helpless and confused. Providing "a context that gives them meaning," as the influential Hutchins Commission on Freedom of the Press recommended back in 1947, makes the world more manageable.

You can place material in context via a variety of strategies:

CONTEXT IN TIME

Note how a little history adds meaning to an article on Sakhalin Island, a remote outpost off the Siberian coast. To stress the surprising extent of change on the Russian island, which is in the midst of a cultural renaissance, this writer began by looking backward:

> *Historians say life was so bad on Sakhalin Island, a czarist penal colony in the 1800s, that Siberian labor camps seem tame by comparison. . . . "Everyone wants to*

escape from here—the convicts, the settlers, and the officials," said Gen. Konovich, military governor of Sakhalin, in 1890.

CONTEXT IN SPACE

If you consider time a vertical line reaching from the past into the future, then space is a multitude of horizontal lines reaching out across the present. Context in time enriches meaning by comparing what is to what was or what might be. Context in space enriches meaning by comparing the thing at hand to similar things elsewhere.

A financial officer who's writing about marketing costs for one of her company's products, for example, probably will want to compare her company's costs to those for competing products. A fashion writer might compare current styles in New York, London, and Paris. A civic activist might compare the local parks budget with the amounts similar cities spend on parks. A report on methamphetamine describes how it has spread across the globe:

> *Methamphetamine addiction has plagued the West for three decades, but it barely existed in the East until a few years ago. In the meantime, however, the problem has reached significant levels in India, Mexico, and other parts of the Third World.*

CONTEXT BY CATEGORY

Another way of expanding meaning with context is to draw other examples from the same category. Movie reviewers often use the technique, which gives their readers a good idea of how a new film might compare with something familiar. For example:

> *It's rare to see a war film you can truthfully label poignant. But* The Last Full Measure *combines the heart-pounding excitement of* 1917 *with the emotional honesty of* Saving Private Ryan. . . .

You can describe many categories numerically, too. Averages or statistics that describe the larger class to which something belongs are what the statisticians call parameters:

> *Some form of lottery is run in thirty-two states . . . with a total of about sixty-five percent of the population.*

III. Readability

I'll explain, and I'll use small words so you'll be sure to understand, you warthog-faced buffoon.
—Wesley, speaking to the king in The Princess Bride

WRITING TO BE READ

Early in Jonathan Franzen's writing career, a reader sent him a letter: "She began," he remembers, "by listing thirty fancy words and phrases from my novel, words like 'diurnality' and 'antipodes,' phrases like 'electropointillist Santa Claus faces.' She then posed the dreadful question: 'Who is it that you are writing for? It surely could not be the average person who just enjoys a good read.'"

Oops.

But Franzen could have avoided that long-ago embarrassment if he'd known about readability testing. These days most word-processing programs contain a readability application, and you can Google "readability" and access a dozen or so readability tests. Most of them include a Flesch-Kincaid readability score, which is derived from writing characteristics such as word and sentence length. Such scores are often expressed in grade levels. The Flesch-Kincaid for this chapter is nine, meaning that a ninth grader, concentrating hard, can understand it.

In fact, most of us prefer reading that's a couple of grade levels under our top level of schooling. So this chapter should be comfortable reading for anyone who's reached the junior year of high school.

Most writers with Flesch-Kincaid scores of ten or less can engage a large, diverse audience. But hardly any bother to check their scores. That's partly because of ignorance and partly because of prejudice. Most writers just don't know that readability is so easy to measure. Others resent the idea that they should be writing at what they regard as ninth- or tenth-grade level. They think readability tests are a mechanism for dumbing down their writing.

They don't understand that readable writing may be simple, but it isn't necessarily simplistic. Clear, direct writing produces the lowest scores. Simple, widely understood words score better than jargon and gobbledygook. Good readability scores, in other words, reflect some basic traits of good writing.

Critics of readability research often assume that higher scores signal an elevated approach. To write for college graduates, in other words, you should aim at a readability level of sixteen. But a score of sixteen simply means that college grads can understand the copy—it doesn't guarantee that it will engage them. Readers don't always have the energy or inclination to tackle writing that demands intense concentration.

Besides, nothing says that clean, readable writers can't deal with complex subjects. The *Wall Street Journal* manages its daily reporting on the twists and turns of the American economy with an average readability score of eleven.

Most of the best writers I worked with, reporters who won national awards and produced lots of positive reader response, write at Flesch-Kincaid levels of ten or less. Tom Hallman, a Pulitzer Prize winner, usually scored about seven.

Not that readability formulas offer any magic measure of written style. Writing is an art, not a science, and you can't judge its effect via mathematics or with machines. You could write pure nonsense that would score well on a readability test. "'Twas brillig and the slithy toves / Did gyre and gimble in the wabe," the first sentence in Lewis Carroll's "Jabberwocky," scores a four.

Readability may not be the same thing as meaning. But that doesn't mean it's meaningless.

MEET THE PERIOD

A newsroom legend tells of a young, new reporter who flooded the city desk with long, flowery stories. His sentences warmed up slowly, curled around a long phrase or two, eventually ambled up to a weak verb, then trailed off in a thicket of subordinate clauses.

The cigar-chomping city editor (in those days city editors were always cigar-chomping, desk-thumping, and whiskey-swigging) bellowed across the newsroom, summoning the cub. While the kid sat trembling before him, the old curmudgeon rolled a sheet of copy paper into his typewriter and began pounding away with one finger. Eventually he filled the page and handed it to the newbie. It was completely covered with black dots.

"Here," he said. "We call those periods. We have lots of them around the newsroom. Use all you want. Anytime you run out, just come on back and I'll give you some more."

The apocryphal city editor had a point. All the major readability formulas include sentence length as one element in overall readability. Paula LaRocque, formerly the writing coach at the *Dallas Morning News*, urges that writers hold average sentence length to twenty-three words.

That's average sentence length, mind you. LaRocque also notes that the best writers vary sentence lengths, creating a pleasing mix of long, midrange, and short sentences.

Short, punchy sentences are particularly important to summary leads, which should stress a single strong idea. Note how a period or two—along with the minor modifications needed to produce complete sentences—would have improved clarity in each of these examples:

> *Spurred by those complaints and a formal petition filed more than two years ago by environmental group Bluewater Network of San Francisco, EPA finally, reluctantly, is considering the first change since 1984 in how it calculates the fuel-economy numbers pasted on new vehicles.*

> *Supporters of continued commonwealth status for Puerto Rico defeated those who wanted statehood in a vote Sunday that turned back the strongest movement this century for full union with Washington.*

IV. Writing with the Reader in Mind

A writer's style should not place obstacles between his ideas and the minds of his readers.
—Steve Allen

DEFINING YOUR TERMS

Clear writing relies on conversational English. So writers who write to *express*—rather than to *impress*—seldom have to pause for definitions. But the most conscientious communicator occasionally must include a word unfamiliar to some readers. That calls for a definition. Dewitt Reddick, the University of Texas journalism professor who wrote a classic book on science writing, says that a good definition contains at least two of three basic elements.

1. A reference to the larger class of things to which the defined object belongs
2. An explanation of how the thing defined differs from other members of the larger class
3. An illustration

Let's say you want to define "wallaby." You might say that a wallaby is (1) a kangaroo that's (2) generally smaller than the large gray and red kangaroos most Americans think of when they imagine kangaroos, and that (3) most wallabies stand about as tall as a fire hydrant.

Most journalistic definitions are briefer. A reference to my city's articulated buses, for example, as "the ones that bend in the middle," places the articulated variety in the larger category of buses and explains what sets them apart. A reference to the tiny keyboards on handheld computers as having keys "comparable to Chicklets" accomplishes the entire definition with an illustration.

Still, some arcane terms slip into print with no explanation. In a news story on the Supreme Court's decision to ban race as a consideration in jury selection, for example, the reporter quoted Justice Clarence Thomas's warning that the decision "inexorably will lead to the elimination of peremptory strikes." But what's a peremptory strike? Nowhere did the report even hint at the legal meaning of the phrase.

Reddick's formula would have rescued readers from that confusion. A peremptory strike, according to that three-part recipe for definitions, is (1) a lawyer's motion to dismiss a potential juror from a case (2) without any stated cause. And, we might add, (3) some prosecutors have been accused of using peremptory strikes to make sure that Black jurors don't judge Black defendants. And, conversely, some defense lawyers have been accused of using peremptory strikes to make sure that Black jurors don't judge White defendants.

GOOD EXAMPLES

When you can't find a way around a term that's known only to a narrow slice of society, it's time for a definition that clarifies the new concept by comparing it to something found in almost every household. One of the first reports back from a huge tanker spill in Alaska described the crude oil fouling beaches there as "the texture of mayonnaise."

But the writer who noted that "an adult Clydesdale can stand as tall as nineteen hands" probably left most readers shaking their heads. Measuring according to hands will connect with the ranchers and horse buffs in the audience, but these days hardly any urban readers know that the "hand" used to measure horses equals four inches, or that the measurement is from the bottom of the front hoof to the top of the withers. For that matter, not many readers will be altogether clear on "withers." Inasmuch as a hand is one-third of a foot, the writer might better have said that a Clydesdale can stand more than six feet tall at the shoulder.

The magazine writer who described research on the low-pitched sounds elephants make was far more considerate. She noted that researchers recorded the inaudible sounds and detected them by speeding up the tape. That increased the pitch of the sound "like the chipmunk talk of an LP record played at forty-five rpm."

A travel writer was equally descriptive when she described the minuscule portions served in the dining rooms at some health spas. They are, she wrote, "meals that could fit into the palm of your hand," a reference to hands that we all can understand.

INSULTING READERS

When you write for a mass audience, you're like a teacher in a one-room schoolhouse. Somehow, you must make yourself intelligible to both third graders and high school seniors. Similarly, any mass audience will include readers, listeners, or viewers who are well educated and knowledgeable and others who have bricks for brains. Somehow, you must inform the ignorant without insulting the informed.

You can err in both directions. A typical metropolitan news source, for example, will publish complicated international reports that score sixteen or eighteen on the standard readership tests. Only a college graduate can read them comfortably.

On the other hand, news reporters and copy editors are prone to silly definitions that would draw groans from third graders. My newsroom once defined fog as "a cloud that forms near the ground" and tar balls as "oil that has hardened into lumps of asphaltic residue." We even identified Peter Pan as "the boy who could fly."

Most decisions about definitions are more complex. Any mass audience is divided not only by intelligence, but also by other factors that bear on knowledge. Easterners share cultural knowledge unknown to Westerners, and vice versa. Women are likely to understand parts of our culture foreign to most men. Blacks know terms unfamiliar to most Whites.

Age divides audiences, too. Many younger readers have never heard of Neville Chamberlain. So it's not surprising that a wire service chose to identify him as "the British prime minister who proclaimed 'peace in our time' after negotiating an agreement ceding portions of Europe to Adolf Hitler."

Many readers born before and after the post–World War II baby boom have never heard of Jim Morrison. So you can understand the impulse to identify him as "the lead singer for the Doors, a band that flourished in the sixties."

But anyone who lived through World War II will be insulted by the encyclopedia entry on Chamberlain. And anyone young in the sixties—and lots of today's rock fans as well—will be insulted by the assumption that either Morrison or the Doors need explanation. So what to do?

One trick almost always works when a large part of the audience knows a term that's foreign to the rest of it. You define the term obliquely, without suggesting that you're defining anything at all.

In the case of Chamberlain, for example, you might handle a definition this way:

> The next speaker compared Clark to Neville Chamberlain. But Clark himself then stood and stressed traits that set him apart from the discredited British prime minister. He was a fighter, he said, suggesting that he was a man quite different from the appeaser who caved in to Hitler.

An oblique definition of Jim Morrison might go something like this:

> Flowers covered Jim Morrison's grave. The Americans paused at the simple monument to the sixties rock icon and then moved on.

The oblique approach borrows a fiction-writing technique that subtly introduces background information about character and setting in the early parts of short stories and novels. Often such exposition reserves the main clauses of sentences to advance the action line. The necessary background slips into the narrative via subordinate clauses, appositives, and modifiers.

When done right, exposition allows readers to soak up background without realizing it. That kind of quiet approach is the secret to avoiding insults in any language.

V. One Meaning at a Time

See a thing clearly and describe it simply.
—Arthur Brisbane

FINDING OUR MISPLACED MODIFIERS

Years ago broadcaster David Brinkley told his audience a story about a Small Business Administration form that supposedly asked loan applicants to "indicate in Box 3A the number of employees broken down by sex." One applicant, according to the anchor, responded with "none," but added that he had "two with alcohol problems."

Some variation on the gag must be nearly as old as language. The first misplaced modifier no doubt came not long after the first complete sentence. "Trog kill mammoth" became "Trog kill mammoth with big spear."

Dangling modifiers are among the most frequent—and funny—errors writers make. If you write "Relaxing on the veranda, a fly landed in my drink," you've created the dreaded dangling participle. *You* were relaxing on the veranda, after all, while the fly swam for its life. "Relaxing" is a participle (a verb converted to an adjective by adding "ing") that dangles because it modifies the wrong thing. You can easily solve the problem by including the person who is doing the relaxing: "As I relaxed on the veranda, a fly landed in my drink."

"The Lower Case," a regular humor feature in the *Columbia Journalism Review*, prowls the nation's newspaper headlines looking for laughs. More often than not, dangling modifiers supply them: "Teens can't talk about sex with mom." "Legislators hold forum on electric grid."

But most danglers contribute confusion—not humor—to the news columns:

> *Former Mayor Tom Bradley suffered a stroke Thursday while recovering from heart surgery that affected his ability to move the right side of his body, doctors said.*

Clearly, the writer meant to say that the stroke—not the surgery—affected Bradley's ability to move the right side of his body.

We seldom make such mistakes with simple modifiers, which jump off the page when they're in the wrong place. If the man is a brunet and the chair is green, only a serious dyslexic would write that "the green man sat in the brunet chair."

But phrases and clauses act as modifiers, too. In the Bradley reference, for example, the misplaced modifier—"that affected his ability to move the right side of his body"—was a subordinate clause. It was intended to act as an adjective modifying the noun "stroke." Instead, it seemed to modify "surgery," the noun appearing immediately before it.

Such errors account for most misplaced modifiers. Two tricks help avoid them:

- Read copy aloud. When we read silently, we tend to interpret copy the way we intended it. When we read aloud, we often hear what it actually says.

- Pay particular attention to clauses and phrases, especially when they come at the beginnings or ends of sentences. In addition to their internal content, all clauses and phrases also act as modifiers, single units that function as adjectives or adverbs.

In the preceding sentence, for example, "in addition to their internal content" is a pair of phrases that serve as an adverb modifying "act."

If the phrase or clause begins the sentence, check the first noun or verb that follows it. That's the antecedent. If it isn't the one you intended, recast the sentence to get the modifier next to its true antecedent. If the phrase or clause comes toward the end of the sentence, check the noun or verb that comes before it. If that isn't the intended antecedent, move the modifier.

Dangling modifiers fall into a couple of common categories.

Dangling Subordinate Clauses

The transfer is done with a pipette to hold the egg and special glass needles for injecting the sperm, which are washed in solution before they are used.

Making for especially clean sperm, apparently. Or, more likely, an especially clean needle.

Other large creditors include five local television stations that ran Tom Peterson's ads, which collectively are owed $517,672 and various suppliers.

We have to assume the money was due the creditors and suppliers, not the ads.

. . . a two-story wagon with a built-in iron stove, spring-cushion seats, and sleeping bunks that took eight oxen to pull.

Presumably, the oxen pulled the wagon and the bunks came along.

Dangling Prepositional Phrases

Still another member drew laughter when he asked for advice on how to rid a neglected historical building that is being eyed by a local beer brewer of bothersome birds that are roosting in the rafters.

Don't we have enough bothersome birds without brewing more?

Iowa State sophomore Troy Davis became the fifth player in NCAA Division 1-A to rush for 2,000 yards in the Cyclones' 45–31 loss to Missouri on Saturday.

What a game! Five players rush for a total of more than ten thousand yards. It's hard to imagine that the score wasn't even higher.

Despite a clean record at the state Children's Services Division, police began investigating the couple based on information from an informant.

At least the cops are clean.

Almost all of these examples consist of sentences that try to present multiple ideas. Several comprise four or more, so it's no wonder their writers lost track of what went with what.

Separating the main ideas into separate clauses or sentences would have helped. The bothersome bird example would have been clearer if the writer had relegated the brewer to another sentence. The last example might have read: "The couple had a clean record at the state Children's Services Division, but police investigated them after a tip from an informant."

As always, simplicity produces clarity.

PUZZLING PRONOUNS

Ambiguity is a prime threat to clarity, and pronouns often contribute to ambiguity. Pronouns acquire their meaning by virtue of their antecedents—the nouns they represent. If a pronoun has more than one possible antecedent, it is by definition ambiguous. Like this one:

Disability insurance premiums . . . are going sky-high for women while they are falling for men. . . .

You could argue that a woman's insurance premiums *should* go up when she falls for a man. But that's probably not what the writer intended to say.

The writer who produced the following sentence probably didn't mean to suggest that foreign countries have disabilities, either:

. . . which included their six biological children plus more than eighty others adopted from the United States and several foreign countries, many with mental or physical disabilities.

Of course, most ambiguous pronouns simply leave readers lost, rather than amused:

> *Dark clouds gather and a few precious raindrops dampen the dusty streets, but it isn't enough.*

What isn't enough? Rainfall, presumably, or some similar noun. But no such noun appears anywhere in the sentence. "Raindrops" can't serve as an antecedent because raindrops are a "they," not an "it."

Wayward use of "it" may, in fact, be the most common pronoun problem. The following paragraph produced a letter from a confused reader. "What should be a police decision?" he asked. "And *what were* citizens doing?"

> *To be sure, a man in a ski mask with a semiautomatic weapon, trying to intimidate by terror, should expect a violent reaction. But it's hard to see shooting at a fleeing suspect as self-defense. In any case, it should be a police decision. When citizens do it, they further endanger themselves and the lives of bystanders.*

A writer's natural tendency is to read what should be on the screen or paper, rather than what is actually on the screen or paper. That makes us especially vulnerable to pronoun problems. We know what the antecedent should be, and we assume the pronoun connects to it.

Reading aloud is one way to counter that tendency. Going over the copy silently lets the intended meaning wash the actual meaning away. Hearing the words brings us back to reality.

HERE THEY COME

Here's a new threat for the paranoids among us. Not only do "they" fly the black helicopters and plan assassinations. But "they" also have infiltrated the language, dropping in to do their mischief in places where they have no business.

Often, they show up connected to singular antecedents. Many publications are full of these interlopers, which often pop up after the name of a business or organization, improperly joining the singular with the plural.

> *While the **bureau** is now struggling to make up for lost time, **they** are doing it in an atmosphere of increased gunplay between its officers and the public.*

The bureau is a singular thing, properly designated by "it," not "they." Unfortunately, the gremlins that put "they" in the wrong context are equally adept with "their."

> *The . . . Store of Knowledge reflects the public broadcasting* ***industry's*** *efforts to seek financial support for* ***their*** *radio and television stations. . . .*

The times are changing on this issue in some cases. The *AP Stylebook* now allows "they" as a singular pronoun when the antecedent refers to a nonbinary person who prefers this pronoun, as does the *Chicago Manual of Style*. Both also cautiously endorse the singular "they" as an alternative to the clunky "his or her" when an antecedent's gender is unclear or ambiguous. Those are relatively rare occurrences, however, and the agreement rule still holds under circumstances when gender isn't an issue.

MAROONED MODIFIERS

Question: What's wrong with this sentence?

> *Oregon Steel is experiencing a hiccup this quarter, but most believe it's not a dangerous one.*

Answer: Nothing, technically. And yet something's not quite right. To readers with sensitive inner ears the sentence lacks punch. And to writers with naturally skeptical mind-sets, it makes the kind of sweeping assertion that demands evidence.

The problem, in both cases, lies with the word "most." Ordinarily the word serves the same function as sister modifiers such as "many," "few," and "some." They're all adjectives of relative quantity and, as such, modify nouns. Remove the noun and you're left with a marooned modifier, a wayward word that lacks both substance and credibility.

When you run into a phrase such as "most believe," the natural reaction is "most what?" Most economists? Most company officers? Most writers within shouting distance of the author?

Marooned modifiers, in other words, lack an edge. They're meant to be joined with the tangible reality of a noun. When they lack that anchor, they drift, soft and aimless. Like this:

Taking the leadership role seems to be part of the natural maturation process that has taken him from his days as a talented, if sometimes enigmatic, young player to a leader respected by **most** *as one of the greats of the game.*

The real thing is preferred by **most**, *however.*

Not only do such sentences lack the strong, assertive quality that marks most good writing, but they also call the writer's credibility into question. Sweeping assertions demand evidence. Who says that "most" prefer the real thing or that "most" respect an athlete as one of the greats?

Compounding the Confusion

Dangling modifiers may be a major source of unintended meaning, but they're not the only one. Writers produce plenty of statements that are just plain ambiguous. Like these:

Van Nuys, California, man convicted of sexual assault on plane.

Shame on the federal prosecutor who put that headline on a press release announcing the conviction of a man who attacked a woman on an airliner. And shame would surely have followed if the prosecutor ever found out that the headline had gone viral among journalists all around the country.

Victim of attack tells parents to beware.

Was the message intended for the victim's parents or for all parents?

Which is rather remarkable since his competition included the state's Spam-carving champion, as well as a Kent man who creates life-size cake sculptures and the Outhouse Races in Spokane.

Presumably, the writer didn't mean to say that the Kent man created cake sculptures *and* founded the Outhouse Races.

Mikhail Gorbachev starts writing column.

So is the former Soviet president writing a column about writing? Or is he sticking closer to his actual expertise?

The Chapter 6 Cheat Sheet

FIVE SHORTCUTS TO WRITING MORE CLEARLY

1. **Read your rough draft aloud.** Confusing constructions and ambiguities that were invisible when you silently read your manuscript become obvious when you hear your copy spoken.
2. **Add some periods.** Most clear writers produce sentences that average twenty-three words or fewer. Check your own average by counting the number of words on a single page and dividing by the number of sentences. If the resulting number is more than twenty-three, add four or five periods and some capital letters at appropriate places, modifying the wording as necessary to create additional sentences. Then calculate the average again.
3. **Define your terms.** Pick an unfamiliar word and define it in terms of (*a*) the larger class to which it belongs, (*b*) the way it's different from other members of the class, and (*c*) an illustration or description. A jack, for example, is (*a*) a salmon that (*b*) returns to fresh water a year before it's sexually mature and (*c*) looks like an adult but is much smaller.
4. **Think about context.** Help your readers understand concepts by placing them in historical, geographical, or categorical context. You might, for example, explain how a style of painting differs from those that came before and after it, how the plan of one city resembles others, or how a new movie about two cops departs from the formula for buddy movies.
5. **Attach your pronouns.** Puzzling pronouns contribute a disproportionate amount of cloudy meaning. "It" and "they" are among the worst offenders. When you're polishing a rough draft, pause every time you encounter either "it" or "they" and check to see what it's supposed to represent. Is there a noun or another pronoun that's clearly connected to the pronoun? Do the two words agree in number? Or have you written something like "the fishermen forded the streams, but it didn't make any difference in the results"? If so, substitute the appropriate noun for the confusing pronoun. "The fishermen forded the streams, but the new location didn't make any difference in the results."

7
Rhythm

Writers are in the music business.
—Don Murray

THE MUSIC IN THE WORDS

Fiesta celebrants gather around a mariachi band in a Jalisco village square. Angelinos cluster around a jazz combo on Santa Monica's Third Street Mall. Oktoberfest revelers follow an oompah band pounding away in a Munich park. The magnetism of rhythm can draw an audience anywhere.

But rhythm's primal appeal reaches far beyond its most obvious manifestations in music. A pleasing fabric design has its own kind of rhythm. So does the chirp of a cricket, the beat of waves breaking on a beach, and patterns of human language, written as well as spoken. Words can be appealing for the beat they produce, regardless of content.

How often do we find ourselves reading something with no possible application to our own lives? A die-hard urbanite reads an article on sagebrush, or a rancher gets caught up in an essay on New York rent control. If the words flow lyrically, they attract and hold our attention.

Language that lasts almost always resounds with deeply appealing rhythms. In *The Elements of Style*, William Strunk and E. B. White illustrate the power of rhythmic writing by referring to *The Crisis*, Tom Paine's classic Revolutionary War essay. *The Crisis* sold more copies per capita than any other commercial publication ever printed in the United States. It is best remembered for its most lyrical line: "These are the times that try men's souls."

That's a masterpiece of syncopation. The *t* sounds cycle through the words in perfect counterpoint to the *s* sounds. The syllables collect in beautifully balanced groups. The sentence rolls off the tongue with the appeal of waves breaking on a beach.

But, as Strunk and White point out, Paine could have easily botched the job. Who would have remembered "How trying it is to live in these times"? Or "Times like these try men's souls"? Or, worst of all, "Soulwise, these are trying times"?

Prove the point yourself by juggling a few other memorable lines. Would we remember "The early bird gets the worm" if Poor Richard had written "The worm is gotten by the early bird"? Would a simple injunction to "be selfless and patriotic" have inspired Americans in the same way as John Kennedy's appeal that you "ask not what your country can do for you; ask what you can do for your country"?

The emerging brain science of storytelling reveals how closely language links to music. Half of the Americans tested imagined a narrative story line when they heard a musical score played without lyrics. Smaller but still substantial percentages of subjects did the same in China.

Despite its obvious value, some editors ignore rhythm as they strive to enhance accuracy, precision, and brevity. If you're a writer who chooses the word "kid" because it makes just the right sound in just the right place, and your editor changes it to "youngster," it's time to talk. Editors need to know if you have particular rhythms in mind so that they don't disrupt them with changes aimed at improving other aspects of your writing. A responsible editor will honor a writer's intended rhythms if he can.

Whatever you do, don't let tin-eared editing persuade you to give up your quest for pleasing cadences. Seductively rhythmic writing can add value that often transcends content. Dan Neil, then with the *Los Angeles Times* and later at the *Wall Street Journal*, won the 2004 Pulitzer Prize for commentary with the unlikeliest of material—a series of automotive reviews. Despite Neil's prosaic subject, the sound of his writing gives it an appeal that reaches beyond the gearheads who typically read about cars and motor sports. Consider the way he turns from damning a Rolls-Royce for its bulk to praising it for its roadworthiness:

> *Yet from the driver's seat, the Phantom is a sensational automobile. There's magic and mystery here, fistfuls of romantic motoring. I could drive it to the crack of doom.*

As the Pulitzer jurists discovered, you could read Dan Neil to the crack of doom, too. There's magic and mystery in his written rhythms, which is eloquent evidence of the rewards that come from hearing the music in the words.

I. Elements of Rhythm

A story can be wrecked by a faulty rhythm in a sentence—especially if it occurs toward the end—or a mistake in paragraphing, even punctuation.
—Truman Capote

BALANCE

Poets and lyricists often organize their work in stanzas. The form of one line matches another, and patterns repeat in the simplest rhythmic forms. What is rhythm, after all, but a pleasing sequence of patterns?

Many college students can cite a classic example, John Donne's seduction line from "The Flea":

Marke but this flea, and marke in this,
How little that which thou deny'st me is.

A prose writer with a great ear instinctively reaches for similar matched elements. Consider Cynthia Gorney, who won an American Society of Newspaper Editors writing award at the *Washington Post*. After interviewing Robert Kennedy's killer, she wrote:

Sirhan Sirhan, who wrenched aside the 1970s with the force that history gives only to political assassins, wants to go home.

Note how the first element—"Sirhan Sirhan"—balances the last—"wants to go home." Each has the same number of syllables. The last element echoes the beat of the first by shifting the emphasis to second syllables. The subordinate clause in the center acts like a fulcrum, supporting the parallel elements at either end.

Notice the balance in Gorney's description of an entry in the Calaveras County Jumping Frog Contest:

Willie was a dark frog, in his way; he was young, and exquisitely muscled, in the upper leg, where it mattered.

Gorney places a high value on cadence, and she will break the normal rules of syntax, punctuation, and grammar to get it. In her description of Willie the jumping frog, she put a comma after "muscled" to create a balanced element that pleased her ear. In the following example she substitutes an adjective set off by commas—"expansive"—for what ordinarily would be an unpunctuated adverb—"expansively."

Sirhan smiles, expansive, touches his chest.

Rhythm can help build an argument. *Boston Globe* columnist Ellen Goodman often advances her logic in clause after carefully balanced clause. The repeated rhythms underscore the sequential thinking:

Adolescence isn't a training ground for adulthood now; it is a holding pattern for aging youth.

The person we thought we might be still challenges the person we are.

Hear the patterns? The structure of each clause comes close to matching the clause that comes before. Phrases such as "the person" repeat. "Aging youth" echoes "training ground," and the rhyming syllables of "we" and "be" punctuate the second sentence like a downbeat.

Read rhythmically gifted writers such as Goodman and Gorney aloud. Listen to their music, study the patterns that create it, and think about ways to apply those lessons to your own work.

CYCLES OF SOUND

Truly rhythmic writing balances not only the beats of words, phrases, and sentences, but also the sounds they contain. To reach the pleasure centers of the brain, they, too, must appear in satisfying cycles.

Alliteration creates such cycles by repeating two or more initial sounds, usually consonants, in the same phrase. A *Wine Spectator* headline on cheap champagne—"Bubbly on a Budget"—is one example. And here's another from Bill Blundell, describing the scene around a Washington State logging camp:

> *Nine miles east, Mount St. Helens rises like a white wall, its shattered summit banked in mist.*

The strict alliteration of "white wall" contrasts with the looser repetition of *m* sounds throughout the sentence. "Shattered summit" adds another alliterative element that builds on "white wall" with two-syllable elements that work like a jazz variation on a theme.

Here's a sentence from *Image* magazine that balances alliterative elements just as precisely:

> *Is this mere marketing hype, a faddish flash in the promotional pan?*

In the next example, "part" and "art" create a gentle internal rhyme and a perfectly balanced center for Paul Trachtman's *Smithsonian* magazine description of a sculptor's work:

> *Illusions and shadows, light and dark, have been part of Bontecou's art from the beginning.*

One caution: It's easy to overdo rhyme and alliteration. When Nixon's vice president, Spiro Agnew, denounced his media critics as "nattering nabobs of negativism," the phrase drew attention not in admiration, but in ridicule.

CLUES TO THE CADENCE

Much writing ignores the rhythmic possibilities inherent in punctuation. Tom Wolfe aside, most of us seldom stray far from commas and periods. But most punctuation marks indicate pauses, and pauses create the measured movements of rhythmic sounds that we call cadence.

Each of the pause markers we customarily use—commas, periods, dashes, ellipses, exclamation points, question marks, parentheses, colons, and semicolons—suggests a different kind of beat. Victor Borge built a career on illustrating the differences among them with a comedy routine he called "phonetic punctuation." As he spoke, he'd sound out the punctuation marks we usually glide over silently. A period was a loud *thwok*, an explanation mark was a descending squeak followed by a *thwok*, and so on.

Maybe you had to be there. But from a writer's point of view, Borge made an important point. Try following his lead and sound out each punctuation mark in your mind. Periods create the sharp, crisp break of a karate chop. Commas suggest the smoother rise and fall of a speed bump. Semicolons hesitate for a second and then flow forward. Dashes call a sudden halt. Ellipses ooze along like spilled honey.

Punctuation marks are like the drum set in a pop-music combo—they lay down the beat that lies at the heart of each tune. And that's what turns the sounds made by all those different instruments into a dance.

RHYTHMIC STRUCTURES

As in music, the rhythms of writing occur at multiple levels. The most basic musical unit is the cycle of beats known as a measure. That's analogous to the cadence writers create within individual sentences.

But a musical score contains higher-order rhythmic elements, too. A pop song may have an introduction, a bridge, and a chorus that repeats through a number of stanzas. Jazz compositions can get far more complicated, and they sometimes overlay beats in swirling patterns of incredible complexity.

The simplest structural element in prose rhythm is sentence length. Writers with sensitive ears deliberately vary the lengths of their sentences as they strive for variety and balance.

Sentences of similar lengths can become structural elements that repeat rhythms and play off sentences of different lengths. Notice, for example, how the three short sentences that conclude this Jonathan Susskind paragraph from a travel story serve as counterpoint to the long opening sentence:

> *Decades later, the strawberry fields on Vashon have dwindled to a couple of patches on farms that mostly serve the U-pick trade. The peaches succumbed to diseases. The currant fields are overgrown. Cherries go to the birds.*

When short, punchy sentences follow long, languid ones, they act as points of emphasis, like the clash of cymbals in an orchestral crescendo. Sonny Kleinfield of the *New York Times* used the device when he described the aftermath of the 2001 World Trade Center attack:

Many people were busy on cell phones, trying to reach friends and relatives they knew in the buildings to alert their own loved ones that they were all right. But the circuits overloaded. Fear mounted.

Paragraph kickers are yet another tool of structural rhythm. A good kicker ends a paragraph with a final word that is short—preferably a single syllable—and crisp. Good graf kickers, as they're known in the newsroom, typically end with a hard consonant sound, a *t*, for example, or a hard *g*, *d*, *p*, or *k*. Such words close a paragraph like the downbeat that ends a stanza of dance music. They leave readers leaning forward, ready to take the next step. Like this:

Conservatives complain that the Supreme Court is too liberal. Liberals complain that it's too conservative. Both charges are inaccurate: in reality the Court is a careful political actor that arguably represents the center of gravity of American politics better than most politicians do. The real problem is not the Supreme Court's politics, but the depressing quality of its work. (Benjamin Wittes, *Atlantic*)

THE RULE OF THREE

A venerable rule of flower arranging is that you avoid even numbers. One rose in a bud vase is fine. Two is tacky. Three looks great. The rule isn't absolute, and tasteful flower arrangers can create beautiful exceptions. But it still hints at some innate aesthetic.

Something similar applies to writing. The inner ear seems to prefer a three-element series. Two sounds blocky. Four sounds busy. But three sounds just right. So when you put together a series, look for ways to sort the available material into elements of three:

Playing games at the office used to mean working smart, dressing for success, and swimming with the sharks.

The other three years they plant, grow, and harvest popcorn on those huge 125-acre circles that give people in airplanes something interesting to look at.

Probably not any kind of a record, but not bad for a five-year-old. No messed-up hair, no untied shoelaces, no problem.

II. Sentence Variety

True ease in writing comes from art, not chance.
As those move easiest who have learn'd to dance.
—Alexander Pope

SENTENCE SHAPES

The ability to exploit a variety of sentence forms expands a writer's range. Mixing it up a little with alternating sentence forms adds interest. So an occasional review of grammar school sentence classifications can help just about any writer:

1. The Simple Sentence

For clarity's sake, simple sentences should dominate your writing. At their best, they're short, to the point, and move ahead with a steady, logical progression.

A simple sentence contains one or more subjects and one or more verbs, but it contains no more than one clause—a group of words containing both a subject and a predicate. For example:

> *For one thing, the advantage can clearly exist.*

> *The wind stirs whitecaps on the brackish estuary.*

> *With his Yasser Arafat beard and an outfit that made him look more like the manager of a dinosaurian rock band than the head of a billion dollar enterprise, Knight was the quintessential high-powered Webfoot—charming, casual, absolutely no sense of self-importance.*

All three examples are simple sentences—each contains only one basic statement—"advantage can," "wind stirs," "Knight was."

You can add subjects and verbs ad infinitum without leaving the confines of the simple sentence. "We and the Browns can serve tea and eat crumpets. . . ." But the more you tart up a simple sentence with additional elements, the more you lose the virtue of its simplicity.

2. The Compound Sentence

A compound sentence combines two or more simple sentences. Independent clauses—the basic language unit that can stand alone as a complete sentence—can only be joined by coordinate conjunctions. So the independent clauses in a compound sentence will always be connected by "and," "or," "for," "yet," "but," or "nor."

Compound sentences are not necessarily complicated. Combine two short simple sentences and you end up with a clear compound sentence:

He opened the door, and she walked in.

Most compounds are more complicated. They may, for example, use three or more elements in series, substituting commas for most of the coordinate conjunctions. Still, they can be perfectly clear and to the point:

He walked down the long hall, slowly opened the door, and she walked in, looking like a prom queen.

3. The Complex Sentence

Despite its name, this form doesn't have to be complicated. The term merely means that the sentence contains at least one subordinate clause—a clause that can't stand alone. For example:

Her boyfriend, Tony Weiss, who is also a server, nodded knowingly.

And when the evening was over, they said good night.

"Who is also a server" and "when the evening was over" are the subordinate clauses in these examples. Without them, you're left with simple sentences built around the basic statements "Weiss nodded" and "they said."

Most complex sentences carry a little more freight. But good ones still are perfectly clear:

When Children's Services Division workers seized Diane Whitehead's six children last month, it wasn't the first time the agency and the Aloha mother had crossed swords.

4. The Compound-Complex Sentence

This form is a permutation of the other three. It hangs a subordinate clause onto a group of two or more linked independent clauses.

> *The chief factor cherished the seeds, and he later transplanted the seedlings to the company gardens, where they thrived until the Great Flood of 1894.*

Compound-complex sentences get unwieldy in a hurry. So clear writers minimize their use, generally restricting them to no more than 10 percent of their work.

But varying the sentence structures in a piece makes it more interesting, and writers who care about rhythm will stray from the simpler forms to mix in compound sentences now and then. Or they will add a complex sentence, which slows the pace when the reader drops into the subordinate clause. They think about the position of prepositional phrases. And they use other structures, such as participial phrases, thereby adding interesting new dimensions to the basic form.

They're continually aware of sentence structure, in other words, and they will probably realize that each sentence in the preceding paragraph illustrates the very point it makes.

PACE

Endless hours at the speed limit on an American freeway spell certain boredom. So do hours spent creeping along in a traffic jam. And survivors of the Trans-Siberian Railway say that day after day of clackety-clacking across the steppe is a recipe for madness.

Reading, too, is a journey. And, as with all journeys, changes of pace help keep things interesting.

The proper use of pace is important in any kind of writing. In an expository piece—the typical newspaper report—pace should slow when a writer wades through a difficult bit of material. In a city council story, a good reporter doesn't rush past the city manager's explanation of a difficult land-use regulation. On the other hand, a fast-paced "flash-by graf" is a good way to blow past mundane "in other business" aspects of the meeting.

Pace is especially critical to storytelling. Not only does varied pace keep the audience awake, but changing pace at critical moments also adds drama.

When the killer creeps into the victim's bedroom, time almost stops. The door creaks. The knife slowly rises. The victim rolls over . . . and the killer freezes. Then quiet footsteps resume their slow approach to the bed.

But when the knife plunges to its mark, the story breaks into a run. The killer slashes and stabs. The victim writhes and screams. Doors fly open. Sirens wail. The murderer dashes for the street.

As I explain in *Storycraft*, the sequel to this book, the pace of a good nonfiction narrative usually follows the story's narrative arc. Most tales begin with a languid opening devoted to exposition—the segment that explains the background necessary to understanding the story's core conflict. Then the pace picks up as the protagonist confronts the complication in a segment devoted to rising action. Eventually, the pace reaches its most fevered pitch as the collision of forces produces the climax. Then the pace falls off again as the writer wraps up loose ends in the denouement.

III. Attribution

The right word may be effective, but no word was ever as effective as a rightly timed pause.
—Mark Twain

SAYING IT WITH RHYTHM

In his classic text, *On Writing Well*, William Zinsser advised placing the attribution at the first natural pause in the quotation, rather than at the beginning or ending. Cynthia Gorney follows Zinsser's tip religiously. In her profile of Theodore Geisel—aka Dr. Seuss—she used the technique as a way of adding punch to Geisel's flustered response when she asked him to read one of his own tongue twisters:

> *"Not wearing the right glasses," Geisel says quickly, "I can't."*

Mark Bowden, the newspaper police reporter who broke onto the national scene with his book *Black Hawk Down*, adheres to the same technique. He used it as a way of adding drama to a story on an elderly woman trapped in her apartment by housing-project violence. Bowden and the woman talked about added security. He asked if that wouldn't make the place feel like a prison. And then . . .

She leans forward in her chair, smiling, and reaches out to put one hand on his knee. "Honey don't you know?" she says. "This IS prison."

Well-placed attributions are especially important for quotations that end paragraphs or entire articles. Kickers should never trail off with "said." The attribution lacks the sense of sharp finality that's required to close the door on a piece of writing.

Consider this example from Tom Hallman's "The Boy behind the Mask," which won the 2001 Pulitzer Prize for feature writing. The climax of the story occurs when the protagonist, a boy with a terrible facial deformity, rejects a school administrator's offer of special treatment. Instead, he stands in a slow-moving line with his fellow students.

"I'll wait," Sam says firmly. "This is where I belong."

Now consider how that kicker, which ended the segment that served as the climax of the entire series, would have read in the more conventional form:

"I'll wait. This is where I belong," Sam says firmly.

IV. Keeping the Beat with Prepositions

All the fun's in how you say a thing.
—Robert Frost

THE ROAD BEST TAKEN

One of the major choices our language offers involves the way it expresses relationships between things. On the one hand, our language is inflective—it can express relationships by changing the forms of words. To show that a roof is connected to a barn, we change the word "barn" by making it possessive: "the barn's roof."

But English is also distributive. Instead of changing the forms of words, we can express different relationships by changing the forms of phrases. Rather than "the barn's roof," you can speak of "the roof of the barn."

Knowing how to substitute one approach for the other can help you maintain pleasing rhythms. You can avoid the unpronounceable plural possessives—such as Joneses'—that inflection can produce. And you can steer clear of awkwardly repeated prepositional phrases—such as "of the roof of the barn"—that sometimes result from distribution.

Fortunately, what twists tongues in one way may get right to the point the other way, which suggests a way of avoiding repetitious strings of prepositional phrases, a common fault that can bog a sentence down with excessive length and singsong rhythms. Try reading the following sentence aloud:

> *Encouraged by the murky outcome, Mr. Bloomberg authorized his campaign team to double his spending on television commercials in every market where he is currently advertising and (to) expand his campaign's field staff to more than two thousand people, strategists involved in the conversations said.*

The best you can say for such sentences is that they should never happen in the first place. No sentence can safely carry more than three prepositional phrases. The example has four, each underlined.

Several computer grammar checkers generate preposition counts. When a computer readability check reveals that prepositions make up 15 percent of your word choices, you may have a problem. Lean, direct syntax seldom contains more than 10 or 12 percent prepositions.

You can easily eliminate unwanted prepositional phrases—you simply make the preposition's object modify its antecedent directly. "A neighbor of Chan" becomes "Chan's neighbor." "A shelter for the homeless in the Wheeler neighborhood" becomes "a Wheeler neighborhood homeless shelter." And "spending on television commercials" becomes "television spending." The tactic doesn't eliminate every prepositional phrase. Nor would you want to. The point is to reduce the number to no more than one or two per sentence, eliminating the singsong effect that disrupts the writing's cadence.

DEAD WEIGHT

Most old-timers remember the commandment against splitting infinitives, meaning the verbals formed by combining "to" with the root verb. Once you wrote "to go," according to the rule, you didn't dare add an adverb between the "to" and the "go." But that was the law back in the days before "to boldly go" had been repeated ten thousand times in *Star Trek* syndication. Nowadays, nobody loses sleep over an infinitive split by an adverb or two. In fact, few writers seem to worry about infinitives for any reason. Which is too bad, because a few infinitives can do a lot of damage.

The problem is that infinitives are self-contained little units that sit in the middle of a sentence like bricks. Rather than adding to the flow, they break it up, creating sentences that lurch along in fits and starts. In addition to the four prepositional phrases slowing the clunky sentence about the Bloomberg campaign, two additional bumps—the infinitives "to double" and "to expand"—make what should be a smooth ride even rougher.

Out-of-control infinitives do their dirty work everywhere, as in these examples:

> *. . . said his group wants chiropractors* **to continue to have** *the right* **to authorize** *temporary disability payments for injured workers and* **to rate** *whether they have been permanently disabled.*

> *The Sweet Home school board says Bible teachers may no longer go into local public schools* **to hand** *out slips seeking parents' permission for schoolchildren* **to skip** *classes* **to attend** *Christian education classes.*

When you see infinitives piling up in a sentence, consider replacing one or more of them with:

1. a subordinate clause—"to skip classes *so that they can attend*"
2. a gerund—"*handing* out slips."

Of course, you don't want to pile up the subordinate clauses or gerunds, either. Variety is the key.

V. Parallel Construction

How lovely are the wiles of words.
—Emily Dickinson

THE SWIRLED SERIES

Rhythm, as we have seen, stems in part from symmetry that balances one element with another. A writer with a good ear for the language may begin a sentence with a phrase made up of two-syllable words, for example, and then conclude with another phrase containing the same number of two-syllable words.

Balance is most important with closely related structural elements. Windows in well-designed buildings usually share similar shapes, and so should sentence elements that appear in a series. A well-written series of words, phrases, or clauses is parallel.

Parallel construction does more than create pleasing design. A series is easier to understand in parallel form. And elements in series have far more impact in a crescendo of repeated forms. Take this subheadline:

Abortions Would Be Allowed Only in Cases of Rape, Incest, or to Save the Mother's Life

The last element in the series falls flat. It dashes the expectation created by the first two elements, which are perfectly parallel. "Rape" and "incest" are nouns. The third element—"to save"—is an infinitive. It acts as a noun, but it's not in the form of a noun. The series becomes much more palatable if the third element is parallel to the first two. "Abortions would be allowed only in cases of rape, incest, or a *threat* to the mother's life."

Infinitives aren't the only verbals that cause problems with parallel construction. Note this example, which mixes nouns with a gerund:

The young people who are graduating with highest honors this month and next from metropolitan-area high schools dwell instead on valued ***friendships****, on* ***teachers*** *who challenge and inspire, and on the* ***getting*** *of knowledge.*

The writer needed to substitute a noun for "getting." She might have used "knowledge" by itself. Or she might have preserved the original meaning by writing about the *acquisition* of knowledge.

Remember that a series should be parallel according to voice, too. This one lapses into passive for the last item:

The nation's worst ***oil spill spread*** *out of control Monday as a* ***supertanker remained*** *impaled on rocks, wind gusts topping seventy mph forced postponement of already-delayed cleanup efforts and* ***questions were raised*** *about the ship captain's drinking.*

Here, on the other hand, is a tricky series that the writer successfully negotiated with his unwavering commitment to nouns:

. . . crime fueled by drugs, unemployment, educational failures, racism, low self-esteem among many of the young, large numbers of single-parent families living in poverty, shoddy housing, and indifferent landlords.

And this perfectly controlled *New York Times* series of sentences describing the fall of wreckage from the space shuttle *Columbia* on Nacogdoches, Texas, gains narrative authority from its rhythmic power:

> ***It sounded** like a freight train, like a tornado, like rolling thunder—and then a gigantic boom.*
>
> ***It fell** from the sky in six-inch chunks and seven-foot sections of steel, ceramics, circuit boards, and who-knows-what.*
>
> ***It tore** holes in cedar rooftops, scorched front lawns, ripped a streetlight from its pole, and littered the parking lot behind the Masonic hall downtown.* (David M. Halbfinger and Richard A. Oppel Jr., *New York Times*)

VI. Recipes for Rhythm

I think I could pick out the best writers in a strange city room by those who write with their lips moving. . . .
—Don Murray

Finding the rhythmic elements in somebody else's writing is one thing. Creating them in your own is something else.

You can start by reviewing your rough drafts with an ear tuned for balance, alliteration, attribution placement, sentence variety, and the effect of the pauses created by various types of punctuation.

If you have a three-beat element at the beginning of a sentence, for example, is there a way to balance it with a three-beat element at the end? Can you replace one modifier with another more pleasing to the ear? Are you damaging rhythmic variety by stacking repetitive twenty-word sentences in big blocks or backing into most sentences with the same kinds of prepositional phrases?

But the best thing you can do is to start reading your work aloud. Broadcast writers, who consciously write for the ear, know that you must actually hear the words if you hope to avoid the awkward phrasing that produces embarrassing on-air stumbles. Reading aloud is part of the culture in most broadcast newsrooms.

Not so in print newsrooms. Reporters have an amazing reluctance to speak the words they write. Their copy sometimes reaches hundreds of thousands of readers the minute they hit "send," yet they hesitate to let the two or three reporters sitting around them hear a mumbling rendition of it before making final decisions about phrasing and sentence structure.

Freelancers and other writers who work alone have even less excuse for failing to read their work aloud. Why pass up a simple step that pays such rich dividends when nobody's around to hear anyway?

Whatever your genre, reading aloud is almost certain to uncover possibilities that never would have surfaced in a silent reading. If you work surrounded by people and you're shy about rendering your own writing aloud, you might try picking up the phone and pretending to read your copy to a source.

The point is to read, not to perform. You don't have to sound out every syllable for dramatic effect. Movie director John Sayles says he likes to read script dialogue in a perfectly flat voice so he can judge it unadorned by what an actor will add.

So mumble. Whisper even. If you listen to the sound of what you've written, you'll hear all the notes, whether they're false or true.

The Chapter 7 Cheat Sheet

FIVE SHORTCUTS TO MAKING YOUR WRITING MORE RHYTHMIC

1. **Listen for the cadence.** Pay particular attention to the flow of your writing when you read it aloud. Does it roll along smoothly, without long, unbroken torrents of sound, awkward pauses, and tongue-twisting miscues? If not, tinker with the syntax to improve the beat.
2. **Look for alliteration.** If you write something clunky in your first draft, cast about for something that repeats a key sound. Can you turn "contours of the bend" into "contours of the curve"? How about converting "secrets of the experienced" into "secrets of the savvy"?
3. **Balance your sentences.** Pleasing sentences display a certain symmetry. The previous sentence, for example, begins with a two-syllable word followed by a three-syllable word. And it ends with a two-syllable word followed by a three-syllable word.
4. **Vary the lengths of your sentences and paragraphs.** Nothing kills interest like sentence after sentence of the same length. Mix things up by following long sentences with short ones, or create pleasing paragraph patterns with progressively shorter—or longer—sentences. And do the same thing with the paragraphs themselves. Paragraphs

that develop a complex argument may contain a dozen sentences. Paragraphs that make a key point may contain only one.

5. **End with a bang.** The last word in a paragraph, chapter, or story should slam the door. Search for crisp final words with single syllables and hard consonants. Can you substitute "beat" for "rhythm," as I did at the end of the first suggestion on this list? Can you figure out a way to end on a word like "click," "dupe," "pit," or "dead"?

8

Humanity

The mystery lies in the use of language to express human life.
—Eudora Welty

One of the working principles of American journalism is that you should "get people into your stories." Young reporters learn that what that actually means is that you should get lots of direct quotations into stories. The quotes generally come from athletes, politicians, promoters, and various brands of activists. On the whole, they're practiced and vacuous, filled with more self-serving hot air than humanity.

Other forms of nonfiction capture humanity more successfully. The best profile writers place their subjects in believable environments that evoke real life and show human beings behaving in ways that reveal their core personalities. Top feature writers bring the same humanity to stories about food, travel, sports, and the arts.

Fiction writers work with the richest palette. Novelists have been honing their craft for centuries, and they've developed an impressive array of techniques for bringing characters to life. We barely have room to skim the surface here, which is why I devoted a full chapter to character development in *Storycraft*, this book's sequel.

Recent brain research shows that the audience is most engaged by the protagonist's emotions, intentions, and beliefs, and the scientists who conducted one such study concluded that their findings resolved the old debate about the importance of plot versus character. "Aristotle proposed 2,300 years ago that plot is the most important aspect of narrative, and that character is secondary," the study's lead author wrote. "Our brain results show that people approach narrative in a strongly character-centered and psychological manner, focused on the mental states of the protagonist of the story."

Still, the challenge of capturing the complexities of human personality, motivation, and behavior remains daunting. Novels, films, television dramas, and short stories are peopled with far more cardboard characters than fully rounded human beings.

Larry Leonard, an Oregon writer who created everything from magazine-style profiles to children's books, reduced the challenge of capturing humanity on the page to profound simplicity. "It is very difficult," he says, "to make people out of words."

I. Anecdotes

You have to tell stories to get stories.
—*Ken Metzler*

INSIDE STORIES

One of the best ways to "get people into your stories" is to show sources and characters actually doing something. Specific descriptions of action allow readers to visualize human beings as living, breathing characters operating in their natural environments. And one of the most efficient tools for creating those kinds of images is the anecdote.

Effective anecdotes usually contain little protagonist-complication-resolution action lines. In such stories the central characters face challenges. They do things to overcome them, and readers keep reading to see how things will turn out.

The anecdotal action line can lead readers through entire magazine stories. Gay Talese's classic *Esquire* magazine profiles often contained twenty or more. One anecdote leads to another, which leads to another, and so on.

Good anecdotes not only entertain, but they also offer evidence that relates to the story's overall point. That helps create the thematic quality that's a hallmark of good feature writing. And they do so by showing, rather than telling. Pure quoting is likely to conceal because few of us are totally candid about ourselves. But behavior is more likely to reveal. So anecdotes often remove facades to show real human beings.

Some anecdotes are better than others, of course. So what makes for good ones?

They're short, for one thing. The best anecdotes consume only a paragraph or two. In almost no cases do they run on for more than four paragraphs. One of the first rules of joke telling also seems to apply when it comes to anecdotes—the better the punch line, the longer the story it can support. Which may be why a Henny Youngman gag is worth no more than one line . . .

Most anecdotes begin with a cue that tips readers off to the fact that exposition has ended and an anecdote is beginning. Such cues serve the same function that "once upon a time" does for fairy tales. They usually deal with time, too. A phrase beginning with "during," for example, will alert readers to the fact that an anecdote is about to begin. So will a clause that begins with "when." Or if somebody other than the writer is telling the tale, revealing that fact sets the stage: "So and so likes to recall the time when . . ."

The beginning reference to some point in the past suggests something else about anecdotes: They're told from the viewpoint of somebody looking back from the present, and as a result they're almost always in the past tense, even if the surrounding copy is in the present.

Good anecdotes frequently end with a strong kicker, the kind of tagline that lets readers know the story is over by creating a sense of closure. If the story's funny, the kicker's the punch line. But whether it's funny or not, almost any anecdote should end with a line that's punchy. A good one never ends with an attribution.

Each of the following anecdotes illustrates one or more of the characteristics that make the device such an effective narrative tool.

From a Calvin Trillin article about the South African obsession with kabeljou, a local fish:

> *Patricia Suzman, who grew up in Johannesburg and now lives in Bean Town, happened to be in South Africa while I was there, and she told me that when the immigration inspector at the Cape Town airport asked her the purpose of her visit she answered, "I am here to eat kabeljou."*

Just so! The anecdote, which appeared in the *New Yorker*, is wryly humorous in the patented Trillin fashion, and it illustrates the article's central point—a South African would travel halfway around the world to once again sample the fishy taste of home.

From a *Los Angeles Times* editorial, by Andrew Malcolm, praising a famous scientist's drive to achieve:

> *One day many years ago in a valley not far away, George Marcy's parents gave him a used four-inch telescope. At night he would unlatch his bedroom screen and climb*

onto the patio roof with his new toy. There, for countless hours, the boy toured the solar system and Milky Way. Marcy recalls feeling very small but strangely connected to something much larger and grander as he studied Saturn's rings, monitored the movements of Jupiter's moons, and wondered whether anyone or anything was out there looking back at Granada Hills.

Marcy grew up and defected to Northern California, to a planet called Berkeley. He's taller now but still feels small as he scans the skies with UC Berkeley's computers, $5-million spectrometers, and telescopes with thirty-three-foot mirrors.

A scientist blazing trails on the frontiers of knowledge—in this case discovering planets in other solar systems—would naturally have a story about how he came to discover his passion. Malcolm asked the right question and came up with an anecdote that perfectly illustrated the theme of his story.

From a Mark Mahoney editorial in the *Glens Falls* (New York) *Post-Star*

The doctor walks in to see his patient, who's covered from head to toe in bandages, his right arm in a sling, his left leg raised in a strap attached to the ceiling.

"How'd you hurt yourself?" the doctor asks.

"I was raking leaves," the patient groans through the tiny mouth hole in his bandages.

"How on Earth did you do this kind of damage just raking leaves?" the doctor asks in amazement.

"I fell out of the tree."

Don't laugh.

If you live in Queensbury and you expect to have the town pick up your leaves this year, that guy in the hospital bed could be you.

OK. So you have to write an editorial about the fact that the city is conducting its annual leaf pickup on the usual dates even though it's been a mild autumn and the leaves haven't fallen yet. Hmmmm. Isn't there an old gag about a guy who tried to rake his leaves before they'd fallen? And wouldn't that make exactly the right point?

TELLING STORIES, GETTING STORIES

Nonfiction writers can't manufacture anecdotes, of course. Which means that the ability to recognize and write a good anecdote won't serve much purpose without the additional ability to find great anecdotes in the first place.

Some writers obviously have the knack. Others fill their notebooks with dull, abstract detail. The main difference seems to lie in their interviewing techniques. Ken Metzler, author of *Creative Interviewing*, said interviews that produce good anecdotes are more like conversations than interviews. The interviewers put as much into the discussion as they take out. They relax their sources by getting loose themselves. They provide plenty of support and approval so that sources feel OK about revealing intimate details of their lives. They tell stories to get stories.

When Truman Capote turned to nonfiction, he quickly mastered the technique. His interview with Marlon Brando uncovered details of the actor's relationship with his alcoholic mother that had never before been revealed. Brando's friends were astonished, and one of them asked him why he'd been so open with a gossipy snoop.

Brando confessed that Capote had kept him up most of the night drinking. And he admitted that his judgment had been affected. Moreover, he said, Capote had dominated the conversation, often revealing excruciatingly private things about his own life. He could hardly get a word in edgewise, Brando said. And when he finally did, he damned well wasn't going to let the "little bastard" get away with telling better stories than he did.

You also can collect good anecdotes by interviewing colleagues, friends, and relatives of your subjects. Prime the pump by telling them what personality traits you're trying to illustrate. "I hear," you might say, "that Henry is obsessed about neatness, and that he even organizes his sock drawer. Does that ring true with you, and have you ever known him to do anything similar?"

Your source might oblige by telling you how Henry compulsively organizes his desktop or about the time he restacked the firewood at a remote campsite because it wasn't tidy enough for him.

II. Vignettes

Writing succeeds when it puts pictures inside our heads, when it makes it possible for us to visualize people and landscapes, actions and scenes. We remember what we can visualize. We think about what we can remember.
—Lauren Kessler

LITTLE PICTURES

> *The prison guard took a wide stance, lifted her arms, aimed and fired. Two barbed darts stuck in the foil target as a hook might in a steelhead's mouth, and she hit the Taser's button.*

Zap.

Blue sparks crackled across the body of the foil target. If it had been a prisoner, he'd have been helpless on the floor.

"It gets your attention, jangles your muscles around a bit," explained Wayne Eatherly, Oregon Corrections Department training manager.

They're bigger than an image. They're smaller than a scene. And they don't have the snappy ending or internal story structure we expect from an anecdote.

Vignettes, such as Sarah Carlin Ames's description of a Taser gun in operation, grab readers' attention with vivid action and arresting images. When they make a thematic point, they also work effectively as leads.

Here's another example, this one by Dick Cockle:

Fifty feet above houndsman Gale Culver, an eighty-five-pound female cougar snoozed away a gray afternoon in the spreading limbs of a fir tree. A dozen yards down the bluff, a smaller mountain lion lay concealed in another tree.

For the tired Culver and two rain-soaked wildlife biologists, the brace of treed cats made the last two hours' chase through the deep snow worth the effort.

Dick's vignette introduces a story about researchers and mountain lions by showing us researchers and mountain lions. The point is obvious, and it needs no explanation.

But some vignettes have symbolic value. The writer sees some small thing and—because of experience, analysis, and understanding—it takes on meaning that doesn't exist for the casual observer. A novelist might simply present that kind of revealing detail as part of the narrative flow, leaving it to astute readers and critics to deduce the symbolic content. But a journalist trying to reach a mass audience is wise to include some explanation.

Here's a sterling example from Fred Leeson, a fine courts reporter who was always careful not to get bogged down in his specialty's obscurities:

David Lawrence Olstad strode slowly down the carpeted aisle and paused briefly before pushing aside the little wooden gate.

The swinging barrier in U.S. District court, as in any courtroom, is more symbolic than practical. It separates the court from the gallery. Lawyers, clients, and the judge up front; observers in back.

As a lawyer for 17 years, Olstad, 45, had walked countless times into that privileged territory. But this time the pugnacious, quick-witted former prosecutor had changed positions in the careful geometry of the courtroom.

Now he was the client—a criminal defendant waiting for judgment to be passed upon him.

Many vignettes are barely more than descriptive details or fleeting images. Writers use them for color rather than symbolic impact. They sprinkle them through their text to give a sense of place or mood. These glimpses of landscape or human activity also help to involve readers, who slip into the story on the wings of the writer's descriptive powers.

Here's an example, especially rich in mood, from Ed Immel, a railroad buff, writing about a Chinese train trip:

In the middle of the night, the passenger train pulls into a nameless station. Outside, not seen but heard, a steam engine in the darkness becomes a live animal. Air pumps pound a methodical thump-thump, thump-thump, thump-thump. The turbo generator whines, and the popping and hissing noises that only a steam engine can make fill the stillness.

III. Quotations

I hate quotations. Tell me what you know.
—Ralph Waldo Emerson

TELLING WORDS

Of all the devices that can add humanity to your writing, the direct quotation is the most overused. A sports story or a traditional news feature may contain a direct quote in every other paragraph, a practice that usually produces a parade of inane or merely dull utterances. Great magazine writers repeatedly demonstrate that the direct quote is expendable, writing five thousand words or more without resorting to one single direct quote.

Still, quotations have their purpose. Sometimes a writer just can't improve on the speaker's exact words. He can't match the wit or the rhythm, the economy of expression, the color, the emotion.

Sometimes writers have good reasons for quoting even uninspired utterances. Maybe a direct quotation clearly establishes the source of a controversial opinion. Maybe it makes a fact or opinion credible by linking it with an authoritative source. Maybe it serves as evidence for a writer's claim that a particular opinion exists. Maybe it reveals something of the speaker's character.

But the usefulness of a quotation has its limits.

In fact, little of what most speakers say bears quoting. Speech wanders. It repeats itself. It wallows in the mundane. Unless someone's saying something truly colorful, authoritative, or revealing, let your pencil rest. Nothing dulls up a piece of writing like a stream of boring quotations.

Why quote directly, as my newspaper did, if a source has nothing more controversial, dramatic, or graceful to say than "We're now producing 300,000 pairs of shoes a day" or "The Wilson River is expected to reach flood stage of eleven feet at about 2 a.m. Saturday"? Such utterances add nothing but information, which is why some editors refer to them as "information quotes."

Pro forma quotes—predictable pronouncements by stuffy spokesmen—are even more damaging. They lack the spice that an especially colorful quote adds to a story. They're too cold and remote to reveal anything about the speaker's character. And they seldom deal with controversial pronouncements from a high authority, which means they don't need the word-by-word precision that a direct quotation offers.

Quotations from business promoters are particularly suspect. When one company buys another, for example, the acquiring firm's PR department invariably grinds out a press release. The names change. But the content is always carefully designed to put a cheery face on the transaction:

> *"Our management team is enthusiastic about the prospects for this new relationship," said Kraig W. Karmers, president and a member of the management investor group. "We look forward to achieving GAC's full potential and building a substantial entity within the high-quality commercial printing industry."*

Business types aren't the only offenders, of course. Politicians are masters of the pro forma quote. They can instantly muster a positive—but inoffensive—comment about anything. But when it comes to pro forma quotes, police are some of the worst offenders:

> *"Since no one was injured and the suspect was taken into custody, it may lead people to believe that success can be achieved in aggressive acts directed at armed suspects," said Officer Mark Hyde, police spokesman. "This certainly is the exception and not the rule."*

Sports has its own formulas. Quote-collecting is the essence of sportswriting, and quote-giving is a skill required for sports stardom. One of the best-loved scenes in *Bull Durham* is the rookie's locker-room lesson in delivering the postgame pro forma quote.

Plenty of those make it into print.

> *"Alonzo is a very good player," said Laettner, whose previous career high was twenty points. "I thought about my game, not Georgetown's. I just wanted to do what I did all year, get the ball inside."*

Accomplished sports quote–givers will always think about their games, of course, not the opponent's. Just as sports figures who win always "come to play" and "give 110 percent." Losers have different problems. They "come out flat" and "never find their usual intensity."

Which is a pretty decent description of pro forma quotes in general.

As these examples indicate, it's sometimes best not to quote at all. When somebody takes twenty minutes to provide a minute's worth of information, you perform a valuable service by extracting what's valuable in a short paraphrase.

Sometimes a nugget turns up in what is otherwise a mundane or convoluted sentence. In such cases, you can paraphrase part of the sentence and quote the rest. So long as you're faithful to the speaker's intended meaning, partial quotes serve readers by trimming the fat and leaving the meat for public consumption.

Isabel Wilkerson, a Pulitzer Prize–winning reporter known for her meticulously researched book *The Warmth of Other Suns*, won't even consider using a direct quotation unless it consists of "words spoken by a source that reveal what you could never, ever say yourself—or imagine yourself—told in such a memorable way that you would like to immediately go and tell it to a friend."

She asks four questions before using any quotation:

- Does the quote move the story along? Is it an integral part of the story? What happens to the story if you take it out? Does it fit seamlessly into the story?
- Does it focus, sharpen, and strengthen the section of the story it is in, or merely repeat something?
- Does it say it better than the reporter can paraphrase it?
- Does it provide facts and facts alone? If so, paraphrase. Critical information should not be conveyed in quotes.

"I think of quotes as spices," she says. "Spices in themselves have no nutritional value. They make nutritious things taste better but, like spices, quotes should be used sparingly."

HAZARDS OF THE QUOTED WORD

Nothing riles sources like the feeling that they've been misquoted. All of us are deeply offended when someone puts words into our mouths. In fact, a misquote is serious enough to merit a legal remedy even if it does no harm to the alleged speaker's reputation. That particular sin is called false-light invasion of privacy.

Of course, sources often claim they've been misquoted once they face the consequences of seeing their own ill-chosen words in print. Most public figures know how to beat a quick retreat when their published comments shine a spotlight on their own bad judgment. Nonetheless, sources do have legitimate concerns about the way writers use their words. In response, writers should be concerned about the ethics of quoting.

Any writer should, of course, be scrupulous about the accuracy of anything put inside quotation marks. Most editors will allow minor changes to clean up grammar or the small oral missteps that plague all speech. But beyond that, the speaker's words are inviolate.

On the other hand, writers are under no obligation to present the speaker's words in the exact order in which they were first spoken. "Play with the quotes by all means," says William Zinsser, "selecting, rejecting, thinning, transposing their order, saving a good one for the end. Just make sure the play is fair. Don't change any words or let the cutting of a sentence distort the proper context of what remains."

Neither are writers under any obligation to preserve the punctuation or style of a quote lifted from another printed source. After all, no punctuation issued from the mouth of the original speaker. Neither did the capitalization, abbreviation style, or any other mechanical aspect of the quotation.

Writers *do* need to be sensitive in the way they use quotations. Research confirms that some journalists show their prejudices by polishing the language of sources they admire while deliberately choosing inane, awkward comments from those they dislike.

Realize, too, that you may demean the less educated if you quote their less-than-articulate comments word for word. On the other hand, you don't want to arrogantly convert everybody's speech to your own idea of what's correct.

"I think the American language is pure poetry," said Carol McCabe, an American Society of Newspaper Editors national writing award winner. "I feel very strongly that it is condescending to make everyone sound as if they're speaking Standard English when they are not. I think their speech is just as good as any I could make up for them. I'm not trying to make it ungrammatical or make them sound stupid. I'm trying to let the poetry of the life they've led, the experiences they've had, come out through the rhythms of the speech."

As Mark Twain demonstrated, a skilled writer can make a dialect quote serve as a powerful agent of characterization. When Buck Grangerford tells Huck Finn that "by and by, everybody's killed off an' there ain't no more feud," you know you're dealing with the real thing.

But dialect can be dauntingly difficult. Educated writers who attempt to capture the authentic flavor of regional, ethnic, or class dialects often end up sounding like just what they are—educated writers attempting to write dialect. They can sound like condescending snobs who set themselves above the human beings they're writing about. You certainly don't want to underscore class or racial differences in ways that make you sound self-consciously superior.

Neither do you want to drain great characters of their color. When pioneering bluesman John Lee Hooker came to my town, talked about his early experiences with music, and said, "The blues done grabbed me, and it ain't ever let me go," the music critic at my paper had the good sense to quote him verbatim.

ECHO QUOTES

In the hands of a clumsy writer, even the best quotes lose their zing. And nothing trashes a good quotation more than spilling its contents in the setup, leaving the quote itself a mere echo.

Logically enough, such mishaps generally go by the name of "echo quotes," although some critics also refer to them as "stutter quotes." In any event, they're like telling the punch line of a joke out of order. An example:

> *Elorriaga was born in Jordan Valley, where his father built a home after immigrating from Spain. By the time Elorriaga was born, his parents had turned the home into a boarding house.*
>
> *"I was born and raised in a Basque boarding house in Jordan Valley," he once recalled.*

Echo quotes make writers look foolish, and they betray the knee-jerk quality that characterizes many of the quotations you see in news media and magazines. Writers include quotes out of sheer habit, without regard for whether they're truly needed. The results look like this:

> *Chaney is nervous about that and wants to hear from more victims.*
> *"We need more victims to come forward," Chaney said.*

> *Lawrence Taylor, the New York Giants All-Pro linebacker, had no drugs in his system when he was arrested on an alcohol-related charge, according to police in Newark, N.J., "There were no drugs," a police official said.*

OUT-OF-SEQUENCE QUOTES

A little planning ensures that readers will have everything they need to understand a quotation before they reach the quote itself. If a writer has to backtrack, adding "this is what he meant by that" information after the quote, he failed to sequence the quote properly in the first place.

Parenthetical material dropped into a quotation almost always means the writer didn't take the time to set the quote up properly before presenting it.

Consider a widely published report about new research indicating personality is almost fully formed by age thirty. Parenthetical explanations marred almost every quotation:

> *"For example, the person who suddenly gets married at age forty and changes his job and place of residence . . . after about two years, you can't say anything (about what effect this had)" . . .*

> *"A lot of this (debate) depends on how you define personality. . . ."*

> *"(Positive events) do not challenge our basic notions about living and what our life is about in the degree that negative experiences do."*

Good planning, in contrast, presents lively quotations in an order that makes instant sense. Here's an entertaining passage, by Field Maloney, published in a *New Yorker* piece about city sanitation workers field-testing a gel that's supposed to block even the worst odors. One of them visits a fish market.

> *The market was closed for the day, but a fishiness lingered. "They clean this place up and they hose it down, but you can never get that smell out," Anderson said. He approached some pallets. "All the fish guts soak into the wood," he explained. He bent over a pallet and began to sniff. A security guard came over. "Sanitation. I'm doing a*

survey," Anderson said with authority, and the guard retreated. Anderson bent down again—a few more long sniffs—then said, "This stuff works pretty good."

ATTRIBUTIONS, THEN AND NOW

As a general rule, news media and magazines differ in the way they attribute quotations. Consider this direct quote from *Time* magazine:

> *"When you open a bottle of nutritional supplements, you don't know what's inside," says Jeffrey Delafuente, a pharmacy professor. . . .*

And this one from the *Oregonian*

> *"Lakefront residential property on Lake Oswego is a property valuation 'hot spot' where values are soaring, while the value of property elsewhere in that city . . . generally is stable," the county assessor said.*

Both quotations serve the same purpose: They cite experts offering an opinion about a continuing characteristic of their respective fields. And both cite talking heads who pop up—and then disappear—in reports that trot out several sources and offer a broad view of their topics. The quotations are not part of a chronological narrative. No description of contemporaneous action surrounds them.

But the attribution for the magazine quote is in the present tense. And the attribution for the newspaper quote is in the past. Why the difference?

The answer, I suspect, is simply habit. Most newsrooms attribute the vast majority of quotations in the past tense. Magazines, on the other hand, operate under a system that calls for the present tense in some circumstances and the past in others.

James Stewart, the former *Wall Street Journal* page-one editor, makes a case for the magazine approach in *Follow the Story*, his book on the tools of nonfiction. Stewart, the author of *Blood Sport* and *Den of Thieves*, calls for distinguishing between quotations that appear within the context of a narrative and quotations that are simply responses to a reporter's questions. He calls the former, logically enough, "narrative quotations," and refers to the latter as "contemporary quotations." Narrative quotes, he says, usually play best with past-tense attributions. Contemporary quotes call for present-tense attributions.

This distinction seems to guide most modern magazine practice. When *Time*'s pharmacy professor made his comment on nutritional supplements, he was speaking in a contemporary sense, commenting to a reporter about the general state of supplement regulation. But when the then-mayor of New York made a public statement explaining the city's policy of seizing the cars of first-time drunk drivers, *Time* attributed his comment in the past tense:

> *Giuliani explained that when an accused drunk driver is cleared in criminal court, the city may still use civil forfeiture statutes to take his car.*

My own advice takes a form similar to Stewart's. When you are writing in a historical sense and the attributed quote appears in the context of surrounding action, use the past tense: "The judge stepped down from the bench and said . . ." And the same principle applies anytime your source is dead.

But when you are merely quoting a talking head making some statement about a current condition or fact—something believed yesterday and likely to be believed tomorrow—use the present tense: "The judge says justice delayed is justice denied."

WHEN ASKED ABOUT . . .

Unnecessary use of "when asked about" usually characterizes the amateur. Most of the direct quotations published are, in fact, responses to questions. Tacking "when asked about" onto a quote adds nothing and bogs down the copy.

It's also a way for intrusive writers to jump into a third-person story that doesn't call for their presence. "Look at me, look at me!" they seem to be saying. "I asked a question!"

> ***Asked how they would*** *vote on the recycling measure, 82 percent of the participants said they would vote yes. . . .*

> *"We try not to be real philosophical here," he said* ***when asked about*** *the ramifications of the game.*

The impulse to inject "when asked about" into the equation can reach ridiculous proportions. Consider these three paragraphs about Norma McCorvey, the "Jane Roe" of *Roe v. Wade*, the landmark Supreme Court abortion case:

> ***Asked*** *if she had been in love with the man who fathered her second child . . . she answers, laughing, "I was in love with his body."*
>
> ***Asked about*** *his most outstanding characteristic, she cracks, "He shot a great game of pool."*
>
> ***Asked*** *if she still thinks she should have aborted that baby, she says, "Absolutely," but her face has lost its tough line.*

Remember: Anything that doesn't add to our writing detracts from it. So why not reject the when-asked-about impulse in favor of simple, direct narrative?

> She had little feeling for the man who fathered her second child. "I was in love with his body," she says, before wisecracking that his one outstanding characteristic was that "he shot a great game of pool."
>
> She remains certain she should have aborted the baby. But considering that thought softens her tough expression.

It is true that some quotations exist only because an interviewer asked a question and insisted that the source respond. If readers won't fully understand a quote without knowing that it was in response to a direct question, then the writer should include that information.

But there are ways to do that without using the passive-voice when-asked-about construction. For example:

> *Isn't this a little early in the gubernatorial campaign to flood the airwaves? Barbara Roberts' campaign will not spend a single dime on television advertising in the next two weeks.*
>
> *"Terribly early," said Skip Hinnman, the general manager at KATU. . . .*

IV. Dialogue

Don't say that the old lady screamed. Bring her on and let her scream.
—Mark Twain

Writers venture out, collect direct quotations, and then return to their keyboards, where they sprinkle their prizes into their copy. The quotations are, in fact, physically disembodied from the contexts in which they were uttered. Hence the notion of "talking heads."

Dialogue is altogether different. When a writer records a scene that contains human beings talking to one another, the words are connected to the speakers *and* to the environments where they were first spoken. In a sense, they're not quotations at all, but part of an unfolding action line. And action almost always draws readers more compellingly than exposition.

When Gay Talese began "Mr. Bad News," his landmark profile of veteran *New York Times* obituary writer Alden Whitman, he opened the story at a quiet dinner party, where Whitman bantered with his wife:

> *"Winston Churchill gave you your heart attack," the wife of the obituary writer said, but the obituary writer, a short and rather shy man wearing horn-rimmed glasses and smoking a pipe, shook his head and replied, very softly.*
>
> *"No, it was not Winston Churchill."*

And when Mike Weiss opened a lengthy *San Francisco Chronicle* series on the making of a California wine, he took readers to the posh New York restaurant where a customer would taste the first glass from the new vintage.

> *Kaye was ready to taste the wine. He swirled it in his stemware. The wine was pale gold, the color of California in early summer. He took a tiny taste.*
>
> *"Mmmmm," he said. "Light. Fruity. It's delicious."*

These openings put readers *into* the scene, to let them experience the moment for themselves. The writer selects a few key details to give a conversation a sense of place. Then he reproduces a part of the conversation exactly as it originally took place. Because readers have the illusion of experiencing what they're seeing and hearing firsthand, they're far more likely to respond emotionally.

Tom Hallman used dialogue with powerful emotional impact throughout a story on a mountain camp for delinquents, a place where the worst of the worst get one last chance to turn their lives around. Group therapy is an important part of the treatment there, and this conversation unfolded as a new boy participated in his first session:

"You said you were afraid. Who more, your mom or your dad?"

"My dad. He tied me up and kicked me and hit me. They sex-abused me. Mom tied me in a blanket, and Dad put a sock in my mouth."

"What did Mom do?"

"She humping me."

"Do you know what that means?"

"I was on top . . ."

"Did you run away from her?"

"No."

"Do you dream about your mom?"

"Yes."

"Good dreams or bad?"

"Good."

The Chapter 8 Cheat Sheet

FIVE WAYS TO GET PEOPLE INTO YOUR WRITING

1. **Tell stories to get stories.** Anecdotes add color to almost any form of nonfiction, but they're tough to get. Try priming the pump by telling stories that illustrate the points you'd like to make. "I hear Harry's really fastidious. My dad was that way. He'd blow up if I moved even one tool a few inches out of its place on his workbench. Does Harry ever do anything like that?"
2. **Watch for meaningful vignettes.** Details aren't the only aspects of reality that are sometimes freighted with larger meaning. Short bits of action also can reveal larger truths. Yes, the worn, cracked boots represented the hard working-life of their owner. But so did the way he hobbled over to his bunk at the end of a long day.
3. **Look for little stories that reveal character.** At its simplest level a story is a protagonist confronting a complication and resolving it. And nothing reveals character more than the ways human beings go about dealing with the problems of daily life. So look for anecdotes that illustrate the key personality traits of your characters.
4. **Quote selectively.** Anytime you feel the need to use a direct quotation, ask three questions: Does the quotation (1) lend authority by attaching a highly credible name to a controversial assertion? (2) reveal character?

(3) add spice? If you can't answer yes to at least one of the three, paraphrase.

5. **Let characters talk to one another.** Direct quotations are useful for some purposes, but nothing displays human nature better than dialogue. Look for opportunities to stand aside and let readers eavesdrop on the revealing conversations your characters have among themselves.

9
Color

There are no dull subjects. There are only dull writers.
—H. L. Mencken

SEDUCING READERS

One of the disconnected bits I remember from grad school is a little equation called the fraction of selection, which supposedly explains why an audience chooses one media message over another. According to the equation:

$$\text{Probability of Selection} = \frac{\text{Expectation of Reward}}{\text{Perception of Effort}}$$

For most readers, pulling a phone out of a pocket, touching an app on the screen, and getting instant access to online news feeds is a lot easier than buying an old-fashioned newspaper and sitting down to read it. A shrinking number of readers, on the other hand, cling to the legacy medium. They think the editing that selects and arranges stories according to their importance or the familiar comforts that come from sitting down in a favorite chair with a hard-copy newspaper make up for whatever extra effort they put into the process.

The fraction of selection also helps explain why readers seek out some authors while shunning others. If you want to maximize the reach of *your* writing, maximize your personal probability of selection. You have two ways to make the fraction bigger: Reduce the perception of effort or increase the expectation of reward. Or both.

You reduce effort by making your writing more forceful, direct, and clear. You increase reward by adding nuggets that give pleasure. Think of them as the chips in a chocolate-chip cookie.

Paula LaRocque, the former writing coach at the *Dallas Morning News*, has her own version of my grad school guideline. Think of readers, she says, as hikers on a trail through the woods. They're not sure where they're going, or whether they should keep going at all. To keep them moving you drop goodies every now and then, little gems they can pick up and tuck in their pockets as they march along. Even if the trail gets steep, they'll keep going if they suspect another reward waits around the next bend.

What rewards do writers have at their disposal? What pleasures do mere keyboard pounders have to scatter along the trail? Reading has practical rewards, of course—the knowledge you need to assemble your kid's bike on Christmas Eve, or the directions to your cousin's beach house. Substance goes a long way with readers. But reading offers intangible rewards, too. Most of them involve the writer's willingness to share personal experiences and insights.

An example: I'm writing this on a sunny November day in an office that overlooks a park. Outside the window a yellow-and-orange curtain of vine maples hangs before a wall of green firs. When a burst of morning sun strikes the maples and ricochets through the window, as one just did, the room fills with an intense autumn glow. That's a pleasure worth sharing.

It's also a literal example of how color can brighten an otherwise ordinary moment. The notion of jazzing up a black-and-white background with splashes of color is so apt, in fact, that journalists use the term "color" as a catchall for just about any writing designed to give pleasure in its own right: a surprising comparison, an unexpected modifier, or a revealing detail that's exactly on point.

Writing colorfully involves some risk. Similes fall flat as often as they surprise and delight. Modifiers can state the obvious. Reckless use of detail can produce tedium or confusion.

Some overly cautious writers, fearful of those pitfalls, retreat into bland recitations of facts and abstract opinions. They may get the job done, but they're unlikely to acquire readers who seek out their writing for the sheer pleasure of it.

They miss something else, too. For a writer, color is its own reward, a bit of payback for the extra effort that goes into creating it. Wordsmiths take pride in well-turned phrases, just as athletes savor especially classy moves. Almost all basketball players score at least some points, but only a few of them dunk. And the writer who contents himself with easy layups and ten-foot jump shots misses the exhilaration that truly well-chosen words can spark. So take that risk. You'll blow a few shots, but you'll have fun doing it. And when you score points with style, both you and your readers win.

I. From the Earth to the Heavens

My task, which I am trying to achieve, is, by the power of the written word to make you hear, to make you feel—it is before all, to make you see. That—and no more, and it is everything.
—Joseph Conrad

THE LADDER OF ABSTRACTION

I picked up one of my most useful writing tools from an undergraduate semantics text, S. I. Hayakawa's *Language in Thought and Action*. The book introduced me to the notion that words exist on a continuum running from the absolutely concrete to the cosmically abstract. Hayakawa called that continuum the ladder of abstraction.

The idea is simple, but profound, and it represents a tool useful in almost any kind of writing. Let me illustrate with the lead of a routine news story:

> *A Portland truck driver was hospitalized early Tuesday after he was seriously injured when someone threw a rock through the windshield of his truck near the St. Johns Bridge.*

At first blush, that sounds fairly concrete. But close your eyes and try to visualize what it describes. At least ten thousand truck drivers must live in my area, and the story doesn't offer a clue as to what this one looks like. You can't form a distinct image of "a Portland truck driver" in your mind. To do that, you must get much more specific. In Hayakawa's terms, you must descend to the ladder of abstraction's bottom rung, where you'll find a single trucker.

Let's call him Fred. A description of Fred is as specific as you can get when you're talking about truck drivers. Everything about him distinguishes him from other drivers, and so you can draw on his full range of characteristics for your description. You might mention his full beard. Or his wire-rimmed glasses, his stocky build, and the bald spot on top of his head. Or maybe you'll mention the way he walks with his legs spread a little, swaying slightly.

With a little concrete description like that, you can create a picture of Fred in the reader's mind. Writing that produces mental pictures almost always comes off the abstraction ladder's bottom rung.

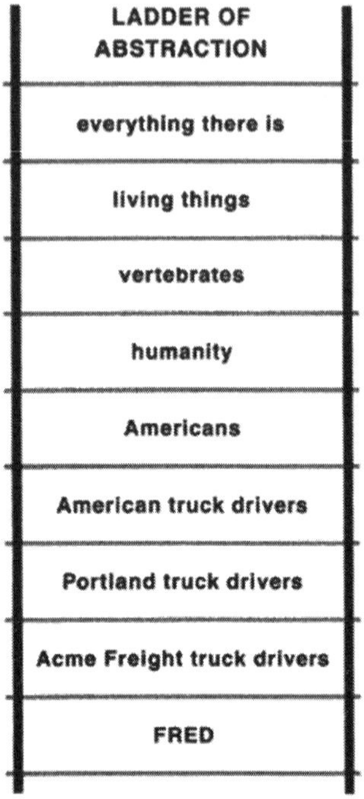

Figure 6. Ladder of abstraction

Your chances of engaging the reader's imagination fade as you move up the ladder of abstraction. Each higher rung represents some larger class containing the thing described at the bottom rung. But progressively fewer characteristics are shared by all the members of the class represented.

Let's say that the next step up from the rung where Fred himself sits is the rung representing the twenty drivers who work for his company, Acme Freight. You can make some general statements about Acme drivers. You might say all of them are men, for example, and that they all wear white coveralls with the company logo on the right breast. But description at that level forms only a vague image, at best.

By the time you get up to the rung representing every American truck driver, you've arrived at a large class indeed. Some are men; some are women. Some are short; others are tall. They actually share only two characteristics—they're American and they drive trucks. Those characteristics aren't specific enough to help you form even a murky mental image.

That's the level typical of most newspaper stories and a great deal of the writing produced in all forms. An article on traffic safety might, for example, report that fifty thousand drivers died in highway accidents the preceding year. An article on autism might note that one in every two hundred children born will suffer some form of the disorder. Both reports describe thousands of cases, with no specific detail relating to any one human being. They offer readers nothing they can see, hear, smell, or taste.

The imagery gets even murkier as you rise beyond that level. Who can form a mental image of a vertebrate? Of a living thing? The classes are too large. The points in common are too few.

Eventually, you approach the top rung, which represents the class containing everything. At that rarefied height, all the members of the class have no characteristic in common, except that they all exist. Writing at that level produces no mental images at all.

Nonetheless, most useful knowledge occupies rungs fairly high on the ladder of abstraction. Things are meaningful to the extent that they apply to large classes of objects. That way, we can generalize our knowledge, applying it in lots of different situations. Einstein's $E = mc^2$, for example, works on the ladder of abstraction's uppermost rungs. You can't visualize mass or energy in the abstract, but the equation is enormously useful because it applies to everything in the visible universe.

Lots of news stories fall short because they never climb the ladder of abstraction to a level that would make them more meaningful. If you're going to do something more than an accident report on Fred the truck driver, for instance, you'd better explain how Fred's example illustrates something about truck drivers, or Americans, or human beings.

But while abstract writing can effectively tap larger meaning, it's almost always an utter failure at generating emotion. Human beings respond emotionally to specific people, places, and actions. Writers who hope to stir emotions have to provide the sensory details that evoke those things. That's exactly what the recent brain research on mirror neurons demonstrates. Only specific detail lights up the "theory-of-mind network," which is where we process our perception of the emotions and actions of others and reproduce them in our own imaginations.

Contrast the news lead on the injured truck driver with John Hersey's *Hiroshima*, which at one point describes a group of soldiers blinded by an atomic bomb flash:

> *When he had penetrated the bushes, he saw there were about twenty men, and they were all in exactly the same nightmarish state: Their faces were wholly burned, their*

eye sockets were hollow, the fluid from their melted eyes had run down their cheeks. Their mouths were mere swollen, pus-covered wounds, which they could not bear to stretch enough to admit the spout of the teapot.

Hersey's words form a horrific mental picture and provoke a wrenching gut response. The passage says nothing about larger issues such as man's inhumanity to man or the dangers of nuclear proliferation, but it engages the deep emotions—generated by mirror neurons—that might open readers to a discussion of those topics. And emotion-generating specificity draws audiences. Best-selling books and blockbuster movies almost always succeed at making audiences laugh, or cry, or shudder.

Purely abstract writing discourages most readers. Who wants to sit through a sermon that drones on about sin without mentioning any dirty deeds, or a long, equivocating speech by a cowardly politician?

Specificity also helps an audience understand what you mean when you ascend the ladder of abstraction and start generalizing about huge categories. You can praise patriotism all you want. But readers will respond differently depending on whether you define a patriot as someone who flies the flag or as someone who protests a popular war.

One of the secrets of good writing, then, is to be both specific *and* general. You engage emotions and illustrate generalizations with concrete detail. You make your writing meaningful by including abstractions that connect your specifics with other examples drawn from different times or places.

Whatever you do, don't get stuck on the boring middle rungs of the abstraction ladder. Every day, writers churn out millions of words that describe mind-numbing bureaucratic processes without mention of individual human beings or larger meaning. They are stuck somewhere between heaven and earth, and their readers never get to sample the joys of either.

UP AND DOWN, UP AND DOWN

Good writers move nimbly on the ladder of abstraction, never staying too long at any one level. None was nimbler than Walt Harrington, a former *Washington Post* writer and University of Illinois journalism professor. Consider the way Walt moved up and down the ladder in "The Shape of Her Dreaming," a *Washington Post Magazine* story that explored the creative processes of Pulitzer Prize–winning poet Rita Dove.

Walt began with a generalization about his subject's working habits.

Twilight is not the time Rita Dove prefers to work. Much better are the crystal hours between midnight and 5:00 a.m., her writing hours when she lived in Ireland the summer of 1978, before her daughter was born, and Rita was young, with only a handful of poems published, before the Pulitzer Prize, before she became poet laureate of the United States.

The opening wasn't on the highest rungs of the abstraction ladder. It said nothing about all of humanity, or even all poets. But it was a good way up the ladder, making as it did a relatively abstract statement about Rita Dove's preferences and summarizing events that spanned two decades of her life. By beginning on the ladder's higher rungs, where abstract terms reach across large, meaningful categories, Walt could quickly tell readers who Rita Dove was and why they should care about the way she created a poem.

But if he was going to engage us in Rita Dove's story emotionally, he had to descend the ladder quickly so that we could experience her world more directly. He did so in the third paragraph:

But this afternoon, for the first time in a while, she sits at her desk in her new writing cabin, which stands down a sharp slope from the back door of her house in the countrified suburbs of Charlottesville, Virginia. . . . The cabin is small—12 by 20, a storage shed with insulation and drywall, a skylight so tiny it's more like the thought of a skylight, a wall of windows whose mullions create miniature portraits of the woods, pond, mountains and sunset to the west.

One person, one place, one time. That's about as close to the ground as you can get. Most readers would have found their interest immediately engaged. They already knew Rita Dove was a big-deal poet, and they knew that they were about to spend time with her in her private writing space.

Then Walt popped back up the ladder a rung or two to give readers some context:

The last few days, Rita has been thinking about three poems she'd like to write. . . .

And then, in his story's fourth paragraph, Walt set the hook, delivering the seductive promise of a bottom-of-the-ladder, hands-on, intimate experience that few readers would be capable of resisting. He revealed his plan to take them along on a seven-week journey with Rita Dove while she created a single poem.

> *It will be a curious, enlightening journey: one poem, one act of creation, evoked from a thousand private choices, embedded in breath and heartbeat, music, meter and rhyme. . . .*

Walt lingered on the abstraction ladder's bottom rungs for a couple of paragraphs. He flashed back to a specific incident a quarter-century earlier and explained how it led to a poem she'd never quite finished. Then, always nimble, he jumped up several rungs to say something general about Rita Dove's writing process:

> *Rita has, after a fashion, a filing system—plastic folders in yellow, blue, red, purple, green, pink, peach, or clear. She doesn't file her nascent poems by subject or title, as a scientist or historian might file documents. She files poems by the way they feel to her.*

The poem she was about to finish, the one that had its genesis twenty-five years before, was in the clear folder. Walt got quite abstract as he built suspense by telling readers they were in for a special experience. The clear folder was reserved for "perfect, clear, pure, lyrical" poems. As Rita Dove described it,

> *"It was a daunting folder. Very few things ever made it out of that folder."*

Once the poet began writing, Walt's narrative continued its adroit movement between the extremely specific and the general. When he described action, he did so minute by minute:

> *February 10, 4:30 p.m. In her cabin, Rita stands at the Schreibpult, the stand-up writing desk that her father, an amateur woodworker, built as a surprise for her two years ago when she turned 40.*

When he generalized, he placed what he was describing within meaningful contexts that sometimes embraced the entire human race:

> *Some people's minds run from point A to point B with the linear determination of an express bus roaring from stop to distant stop. Theirs are minds trained to avoid*

detours, to cut a path past the alleys and side streets of distraction. Rita's mind is more like the water of a stream swirling randomly. . . .

And so it went. Specific action ("March 13, 4:23 p.m."). Larger insights ("But what convinces you is the way the poem influences your breathing, your heartbeat. It becomes a physical thing").

A writer in control of his material doesn't bounce up and down the ladder willy-nilly. Depending on where he is in his story's overall structure, Walt may have spent more time on the ladder's upper or lower rungs. As Rita Dove's new poem began to take shape, the story approached its climax, and Walt knew it was time to immerse readers in the moment-by-moment action. So he stuck to the abstraction ladder's lower rungs, showing us each step toward completion. Finally—on March 26 at 1:43 a.m.—Rita Dove finished the poem.

In her cabin, Rita hears the distant woof of a dog. Outside the open window is a faint wind.

The breeze reminded her of the time her father used the word "zephyr" to describe such a wind. Her imagination engaged. And Walt closed by showing us how Rita Dove's swirling mind was off on an unpredictable journey to another poem.

II. The Telling Detail

The artist, having chosen his theme, picks out only those details that are characteristic and of value for his subject . . . and he rejects all the remainder and puts it to one side.
—Guy de Maupassant

Young writers often learn that detail is important before they understand that good use of detail requires careful selection. Effective writers choose details that serve a larger purpose. Is it important to show readers that a character is obsessively neat? Then by all means describe the meticulously organized pens and pencils on her desk. Do you need to capture the crystalline cold of a January morning? Then the sparkle of sunlight through the icicles hanging from the eaves may suit your purpose.

What you want, in other words, is *telling* details, bits of reality that suggest something larger. At their best, telling details operate as symbols that help make an author's case for a literary theme.

A well-chosen detail can tap levels of human response unavailable to writers who offer only abstractions and generalizations. Abstract writing can inform and persuade, but it cannot light up those mirror neurons in the theory-of-mind network. It cannot, in other words, bring readers to genuine sadness, or horror, or euphoria. Simply exhorting an audience to laugh or cry is pointless, and cheap tricks designed to manipulate emotion are readily apparent to their intended victims.

Abstract thinking originates in the cerebral cortex, the highest and most recently evolved part of the brain. But emotion emerges from the ancient core of the brain as a direct result of external stimulation. Because descriptive writing that's rich in telling detail can approximate experience, it can also reproduce a human being's emotional response to experience.

When readers call or write to tell me a newspaper story that I've edited made them laugh or cry, I know I've helped the writer operate effectively on the difficult bottom rungs of the abstraction ladder. Engaging readers with detail is one of the most demanding—but effective—ways to connect with your audience. At its best, it becomes art.

GETTING OUT OF THE WAY OF THE WORLD

It's the kind of frustrating conversation I had all too often. A reporter would return from the field, sit down in my office, and tell me what he found. The conversation would usually go something like this:

Reporter: The poor guy's in a bad way.
Jack: How so?
Reporter: He's living all alone.
Jack: Where?
Reporter: In a skid-road flophouse.
Jack: In one room?
Reporter: Yup.
Jack: What's it like?
Reporter: Seedy.
Jack: What do you mean?
Reporter: It smells. The plaster's cracked.
Jack: Smells like what?
Reporter: Urine.
Jack: What's the furniture like?
Reporter: I dunno. Ramshackle.

And so it would go. The reporter would give me abstractions; I'd ask for specifics. He was headed for a story that would begin this way: "The onetime golden boy of junk-bond financing has fallen on hard times." I was hoping he'd produce something like:

> *Krystal Wilhelm crouches on the seventh stair of the Merlin Apartments, thin knees pulled against her 16-year-old stomach, insides cramping. She's dope sick. Living in the Merlin, one cracked cement step from the street, the Coeur d'Alene girl knows impure drugs are an occupational hazard. She rocks with cramps. But she needs $2 for a pack of cigarettes and that means going upstairs, finding her shoes, and heading out into the cold for a "date."*

My reporter's story would be immediately forgettable, a speck of gravel in the daily avalanche of bad news. But Julie Sullivan's *Spokane Spokesman-Review* portrait of a young drug addict became a classic, the winner of a national award from the American Society of Newspaper Editors and a favorite example for journalism instructors intent on illustrating the power of detail.

The difference is all in the level of abstraction. Our impulse is to observe specifics, reach conclusions, and report the conclusions. On first meeting, a mother rises from her brood of eight children and gives you a hug. You describe her as "warm." A gas station attendant tells you to "shut off the damned engine before you blow us all to hell." You describe him as "caustic." A metal desk and chair sit alone in a room on a linoleum floor, and you describe the scene as "stark."

You're doing exactly what you've been trained to do. Modern education is all about inductive reasoning—learning how to generalize from specifics. When you start school, you see Spot run. When you finish, you discuss the common attributes of animals that hunt in packs.

Nothing's inherently wrong with that, of course. We built modern civilization out of meaningful abstractions. Einstein thought about streetcars and clock towers and came up with special relativity.

But as a writer, you have a different mission. Reaching readers, drawing them into a world you create on a page and making them experience it with both head and heart, requires that you show them exactly what you're talking about. Before they can get to the same place you are, they need to see what you saw, hear what you heard, and smell what you smelled. You must share your experience, not the conclusions you drew from it.

What made you think the room was stark, anyway?

Step one on the route to increasing your impact through better use of detail is to retrain yourself. Rather than immediately running everything you see and hear through your mental meat grinder, live in the moment and experience the world firsthand, aware of the specifics that are causing your emotional and intellectual reactions. Record the specifics and use them to re-create your reaction in your readers.

"Find what gave you the emotion," Hemingway said. "Then write it down, making it clear so the reader will see it, too, and have the same feeling that you had."

PUTTING DETAIL TO WORK

Among other things, detail can help you develop atmosphere, scene, character, and theme:

1. Atmosphere

An atmospheric detail is one specifically selected to create mood. Thomas Mann, for example, used dark, damp streets to create a foreboding atmosphere for *Death in Venice*.

Notice how my former colleague Spencer Heinz selected detail to re-create the atmosphere of a quiet downtown reading room:

> *Papers rattle softly. When books come back on rainy days, sometimes you can smell the pulp. The room is clean and warm. Other than the silence, there is the creak of the volunteer's chair and the breathing of a man who does not do it easily and the whisper of a comb through hair. Whenever someone opens the door, the window blinds go* clink.

Atmospheric detail doesn't have to appear as part of a full-fledged scene. Individual details dropped into your writing here and there help put readers into the picture, enlivening everything from a novel to a thank-you note. They can create a snapshot of a bitter winter day or a warm afternoon at the zoo:

> *. . . so cold that the chill burns through the soles of boots.*

> *. . . ice cream dripping down bare arms raised to point at giraffes.*

2. Scene

We organize most novels, movie scripts, plays, and books of literary nonfiction as a progression of scenes that eventually tell a full story. (For a full chapter on scene-setting, see *Storycraft*, the sequel to this book.) The writer creates each scene by carefully combining key details. In a play such as *Death of a Salesman*, that may be no more than a kitchen table and three chairs. In a movie such as *Ben-Hur*, it may be chariots, horses, and the dirt track in the Circus Maximus.

This scene, from a 2019 *USA Today* story by Deborah Barfield Berry and Kelley Benham French, painted a picture of Luanda, Angola's capital, as an American Black woman returned in search of her roots:

> *Low adobe huts blurred past, roofs held down by concrete blocks. Then came peeling high-rises with rusty air conditioners. Wash lines with colorful clothes hung from balconies. The city bustled with people, but few of them seemed in a hurry. Children headed to class in white uniforms. On the sidewalks, people prayed, bounced babies, grilled yams, crammed bus stops, peed against walls, braided hair, carried strings of fish.*

Or this drive-by view of Pecos, Texas, for a feature on rodeo cowboys by the *Oregonian*'s Ken Wheeler:

> *It's hot, dry, and quiet in Pecos, where a few calla lilies the shade of Dr Pepper are about the only color at the motel where the cowboys stay. Two-foot-high weeds guard the curb at the closed State theater. The nearest picture show now is 80 miles away, in Odessa.*
>
> *The cook-waitress at Ma Wilson's Texas-Sized Donuts tucks the white plastic fly swatter under her arm while she makes change.*

If you draw on information already stored in the reader's head, you can create a scene with even fewer details. Gustave Flaubert said three would do it, and that's about right. Most of your readers have been to a roadside diner, and you can create a full image of one in their heads by mentioning only the booths with a view of the parking lot, the steamy kitchen visible through an opening in the wall behind the counter, and the waitress who calls you "hon."

David Margolick, a contributing editor for *Vanity Fair*, illustrates this principle in a column he once wrote for the *New York Times*, when he describes the low-rent offices of two lawyers:

> *With its frosted glass doors and their gold-leaf lettering, the offices at 401 Broadway, where Diller practices with his son, Jonathan, are a throwback to the era of Sam Spade and Miles Archer.*

Diller's quarters are furnished in Naugahyde and linoleum, with a business card taped hastily to the door. The only rug in sight is the one atop his head.

3. Character

As Margolick's reference to Diller's toupee illustrates, details reveal character as well as place. The use of detail for characterization draws on a stored inventory of traits that are linked in our minds. If I tell you a male character is slightly built, wears wire-rimmed glasses, and favors bow ties, you will not only form an image based on those traits, but will also expand them to form a more complete picture. This character, you might reasonably conclude, isn't likely to pass afternoons drinking beer and watching NFL games.

Note how Somini Sengupta of the *New York Times* made economical use of character-revealing detail to quickly characterize the ragtag rebel army then besieging the forces of Liberian dictator Charles Taylor:

From rebel headquarters, meanwhile, came threatening words from General Sheriff, the rebel chief of staff, a man missing a couple of teeth and wearing a red beret and gold-rimmed glasses.

Or how Philip Kimball's *Harvesting Ballads* captured class, age, and economic status in this thumbnail description:

Old man unshaven, double-breasted pinstriped, crumpled. Both elbows, hands cradled round an empty shot glass.

4. Theme

All detail should justify its existence by working toward your overall writing goals. Just what are you trying to accomplish, and how does each detail help you achieve that?

Ultimately, those questions return you to your theme—the mission that lies at the core of every thoughtful bit of writing. The theme I sketched out before beginning this discussion of detail, for example, was "detail reveals meaning." So each of the specific elements I've included in the passage should help build the case for that assertion.

When Anthony Shadid, perhaps the finest modern war correspondent, covered the American bombing of Baghdad, he clearly was struck by the way the attack ripped apart ordinary lives. His award-winning reports often juxtaposed the details of family life and images of sudden, horrible violence:

> *Hours later, the 35-year-old day laborer looked out over the detritus of his house. A cracked porcelain plate that read "God" hung on the wall. On the walk outside was the severed hand of Samad Rabai, 17, the owner of an appliance store.*

Rich Read, then head of the *Oregonian*'s Tokyo bureau, wrote a piece on Japanese schools, demonstrating that stultifying policies originating in the national ministry of education produced unimaginative children interested in little but conforming. Among the details he chose was this gem describing the stifling Japanese education bureaucracy:

> *The ministry's detailed requirements extend to stipulating the height of school desks, which has been adjusted upward four times since World War II as students' average height has increased.*

The education ministry's pronouncement on school desks is highly specific, but it stands for something much more universal, a bureaucracy's all-controlling impact. In that sense, the detail serves—as the best details invariably do—as a symbol. The small represents the large; the tangible stands for the intangible.

III. Emotion

No tears in the writer, no tears in the reader.
—Robert Frost

COLOR ME SAD

At their most basic level, stories involve sympathetic characters encountering complications that change their lives. Surely one reason that form has such deep appeal is its potential for provoking emotion.

Spencer Heinz, one of the most intuitive feature writers I ever worked with, had a knack for finding stories filled with the compelling details that produce an emotional response. Studying his technique is a good place to start learning how to get emotion into your own writing.

No matter how many times I read it, I always choke up when I read one of Spencer's most powerful pieces. A ninety-one-year-old Oregon man and his longtime wife were faced with the fact that they had to leave the house where they'd lived for fifty-eight years. Spencer's story took us out to the house, introduced us to old Harold Underhill, filled us in on the necessary background, and then quietly told the story of an ordinary life that was coming to a close. We all can identify with that—Harold Underhill might live next door.

Spencer's topic met the first requirement for evoking emotion: It introduced us to a sympathetic character involved in a challenging situation, the basic story setup that recent brain research confirms as one we're hardwired to find engaging. And the most emotional topics always deal with changes such as the one the Underhills faced—the loss of a child, a brush with death, a rite of passage, an abandonment, a change in a relationship to a loved one.

But where Spencer's story really scored was with specific detail that put readers into scenes, allowing them to experience an emotional reaction directly rather than just hearing about the writer's emotions.

Emotion simply cannot be felt secondhand. Tell a friend that something was really sad, and you are more likely to bore him than sadden him. Explain that you are about to tell a truly funny story, and you're likely to ruin the humor. When it comes to feelings, the map is definitely not the territory.

Writers who succeed in evoking emotion take you to the territory directly. They show you the details that provoked emotion in themselves, and they thereby provoke the same emotion in you.

Spencer's sketch of Harold Underhill was a stream of such details, all smoothly woven into a short narrative. Because of his storytelling strategy, Spencer had to introduce Harold's sixty-one-year-old son, Bill, a California insurance agent. But he kept the focus on Harold himself, and the details that brought him to lovable life. Bill, he wrote,

> *was 637 miles away, but when he closed his eyes, he could see his father on the phone. His father would be sitting by the front window. He would have his cane. He would be wearing, maybe, his functional purple suspenders, and his black buckle shoes, and his good-looking Hamilton watch.*

The watch, as Spencer was astute enough to mention, was a gift from Harold's wife, Patsy, on the occasion of Harold's fiftieth birthday. It was engraved "To Harold From Patsy, 3-26-48."

That alone was enough to raise little lumps in a thousand throats. But the story went on. Harold had back problems. His wife had broken her hip. They couldn't get up and down the stairs anymore. They were too far from their children. It was time to join their son in California.

And always, the touching little details: Harold's breakfast menu—waffles on Monday, chipped beef on Tuesday. The oak floor he installed despite his bad back. The basement workshop with the lined-up jars to hold his nails and screws. The flowers in the yard. The twenty-two-dollar property tax statement from the 1930s. The missing neighbors, familiar faces that gradually disappeared as the years drifted by. Harold's favorite chair.

Spencer made sure we knew that when Harold and Patsy arrived at the airport, two wheelchairs would be waiting to carry them down the long corridor. On the plane they would sit with special bulkhead seating, "for leg room," and they would fly to California, where they would live down the street from Bill. Their son would take care of them for the rest of their lives.

> *Fifty-eight years was a lot to leave and not just for the parents. Bill had grown up in that home. But it was time to start new lives. Once they decided to try, this became the hardest thing for the father to tell his son:*
>
> *"But we can never reciprocate."*
>
> *"Pop," his son replied. "I'm just returning something you've given me."*

IV. Artful Modifiers

Whatever the thing you wish to say, there is but one word to express it, but one word to give it movement, but one adjective to qualify it.
—Gustave Flaubert

WHEN NOUNS AND VERBS NEED SOME HELP

Savvy writers let nouns and verbs do most of the work. Instead of "very deep canyon," they write "chasm." Instead of "walked clumsily," they come up with "stumbled." Still, all those adjectives and adverbs exist for a reason. Sometimes they can express nuances that exist beyond the power of the most accurate nouns and verbs.

An accomplished writer nonetheless turns to modifiers with care. She knows that modifiers can trap her in purple prose that obscures her focus. Flowery writers seldom confine themselves to modifiers that relate to a central point, but more disciplined writers will use only those modifiers that help build a case or advance a story line.

High-potency adjectives and adverbs are original, unlike the knee-jerk modifiers that automatically attach themselves to some nouns. Who needs to hear about one more "spirited chase"? Or another "troubled teenager"? And haven't we all had enough of "angry mobs," "nasty cuts," and "trying times"?

Strong modifiers evoke strong images. The more a modifier suggests a recognizable item, the more it connects with readers, as in these imaginative examples:

> *. . . she pushed a* **burn-scarred** *wooden spoon around the saucepan.*

> *Pollen grains are coated,* **M&M-style**, *with recognition proteins. . . .*

> *. . . but Dixon was pretty pleased his future wife wasn't wearing makeup. The farm isn't a* **face-fiddling** *kind of place, he explained.*

> *Over the road, the Phantom has all the* **glycerin** *smoothness and* **cathedral** *quiet you could hope for.* (Dan Neil, writing about a new Rolls-Royce in the *Los Angeles Times*)

V. The Magic of Metaphor

I love metaphor. It provides two loaves where there seems to be one.
—*Bernard Malamud*

CUTTING FINE FIGURES

"The greatest thing by far," wrote Aristotle, "is to be a master of metaphor."

Why the high praise? Perhaps it's because viewing one thing in terms of another uncorks the human creative process. Combine two previously isolated categories and something mysterious happens. Synapses sizzle. New connections appear. Synergy fashions meaning greater than the sum of the parts.

Metaphor was the clay the great physicists used to mold new theories of the universe. Einstein first talked of trains and clocks, then expanded the images to weave time and space into a single fabric. Freeman Dyson looked to simple earthly things and fashioned them into a workable design for a starship.

Metaphor is a habit of the literary mind, and many writers toss off apparently effortless figures of speech. I once watched Hunter Thompson string together a pastiche of amazing images after decimating a fifth of Wild Turkey. And I still remember the way Norman Mailer zigzagged his way through a series of unlikely—and brilliant—comparisons on a late-night talk show.

What we see in someone like Mailer appears to be a completely different cast of mind. We think "A is like B." He writes "A is like Z," and we suddenly view the world through fresh eyes. The skill is so developed in such minds that we're inclined to credit their rare ability to talent alone. But evidence suggests that metaphorical thinking is a skill you can learn. In *A Moveable Feast*, Hemingway recalls the days when he and Fitzgerald careered through the Spanish countryside in an open car, playing the metaphor game. One would point to an object as it came into view. The other would generate a figure of speech involving it. If he succeeded immediately, the other took his turn. If he failed, he took a drink from a jug of wine and tried again.

We can develop our own skills, too. In all likelihood, none of us will ever match Hemingway or Fitzgerald, but we can nourish metaphor in our writing. To the extent that we succeed, we'll enrich the experience we give our audience. Clever, witty, or revealing figures of speech provide one of the basic pleasures of reading. An especially apt metaphor surprises and delights. It opens new levels of meaning. It gives readers an incentive to keep moving forward, confident that more rewards wait somewhere ahead.

Journalists often reserve metaphor for feature writing, but it's effective in hard-news reports, too. Richard Harding Davis described the advance of the German army's gray uniforms through Belgium as a river flooding its banks, as fog rolling toward someone looking out to sea. William Bolitho described Sarah Bernhardt's funeral as "a playing to the gallery," "a pageant she had planned." Quentin Reynolds described a reporter trapped by the German advance on Paris, and therefore left with no means to transmit his story, as "a jockey without a horse."

However you use metaphor, developing your own metaphorical habits of mind will pay dividends, not only in your writing, but also in your life. The concentration it takes to see the world in metaphorical terms enriches your perception, helping you to see, hear, smell, and feel the details of your environment more intensely.

FIGURATIVELY SPEAKING

Figures of speech take four basic forms, each of them a variant form of metaphor. They are:

1) **The pure metaphor**, which simply describes one thing in terms of something else.

A small school of salmon fishermen working, their boats below the Hawthorne Bridge.

2) **The simile**, which makes an explicit comparison between one thing and another.

Skittering away like a crab from boiling water.

3) **The allusion**, which adds meaning through a reference to a person or thing known to both writer and reader. Allusions often draw their comparisons from literature or the popular arts.

. . . when life stretched out like an endless American Graffiti *summer . . .*

4) **The personification**, which describes an inanimate object in terms appropriate to a living thing, especially a human being.

Classic double-breasted suits by the likes of Gianfranco Ferré and Yves Saint Laurent whisper of well-aged money and Republican voting records.

X-RAY VISIONS

Pure metaphors describe one thing in terms of something else. The most apt identify natural connections, normally unseen bonds that link two apparently isolated things.

> Manhunter*. . . is a dark locomotive of a movie, dragging the audience with it.*
>
> *They will be used as a benchmark to measure future growth in the visitor industry, a sector known for tossing out statistical banana peels.*
>
> *Distance reduced a herd of cattle to a handful of tossed cloves.* (Annie Proulx in the *Atlantic*)

IT WAS LIKE THIS, SEE . . .

Similes are metaphors that make explicit comparisons. They often use the word "like," although that preposition doesn't appear in every simile.

For example:

A police car cruises by, silent, slow, like a porpoise patrolling the deep.

Vaughan chooses his words with the deliberation most people reserve for the dessert tray.

Yet, now, Hollis says, he's straighter than a free-throw line.

MUTUAL ACQUAINTANCES

Allusions forge connections between writers and readers. Writers mention something familiar to their audiences, trusting readers to understand. They mention a name and move on, avoiding long explanations that would belabor a point. Audiences recognize not only the reference, but also the trust and the sense of being included in something unspoken.

A rich allusion will tap dozens of connections in an instant. All that additional information attaches itself to the writing, expanding its content beyond the words that actually appear on paper.

But that miracle happens only when writers pick allusions that connect with most or all of their readers. A literature professor can be fairly esoteric if she's writing for other literature professors. But more diverse audiences require more care. Only the best-known people and objects will resonate for a substantial portion of the audience.

For American audiences, the most widely known references relate to pop culture. Writers aiming for a broad audience will draw most of their allusions from blockbuster movies, best-selling books, and popular television programs. In short, they'll prefer Batman to Barthelme.

The Armada is the Double Whopper with Cheese of SUVs. (Dan Neil writing about Toyota's supersized sports utility vehicle in the *Los Angeles Times*)

. . . the reality landed with the impact of a Tyson uppercut.

. . . he listens to his coach, Pat Foster, as if Foster were John Houseman reading Dickens.

WORDPLAY

Writers who love language like to play with it. They're comfortable with words, and they feel free to horse around with them. The results are often witty and engaging, bits of color that lighten the reader's load and reveal the writer's humanity.

Surprise is the mother of all humor, and words with double meanings have special potential for wordplay. One local film reviewer dismissed a particularly bad movie by writing that "*Frozen Assets* was shot in Portland, a fate some may wish on the filmmakers."

One of the business writers I worked with for years, a woman whose natural exuberance combined with extraordinary writing skills, produced a continuous stream of wordplay. In a Fourth of July feature on the frankfurter business, she noted that "the wiener market is a dogfight these days because of price competition," and that, as a result, a local meatpacker was "the only Oregon-based packaged hot-dog maker left in a market that has become grindingly competitive."

There have been a million dog puns linked (*arrrgggg* . . .) to wieners, of course. But clever wordplay can raise a smile with material that's already been twisted and turned a thousand different ways. The only requirement is that the approach be fresh.

Even the old "roses are red" gambit is good for an occasional poke in the ribs. A clever science writer introduced an item on manipulating DNA to produce oddly colored flowers this way: "Roses are red and violets are blue—unless biotechnology changes the hue."

THE LONG VERSION

One of the virtues of strong metaphors is that you can extend them. As you work your way through a piece of writing, you build on the original image and open up new elements of the subject. At the same time, the extended metaphor provides a framework for other story elements and unifies the writing.

At its most complex, the extended metaphor can contain the central message of an entire novel or book of creative nonfiction. Norman Mailer's *Of a Fire on the Moon* begins with an image of a summer night filled with Americans who've dragged truckloads of high-tech camping gear along with them into the wilderness. He then extends the image to explain the entire American space program as something created by gadget-loving pioneers.

Here are a few more examples of metaphors that clicked more than once:

> *Lee Bontecou, who vanished from the art world in the 1970s after a star-burst of fame, has spent the past few decades working in a remote Pennsylvania barn, producing a series of huge, ethereal, wire-and-ceramic sculptures that hang in midair, like exploding galaxies. . . .* (Paul Trachtman in *Smithsonian* magazine)

The Far East is like a boxcar behind a tired steam engine called Russia, which grinds along a rickety track losing cars even as the crew tries to convert to diesel. The crew could mutiny. The passengers could starve. Conductors could shove the tipsy engineer out the door.

The track is more hazardous here. . . .

Yet if the locomotive doesn't crash first, the Far East could find salvation by coupling with the rest of the Pacific Rim. . . .

SAMPLE SIMILES

As if Eugenie had read Mitchell's thought, she fired a hard glance that struck him like a hurled shot glass. (Annie Proulx in the *New Yorker*)

If the decision to wed was made in haste, their commitment may be as stable as a pup tent in a desert sandstorm.

Maybe it was when the cupboard knob cracked in half and crumbled in my hand, like an Egyptian relic suddenly exposed to fresh air after centuries in the tomb. . . .

Scallions, mushrooms, magenta beets sliced thick as the heels of shoes.

Arnold has grown as an actor even as he has shrunk as a body builder. More important in Hollywood, his box office appeal has bulked up like a rhino on steroids.

APT METAPHORS

Oklahoma's gusher of football crude has spilled onto the cover of Sports Illustrated.

Whelan cuts to the core of the case against apples treated with Alar. . . .

Homer, Alaska, tucked at the end of the North American road system, is a sort of Key West in a parka.

ARTFUL ALLUSIONS

Days disappear like the dwindling dollars in Donald Trump's bank account.

. . . a policy that covers fire, theft, explosion, wind, airplanes crashing into your house, and a plague of calamities even Job couldn't imagine.

As stories of marriages go, John and Betty's is more like a Mel Brooks comedy than an Ingmar Bergman drama.

THE TANGLED WEB WE WEAVE

Like most worthwhile goals, figures of speech involve risk. Figures can fail when they:

1) strain to make the image fit. The elements of good figures often make a surprising match, but once an accomplished writer combines them, they seem like natural partners.
2) mix inconsistent elements of the image, resulting in a mixed metaphor.
3) make no sense. Cautious writers pause after they've written a figure of speech. They close their eyes and visualize what's just been described. The figure should translate to an image of something that could, conceivably, occur in the real world.

Each of these attempts failed one or more of those tests:

The spotlight will focus on more than 100 of the metropolitan area's finest young musicians.

(A spotlight may single out, but it doesn't really focus. And, in any event, it's hard to imagine anything focusing on more than a hundred individuals.)

As he walked up the eighteenth fairway amid lingering twilight Thursday in the opening round of the 118th British Open, Wayne Stephens of Britain was in the process of chiseling his name into the tableaus of this championship and striking a blow for all those dreamers who play golf.

Salmon Task Force Members Lock Horns

TOO MUCH OF A GOOD THING

Even the most creative figures of speech work best in moderation. A simile every three or four paragraphs offers just enough spice to flavor the meat. Much more than that begins to overwhelm. Note this example:

> *The test coupe featured the six-speed manual transmission with a shifter that drops into gear* **like a bank vault closing**. *Massive anti-lock disc brakes almost twelve inches across anchor the 968* **like a stake in the ground** *and keep on* **working like the Energizer Bunny** *even after repeated use.*

Every one of those similes works just fine, although the Energizer reference is tired. Any one of them would have given the paragraph enough extra kick to propel almost any reader into the next passage. But together they're too much.

Let the creative juices run like spilled ink when you're banging out your rough draft. Nothing stifles those oddball connections and serendipitous discoveries like the kind of censorship we impose on ourselves when we're feeling uptight. So let 'er rip. If you end up with three similes in a paragraph, consider yourself lucky. At least you have something to cut.

But then it's time to turn cautious. As Don Fry, the nationally known newspaper writing coach, likes to point out, effective polishing often means killing your babies.

LIKE A BAT OUT OF A BELFRY . . .

A collection of similes allegedly crafted by students in English classes:

> *The little boat gently drifted across the pond exactly the way a bowling ball wouldn't.*

> *McBride fell 12 stories, hitting the pavement like a Hefty Bag filled with vegetable soup.*

> *From the attic came an unearthly howl. The whole scene had an eerie, surreal quality like when you're on vacation in another city and "Jeopardy" comes on at 7 p.m. instead of 7:30.*

> *Her hair glistened in the rain like nose hairs after a sneeze.*

> *Hailstones bounced off the pavement like maggots thrown in hot grease.*

> *John and Cheryl had never met. They were like two hummingbirds that had also never met.*

The thunder was scary, much like the sound of a thin sheet of metal being shaken backstage during the storm scene of a play.

His thoughts were all confused and tangled up, like a pair of underpants in a dryer without Cling-Free.

The Chapter 9 Cheat Sheet

FIVE WAYS TO MAKE YOUR WRITING MORE COLORFUL

Metaphor, wordplay, and other imaginative flourishes add life to your writing. They reward readers, and they make writing more rewarding for the writer, too.

1. **Get in touch with yourself.** Pay close attention to how you feel when you enter a room, meet a person, or watch an event. Then work back to the specific details—sights, sounds, smells, tastes—that produced your emotional response. Jot them down. Then pass the most powerful along to readers in a description of what you experienced.
2. **Pick three.** Describe characters by using the three details that most typify them. A handlebar mustache? Round wire-rimmed glasses? Birkenstocks?
3. **Work backward.** Think about the central point—the theme statement—of something you're about to write. Then ask yourself what specific details would serve as good evidence for that assertion. If you're going to claim that big money warps the values of star athletes, what details would illustrate big money and warped values? Fleeing the scene of a traffic accident in an $80,000 Hummer?
4. **Play the simile game.** Train your figurative ear by playing the game Hemingway and Fitzgerald invented while driving through the Spanish countryside. Point to a random object and create a comparison. "That fireplug looks like a second-grade crossing guard." "That streaked concrete looks like the winner's shirt at a watermelon-eating contest."
5. **Count for color.** Metaphors, similes, and other figurative devices work best when you measure them out carefully. Cram three similes into a single paragraph and you become a parody. Write page after page of featureless prose and you become a drudge. So work your way through a rough draft eliminating and adding color. A figure of speech every third or fourth paragraph is usually about right.

10

Voice

To achieve style, begin by affecting none.
—E. B. White

VOICE TRAINING

Most singers start out in a chorus, their own voice submerged in dozens of others. They take their cues from choral directors and sheet music, obediently following instructions so that they won't detract from a unified sound. They take comfort in the knowledge that the sound of the group will drown out any sour notes they might hit on their own.

So it is with most writers. In school they ape standard forms provided by teachers. As they grow older, they adopt the safe, institutional voices appropriate to their roles in life. Lawyers learn to write in legal jargon. Police officers learn to fill out their reports in "policese." Even print journalists, who write for a living, usually hide themselves in the institutional voices of their publications. The facts may change, but most news reports sound pretty much like other news reports. Their individual authors remain in the background, largely invisible, while the chorus sings with a single voice.

But some singers, eager to develop their own sound, eventually break from the chorus, stepping out on their own and originating unique ways of phrasing and delivery. There's only one Billie Holiday, or Frank Sinatra, or Ella Fitzgerald.

Like a singer's, a writer's voice is an elusive thing, the sum of everything that goes into his or her style of written expression. A distinctive vocabulary might contribute to it. So might a preference for particular sentence forms or syntax. Or voice might emerge from even more subtle dimensions of writing. Unique angles of approach to subjects, maybe. Or a characteristic pace or degree of formality.

Ultimately, voice is the writer's personal style coming through in the writing. It's as complex and varied as human personality itself.

In their early efforts to find their own voices, young writers are often like teenagers who all wear the same antiestablishment fashions—they rebel by copying somebody else. When I was a student, we all wanted to sound like Tom Wolfe, so we slathered sheets of paper with italic type, sentence fragments, and exclamation marks. It never occurred to us that you cannot develop a distinctive voice by stealing one from someone else.

For a reporter, developing a distinctive voice also means avoiding the journalese that cloaks so much newswriting in dull, institutional formality. Likewise, lawyers who hope to craft judicial opinions with the eloquence of Oliver Wendell Holmes must stop writing everything like a product-liability disclaimer.

You won't make yourself one of a kind by wearing a clown suit or dyeing your hair purple, either. In their attempts to stand out from the crowd, young writers all too often replace imitation with ostentation. They lard their prose with garish excess, blitzing readers with adverbs, adjectives, and strained figures of speech. Restraint can make a more arresting impression, and the best writers don't let their voices drown out their messages: "The greatest possible merit of style," Nathaniel Hawthorne said, "is to make the words absolutely disappear into the thought."

Mark Kramer, former head of the Nieman Program on Narrative Journalism at Harvard, says the voices of confident, authoritative storytellers are one of the main things that attract readers to narrative nonfiction. The authority that such voices project emerges from their writers' willingness to develop strong interpretative themes. Top nonfiction storytellers step to the foreground not by jumping up and down and waving their arms, but by confidently offering their personal interpretations of unfolding stories.

To be confident you must be relaxed. The best strategy for developing an authoritative voice is simply to be yourself. Yes, that's easier said than done. Writing is usually more intimidating than giving a speech or socializing in a room full of strangers, two activities that make many of us stiff, uptight, and uncharacteristically formal. I advise writers who produce rigid, lifeless work to start paying attention to the muscles between their shoulder blades. If they can relax those, chances are they can relax their writing, allowing a more personal voice to come through.

That's also one more reason why you should write drafts relatively quickly, without constantly doubling back to futz with what you've already written. If you're loose and rolling, the real you has a better chance of emerging from the words. Rein yourself back in during the polishing phase of the writing process, if necessary, once you've produced a complete piece of writing that's distinctively your own.

You create an individual style once you start to feel like yourself when you write. The words must become as comfortable as your skin. If you're relaxed at the keyboard, your audience will feel a personal connection as they read. "Any writer overwhelmingly honest about pleasing himself," said Marianne Moore, "is almost sure to please others."

THE TONE OF YOUR VOICE

Any piece of writing communicates feeling as well as meaning. It may be warm or biting, formal or conversational. It can relax you, make you angry, or give you the creeps. Or it can be so flat and unemotional that its very lack of humanity sends a message.

That dimension of your writing goes by various names. Nobody has a precise definition for any of them, and they are to some degree interchangeable. But here's one way to define the key elements:

- **Atmosphere**—The imaginary environment created by the writer's images and descriptive phrasing. Blue skies and daffodils; streetlights glowing dimly in fog.
- **Level of diction**—The degree of formality that characterizes a piece of writing. You can incarcerate the miscreants in a correctional institution, or you can throw the crooks in jail.
- **Tone**—The overall "feel" that emerges from a written passage. To some degree, tone incorporates both atmosphere and level of diction. Unlike voice, which reflects a relatively constant personality, a writer may vary tone depending on his subject and goal. You might use crude language, brutally direct syntax, rough-edged detail, and fast-paced action to describe a fistfight in a working-class bar. You might elevate the level of diction, write relatively discursive sentences, focus on fine furnishings,

and slow down the action to depict conversation at a university president's reception.

- **Voice**—The individual personality that emerges in writing regardless of what the words actually say. Mark Twain and Winston Churchill had distinctive voices that could be heard in all their writing. So did Hunter Thompson and Tom Wolfe, classic new journalists who displayed two of the most distinctive voices on the literary landscape.

I. Overinflated Language

The simpler you say it, the more eloquent it is.
—*August Wilson*

To develop your own voice you must rid yourself of the insecurity that keeps you from stepping out on your own. Relaxed confidence typifies writers who chart their own courses.

Insecure writers betray themselves in dozens of ways. Stilted, overly formal language is a tip-off. So is a tendency to cloak individuality in the jargon of specialties such as social or police work, law, or journalism. And reliance on buzzwords, slang, and clichés is a sure sign that writers lack faith in themselves. Avoid cheap imitation, and your own distinctive style has room to emerge.

THE POMPOSITY EPIDEMIC

You pick up the sports page and discover that your favorite baseball player has "sustained an injury." Your bank statement arrives, along with a "funds availability policy." The weather reporter tells you "some precipitation is expected." Why can't they just tell you that your favorite second baseman is hurt, your checks won't clear for twenty-four hours, and it's going to rain?

It's odd. Americans are an easygoing lot, and they strike up warm conversations with strangers of all social classes. Such informality sometimes shocks the Brits, who find it unseemly.

But even the most casual Americans ratchet up their levels of diction when they move from conversation to the written word. The off-duty cop sitting next to you at the ball game keeps shouting "throw the bum out." But when she puts on her uniform and makes her first arrest the next morning, she reports that "the perpetrator was attempting to gain entry to the residence when he was apprehended and incarcerated."

Maybe we learn such stilted English in school, where pretentious formality often confers academic respectability. Maybe stuffiness reflects the fear and tension that afflicts most of us when we sit down to write. Or maybe the pomposity that surrounds us is simply contagious.

Whatever the cause, excessively elevated tone is a major curse of American writing. It obscures meaning, wastes time, and puts off potential readers. It also hides the real personalities of the writers who produce it, submerging them in the kind of stiff formality that afflicts nervous job applicants.

You can avoid that kind of stuffiness by relaxing and writing in a voice that more accurately reflects who you really are. And by avoiding the kinds of words and phrases that seldom show up in everyday speech, like these:

APPREHENSIVE

Many coastal residents are ***apprehensive*** *about the first try at a plan designed to guide development.*

And they're worried, too. . . .

EXPENDITURE

Also included was a $30,000 ***expenditure*** *on the Regional Drug Initiative.*

You don't even need "expenditure" in this example: "Also included was $30,000 for the Regional Drug Initiative." In other constructions, consider "cost" or "expense."

FACILITY

Flames Consume Rickreall ***Facility***

The former Walnut Park Fred Meyer store . . . will house a $7.1 million police ***facility****.*

The best nouns and verbs, the ones most likely to form an image and communicate clearly, are specific. The more abstract you get, the farther you are from punchy, vigorous writing. That's the problem with using "venue" when you're talking about a theater or "people" when you're describing "customers," "shoppers," or "protesters." "Facility" has a particularly unctuous tone, a dash of bureaucratic pretense that you could almost always do without. In our first example, the "facility" in question was a fertilizer elevator. In the second, it was a police station.

FREQUENT/INFREQUENT

> *Cullivan said crack house raids* ***infrequently*** *resulted in large seizures of either cocaine or cash.*

How about "seldom resulted" or "hardly ever resulted"?

FUNDS

> ***Funds*** *Sought for Disease Research*

> *More* ***Funds*** *in Sight for . . . Restoration*

Many headline writers are allergic to the word "money," and they substitute the far stuffier "funds" for it at every opportunity. True, "funds" is a bit shorter than "money," and that may matter if headline space is tight. But "funds" often shows up where "money" would fit just fine. And "funds" usually isn't the right word. The dictionary defines a fund as (1) "a source of supply, a stock," or (2) "a sum of money or other resources set aside for a specific purpose." A fund is, in other words, a designated account. "Money" has the broader meaning we usually are trying to communicate.

GAIN ENTRY

> *. . . someone who could take her home and scale a balcony to* ***gain entry****.*

". . . climb to the balcony to get inside."

INCARCERATE

> *But continuing attention has to be paid to whether* ***incarceration*** *and the post-prison supervision the new guidelines also require are effective in curbing sex crimes in the long run.*

Lots of terms substitute for "incarceration." You can jail somebody, imprison him, or lock him up. Then he completes his sentence, does time, or serves time.

ONE

> ***One** does not have to know the difference between Louis-this or Louis-that style to fall in love with French country furniture.*

> *As **one** nears one of the bogs, water pools up in boot tracks. . . .*

One can't get much stuffier than one is when one uses "one." First look to alternatives that use the third person: "As searchers near the bogs, water pools up in their boot tracks . . ." If that doesn't work, the second person maybe appropriate: "You don't have to know the difference between . . ."

PRIOR TO

> *How diabetics should prepare **prior to** pregnancy.*

". . . *before* pregnancy."

PROBLEMATIC

> *Treatment itself, and who is giving it, can be **problematic**.*

Can be a *problem*. "Problematic" is problematic.

PURCHASE

> *Wine stewards **purchase** and market wines and help diffuse the mystique of their products for customers.*

> *Voorhies said he **purchased** memberships for his wife and two daughters in 1984. . . .*

What's wrong with just plain "buy"? Or, in this case, "bought"?

RESIDES

> *Atwell and Wallace held their first five parties . . . near where Wallace **resides**.*

Resides? When was the last time you told someone where you reside? Most of us talk about living somewhere. That's the logical word to use when we write, too.

SUSTAIN

> *Irvin was taking part in the first of Tuesday's two half-hour scrimmages when he* ***sustained a blow*** *from . . . Duckworth.*

Duckworth hit him.

TRENDSPEAK

> Hip influencers in urban centers may enthuse in it as they salve their angst in the latest hot eatery. And foodies with attitude may opine the same sentiments in their own pricey venues. But that doesn't mean gaslighters won't question its GOAT status.

It's Trendspeak, a pastiche of pretentious abstractions, fad words, breezy syntax, overdone alliteration, and misused sociology jargon. It's as superficial, in its own way, as any other form of groupthink. When a writer insists on calling a gym a venue, he betrays the mental depth of the teenager endlessly repeating variations on "Dude, that was, like, awesome."

Trendspeak, like other fad forms of expression, travels as a contagion. Once one celebrity journalist commented on an actress's "baby bump," bumps started showing up everywhere, a kind of plague of Hollywood fertility. At least "baby bump" is plain English. One of Trendspeak's most annoying characteristics is the way its practitioners strive to inflate their own importance by inflating the language they use. They write to *impress* in other words, rather than *express*. One alternative weekly movie reviewer, for example, actually wrote, "*In Defending Your Life*, his fourth directorial effort, he mocks the typical L.A. denizen's acquisitive soullessness and its concurrent obsession with a secular continuation of consciousness."

No kidding. He actually wrote that.

You can inflate the language with more than jargon, of course. Trendspeakers favor large modifiers and hang them on plain-Jane nouns and verbs in the same way a teen mounts a Mercedes hood ornament on his Volkswagen. So an event becomes a "mega-event," as in "Super-Promoter Bob Walsh: Catching the Tide in Mega-Events." And an empire becomes a "veritable empire," as in "catapulted their chain of taverns into a veritable empire."

Alliteration is overplayed in Trendspeak, too, and it contributes to the glib tone characteristic of the form. "Continuation of consciousness" fits the ideal nicely. So does "feisty fungal afflictions," an alternative weekly's synonym for athlete's foot. Or "bucolic bacchanal" and "mammary mania," the same paper's terms for a rock festival and an obsession with breasts.

Trendspeak is by nature elitist. It's preoccupied with hot restaurants, art films, and the kind of avant-garde literature that seldom sells at supermarket checkout stands. It occasionally thumbs its nose at the masses by appropriating their language and using it in trendy contexts. "Eatery," for example, once denoted the kind of greasy spoon where a real person could find a good chicken-fried steak. Now no newsweekly worth its low-salt cooking column would dare publish an issue without three or four references to "eateries" where the price of the cheapest entrée would buy a week's worth of chicken-fried steaks.

That's a little like Cornelius Vanderbilt's pretentious habit of calling his Newport, Rhode Island, mansion—a multimillion-dollar, gold-plated pile of ostentation—a "cottage."

II. Repetition

All styles are good, except the boring.
—Voltaire

Few of us would eat the same lunch every day. And you wouldn't draw many customers to a zoo filled with nothing but ground squirrels.

So what makes some writers think they can get away with ladling out the same old words, sentence after sentence?

Readers respond with the identical impulse that sends the lunch crowd wandering in search of new restaurants and propels zoo-goers from cage to cage.

Each new word stimulates a new mental response. The more constant and varied that stimulation, the more likely the reader's continued attention.

> *Since his* **death**, *Francke's family has raised questions that his* **death** *may be linked to corruption in the Corrections Department. . . .*

Well, we wouldn't expect them to raise such questions before his death. So the repetition was unnecessary in the first place. Still, we could have substituted "killing" for the second reference to death.

> *. . . organizers continue* ***to attempt to line up*** *television contracts.*

The problem here is a repetition of form as much as it is a repetition of words. One infinitive directly follows another. Remember that participles almost always can substitute for infinitives. We might have written "attempting to line up." Or "to attempt lining up."

> *Already this year, drug investigators have seized* ***marijuana*** *plants worth more than all of the* ***marijuana*** *plants they seized in 1988.*

Why not just drop the second direct reference? ". . . worth more than all seized in 1988."

> *But the remarks by Hershiser . . . seemed* ***directed directly*** *at the Dodgers.*

As is often the case with repetition, the repeated material wasn't necessary in the first place. If the remarks were directed, they were directed directly.

> ***Barbers*** *sat idly outside* ***barber*** *shops, talking quietly.*

"Barbers sat idly outside their shops . . ."

> *They were participating in* ***needlepoint****, mosaics, latchhook, cooking, rocketry, canning, cookies, outdoor cookery,* ***needlepoint****, child development, knitting, crocheting, and child development.*

This list was so boring that it even put the writer to sleep.

THE "ELEGANT VARIATION"

You can follow your efforts to avoid repetition off a cliff, resulting in what H. W. Fowler called "elegant variation." Straining at inappropriate synonyms fools no one, and few readers will long suffer writers who insist on calling snow "the white stuff" or a gym an "exercise venue."

The AP's former writing guru, Jack Cappon, pilloried the practice by tracking its more outlandish permutations: "The house in one paragraph blossoms into an edifice in the next, a structure in the third, a residence in the fourth. Never mind that all have different connotations."

Once they take off in pursuit of variations, writers sometimes lose sight of all sane limits. One writer, Cappon says, referred to Mickey Mouse as the "Disney rodent."

Be particularly cautious about elegant variations on simple attributions. The main noun in an independent clause attracts a lot of attention, and the wise writer avoids running it into the ground with unbridled repetition. But inconspicuous words such as "said" can stand a lot of use. A strained search for synonyms may attract more attention than the sin it was designed to avoid.

The following excerpt, taken from what was an otherwise colorful and engaging piece of descriptive writing, illustrates the problem:

> *"There's nothing more American than tailgating," Jayne* ***noted****. . . . "I love football," Jayne* ***enthused****. . . . "There's a rush to it," she* ***explained****. . . . "Lee* ***says****, 'Can't you ever do anything little?'" Jayne* ***related****. . . . "I was up all night making these," Jayne* ***quipped****. . . . "It's a long day," she* ***emphasized****. . . . "All the more important to pick friends you like. Otherwise it's a real long day," she* ***joked****. . . . "Tailgating takes a lot of preparation," she* ***admitted****. . . .*

In this case, the variation outstripped the original. The words "says" and "said" each appeared only once in a nine-hundred-word report.

III. Speaking Plain English

"It would be political suicide to give that speech," an aide said to his boss.

"He's right, Senator," chimed in another aide. "It's just one clear-cut statement after another."

—Morrie Brickman

PRIVATE LANGUAGES

The journalist finishes a long day in the newsroom, heads home, and happily detours into the corner tavern. He settles onto a stool and glances up at the TV flickering behind the bar. On the screen, tanks roll across sand dunes. The guy hunched over the bar next to him gives him a nudge. "Whaddaya think about this jerk who's been pullin' our chain?" he says, his eyes locked on the screen.

The journalist clears his throat. "The administration," he says, "is known to believe that the time is fast approaching when a decision about a military option must be considered."

"Really!" says the reporter's new drinking buddy. He pushes his baseball hat back on his head and swivels on his stool, staring at his unusual companion. "So what else is new?"

The journalist sits up and turns to face him. "Increasingly concerned about Hindu-Muslim violence in the disputed territory of Kashmir, at the border between India and Pakistan, the State Department has moved to expel the leader of a Kashmiri separatist group visiting the United States."

"I'll be damned," he says, taking another drag on his Camel. "I never wudda guessed."

The journalist decides to change the subject. "In arguing for passage," he continues, "supporters of the resolution said the availability of health care, including rights to abortion and family planning services, have a serious impact on the family and work lives of union members."

"Yeah," says the journalist's new companion. "I kinda figured that." Then he rises from his stool, slowly pours his beer in the journalist's lap, and saunters out the door.

Who could blame the irritated barfly? Hardly anybody would suffer such nonsense in a face-to-face conversation.

Yet the news media routinely inflict it on readers, viewers, and listeners. Each of the responses our imaginary drinker unloaded on his bar partner actually were distributed by American wire services. They were, presumably, passed along by hundreds of local news outlets.

They're all examples of journalese, a pattern of language that William Zinsser defined as "a mixture of cheap words, made-up words, and clichés," word forms "that have become so pervasive that a writer can hardly help using them automatically."

News reports are filled with references to "heated debates," "hot pursuits," "stormy sessions," "clashing protesters," and "trendy eateries." The shooter in a murder-suicide never kills himself; he "turns the gun on himself."

The result is a bland, institutional sameness that Tom Wolfe, who got his start in newspapers and then rebelled against newspaper conventions, condemned the "pale beige tone" that surrounded him in newsrooms. That voice, he said, signaled to readers that "a well-known bore was here again, 'the journalist,' a pedestrian mind, a phlegmatic spirit, a faded personality, and there was no way to get rid of the pallid little troll, short of ceasing to read."

Journalese is far more than this week's onslaught of clichés and automatic modifiers. It's any form of language unique to journalism and distinct from the common speech that holds the English-speaking world together. It's not only headlinese and hype, but also strange forms of syntax that trash the natural rhythms of everyday conversation.

Consider this all-too-typical example:

> *Eduardo Martinez Romero, a reputed Medellin cartel money launderer, was flown Wednesday night by U.S. officials out of Colombia bound for the United States, an administration official disclosed.*

If that example sounds normal to you, you've spent too much time reading journalese. Conversational English never would describe somebody being "flown Wednesday night by U.S. officials out of Colombia." We might say "flown out of Colombia Wednesday night." But we'd probably use both conventional syntax and active voice, resulting in this sentence: "U.S. officials flew Eduardo Martinez Romero, a reputed Medellin cartel money launderer, out of Colombia Wednesday night."

Speakers of journalese also favor long introductory phrases that back into sentences, sometimes withholding the actual subject of the sentence for twenty or thirty words, like this:

> *In its most sweeping declaration of policy since leadership changes in June, the Communist Party acknowledged some mistakes Friday but called for vigilance against . . .*

"In" isn't the only preposition used to pile information onto the front of a sentence, although it's the most common. Prepositions such as "with," "between," and "around" serve the same purpose. One of the form's most popular prepositions—"amid"—hardly ever appears in conversational English.

> *Amid a campaign of terror by Colombian cocaine barons, bombs exploded Sunday at nine banks, one of the blasts killing a . . .*

Another popular form substitutes a participle for the introductory preposition. Other than that minor change, the structure is almost exactly the same:

Bowing under intense pressure from members of their own party, House Republican leaders agreed Thursday to accept a temporary extension of the payroll tax cut, beating a hasty retreat from a showdown that Republicans increasingly saw as a threat to their election opportunities next year.

A closely related form is a version of Timestyle, the backward-ran-sentences-till-reeled-the-mind affectation pioneered by Henry Luce in the early years of *Time* magazine. Here's one:

Arrested there on an accusation of distribution of a controlled substance was Uchechi D. Loud, twenty.

Like jargon and regional accents, occupational languages are contagious. Journalese quietly spreads through newsrooms, sneaking up on journalists, who come to think of it as normal.

But nonjournalists don't. They may not be aware of the specific malady. They probably don't tell their friends that they quit reading news stories because they couldn't abide the writing. But why would they choose to spend time with writers who don't speak their language?

The same is true of any other specialized language. Tax forms written in bureaucratese don't do a terribly good job of collecting taxes; they just frustrate taxpayers. Jurors puzzle through opaque police reports, parents scratch their heads as they try to decipher school announcements sent home with their kids, and contractors go crazy trying to figure out building codes.

If you want to communicate with the written word, use the words your readers are most likely to recognize, and use them in sentences constructed like the ones you hear in everyday conversation.

DREAMING JOURNALESE

An excerpt from *Miami, It's Murder*, by novelist Edna Buchanan, a former *Miami Herald* police reporter:

When I finally slept I dreamed in headlines and bad newspeak: Predawn fires . . . shark-infested waters . . . steamy tropical jungles . . . the solid South . . . mean streets and densely wooded areas populated by ever-present lone gunmen, fiery Cuban, deranged Vietnam veteran, Panamanian strongman, fugitive financier, bearded dictator, slain civil rights leader, grieving widow, struggling quarterback, cocaine kingpin, drug lord, troubled youth, embattled mayor, totally destroyed by, Miami-based, bullet-riddled,

Table 1. Journalese: A Glossary

arguably:	It may not be true, but you could argue that it's true.
assassins:	Must have three names (Lee Harvey Oswald, John Wilkes Booth, James Earl Ray).
brave:	Rescuers brave the elements. Firefighters brave the conflagration.
call for:	Senators call for reform. Protesters call for action. Citizens call for tax relief.
clash:	Just about any disagreement results in a clash.
closure:	Nothing closes. It achieves closure.
crisis:	Anything out of the ordinary. Unless, of course, it is especially bad—a crisis situation.
crucial:	Issues are invariably crucial, as are developments and consequences.
eleventh hour:	When every agreement is reached.
escalate:	What happens to feuds, hostility, and animosity.
dampen:	What fails to happen to spirits when it rains on a parade.
embattled:	A politician or agency taking criticism from outsiders, often the press itself.
flare:	Tensions flare, as do tempers.
frigid:	Rescuers brave frigid—never cold—temperatures.
fuel:	Escalating tensions fuel the possibility of war.
grim:	Highway accident tolls are grim. Possibilities may be grim, too.
hammer out:	Negotiators hammer out—never reach—an agreement. At, of course, the eleventh hour.
historic:	Pacts are historic. So are many achievements.
hunker down:	What embattled politicians and agencies do when under siege.
ink:	The verb. Embattled politicians ink a historic pact.
launch:	Others may launch ships or missiles. But journalists also launch garden parties, holiday celebrations, and marathon bargaining sessions.
marathon:	Bargaining sessions, of course. Is there any other kind?
massive:	A journalistic synonym for "big."
modest home:	Where everybody lives who doesn't live in a "stately home" or a "palatial mansion."
narrowly averting:	Fill in the next word or phrase. A crisis, no doubt. Perhaps even a massive crisis.
pack:	Most of us pack suitcases. But in journalese, storms pack winds.
palatial mansion:	The only kind of mansion there is.

(*continued*)

Table 1. *Continued*

plunge:	What the mercury does when storms packing high winds arrive during a blizzard. Thermometers no longer contain mercury, of course. But never mind.
prompt:	When senators call for reform, the resulting eleventh-hour agreement prompts a historic initiative.
serial killers:	Like assassins, they must have three names (John Wayne Gacy, Henry Lee Lucas).
signal:	You might say the senators sent a signal. Or a message.
sparked:	The agreement sparked reform, narrowly averting a crisis.
spawned:	What a cause does to produce an effect. "The conference spawned a historic pact."
spry:	Anybody drawing Social Security.
spur:	Actions within embattled agencies may spur, spawn, or prompt reform.
stately homes:	Aren't quite as big as palatial mansions.
stunning breakthroughs:	The only kind of breakthrough permitted.
threatened walkouts:	Always lead to round-the-clock negotiations.
trigger:	A possible alternative to "spur," "spawn," or "prompt."
weary negotiators:	The human toll for eleventh-hour agreements following round-the-clock negotiations.
white stuff:	Second reference to snow.

high-speed chases, uncertain futures, deepening political crises sparked by massive blasts, brutal murders—badly decomposed—benign neglect and blunt trauma.

I woke up, nursing a dull headache. . . .

IV. Clichés

Adam was the only man who, when he said a good thing, knew that nobody had said it before him.
—Mark Twain

YOU CAN SAY THAT AGAIN

The noun is "hack." The adjective is "hackneyed." The noun refers, according to the *American Heritage Dictionary*, to "one who hires himself out to do routine writing." The adjective identifies something "overused and thus cheapened, trite, banal."

Yet clichés tempt the best of us. In fact, research shows that the better educated are the most likely to pass along timeworn expressions. Maybe that's because they're better read, and are therefore more exposed to the multitude of overused phrases that deaden popular writing.

Clichés are a bane of the newsroom, where verbally oriented, socially involved reporters and editors are especially vulnerable to the latest semantic fad. Here's a small sampling:

> *Maeda said the* ***window of opportunity*** *for securing top candidates after Aug. 20 shrinks each year.*

> *The task force was formed, but it was still like looking for* ***a needle in the proverbial haystack****.*

> *. . . Wood said after his unsung but hungry Broncos pulled* ***a rabbit out of their hats*** *and scored a 63–58 win over defending state champion Grant. . . .*

> *. . . stardom may be* ***just around the corner****.*

> *By the end of his speech,* ***there wasn't a dry eye in the house****.*

> *Five years later, battling* ***a raging blizzard****, I crossed an 18,000-foot pass in the Himalayas and made my way down to a remote Tibetan village.*

> *The decision was greeted by* ***a storm of protest*** *from citizens. . . .*

Don't worry about clichés in a first draft. If you're loose and productive, confidently charging through your first run at your material, you don't want to agonize over every figure of speech. But you should have no mercy when you're polishing your work. Seize on each cliché as an opportunity for something fresh. Instead of writing that a hockey player picked up the pieces, say that he packed his pucks. Let "storm of protest" be the key to some hard thought about the images that a vigorous protest conjures up in your mind. Reject the blizzard that rages—or howls—in favor of one that suffocates or strangles.

Above all, surprise your readers.

THE CLICHÉ WATCH

Been There, Done That

*Before his kidnapping March 16, 1985, by Islamic radicals in Beirut, Anderson, 49, had run aground in the "**been there, done that**" doldrums of his career at The Associated Press.*

The Buzz

*As Gina, the good-girl virgin intent on bedding the washed-up teen idol (Maxwell Caulfield) doing a meet-and-greet at the store, Tyler proves **the media buzz** around her is warranted.*

Closest Friends

*So they invited 600 or 700 of their **closest friends** and associates.*

Cut to the Chase

*Let's **cut to the chase**: In the debate between two men trying desperately to lower their negative ratings, who won?*

Drop in a Bucket

*The study . . . predicts the city's revenue shortfall will be $2.9 million next year, **a drop in the bucket** compared with the $17.7 million estimated by the Office of Finance and Administration.*

Famous for Fifteen Minutes

*Andy Warhol was right: Everybody's **famous for 15 minutes**.*

Everybody may be famous for only fifteen minutes, but Andy's phrase lives on and on.

Get a Life

*Wake up and **get a life** before you die. Leave the smokers alone.*

Get Your Arms Around

*But if they see a need and they can **put their arms around it**, like a building or computers, then they are supportive of education.*

Go Figure

*"We do this [exercise] because we want our guys to find us attractive. **Go figure**."*

Good News/Bad News

It is too early, of course, to make definitive pronouncements about the Sixers, but there was plenty of ***good news*** *and some* ***bad news*** *to sprinkle about.*

Good Times/Bad Times

For Dunning, it was the ***best of times*** *and* ***the worst of times****.*

*It has been—to crib a bit from Charles Dickens—****the best of times*** *for cheats and crooks,* ***the worst of times*** *for honest people.*

Attributing a cliché doesn't freshen it.

Hard-Earned Money

. . . it hadn't forked over its ***hard-earned money*** *to hear the sounds of musical barriers tumbling. . . .*

Funny how money is always hard-earned. Does anybody ever surrender cash that came easily?

Hearts and Minds

It is a case that is in the ***hearts and minds*** *of Wilsonville residents who were shocked by Crawford's violent death.*

Hell Hath No Fury

Hell hath no fury *like a reader scorned on the comics pages.*

In Your Face

. . . the hyped-up dissonances, the cheeky, ***in-your-face*** *spirit of kids on the street.*

Inquiring Minds

So what's troubling Roseanne Barr? ***Inquiring minds*** *want to know.*

Jump-Start

Others say efforts to ***jump-start*** *that weak economy will require further rate cuts.*

Lap of Luxury

That's just one example of the program that operates in the ***lap of luxury****.*

Like, Well

The Cowboys have won five straight and are looking **like, well**, *the Cowboys again.*

. . . an after-shave we presume that smells **like, well**, *a wet gun dog.*

Little Did He/She Know/Imagine/Dream

Little did he know *in 1964 that he would return 30 years later as secretary of the Navy.*

The "little did he/she know" lead is one of the laziest devices in writing. It serves to start almost anything written on anybody who's ever accomplished anything. And it inevitably goes without saying.

Mantra

He repeated what has become a **mantra** *for him It is possible to enact a tax cut that will reduce federal revenue by $548 billion over six years. . . .*

Mean Streets

And like a lot of strangers who wander into New York's **mean streets**, *the show is getting mugged.*

No-Brainer

In normal use, however, operating the top is a **no-brainer**—*lift two latches and push a dashboard toggle to lower it.*

For the average NBA coach, this is a **no-brainer**—*back up the moving van again and load everybody up.*

Only One Thing Is Certain

Currently, **this much only is certain.**

This clause is a variation on the classic broadcast news cliché: "One thing is for sure . . ." It's a cop-out that prevents real thinking. And it's patently false—far more than one thing is sure in almost any situation.

Or What?

Boy is it weird out there **or what**?

Over the Top

McGillivray and Zerlin once considered having the Farndale company produce a Christmas panto, but they figured such plays were so ***over-the-top*** *to begin with that the parody factor would be wasted.*

Path to Someone's Door

Among the people who beat ***a path to her door*** *were former Interior Secretary James Watt. . . .*

Poster Boy

These days, Gilliam might even be considered a ***poster boy*** *for healthful living.*

Radar Screen

*But Thursday he was gratified that the plan at least was on the congressional "****radar screen****" and had support from the Republican leadership.*

Ready and Willing

Now, almost three months after the operation, she is ***ready and willing*** *to share her story.*

Reinvent

Likewise, the administration's plan to ***reinvent*** *the federal government might save $108 million.*

It's not too late to restructure the package or to ***reinvent*** *the agency to make the package work.*

Rocket Science

Not that those of us who work for this newspaper are all ***rocket scientists*** *in the consumer-warning department.*

Same Old, Same Old

But I'm glad I chose to come here. I've met a lot of new people. It's like starting over, and not the ***same old, same old****.*

Send a Message

China's leadership aims to ***send a message*** *to the country's prodemocracy movement.*

Shot in the Arm

Cardroom operators here say they are just offering folks a place to play a friendly hand of cards and give the local economy a **shot in the arm**.

Slings and Arrows

While this battle of words is tame compared to the **slings and arrows** *of the past . . .*

Slippery Slope

But until my kids slide a little farther down the **slippery slope** *to Satanism, count me out of the campaign to blackball Halloween from our October routine.*

Step Up to the Plate

This past year when marionberry growers wanted 59 cents a pound for their crop, one of the first processors to **step up to the plate** *was RainSweet Inc.*

Strutting Stuff

Eight official Lassies have **strutted their stuff** *on camera. . . .*

Take a Backseat

. . . have **taken a backseat** *to worries about the deadly AIDS virus, she said.*

Take . . . Please

Take *state government, for instance.* **Please**.

Tale of the Tape

We enjoy the peacock-primping before the gun goes off, but we can no longer believe the **tale of the tape** *for too many victories come with an asterisk attached.*

Terminally

Along with roadside espresso carts, grunge turned the Northwest **terminally** *hip.*

Think

Think *May to June for this spawn, though some rainbows remain silvery and with that pale hue approaching magenta in some fine examples.*

To Be or Not to Be

To buffer or not to buffer? *That is the question.*

The bit from *Hamlet* is so well worn that even a play on words is tired. Wise writers will avoid *any* variant on any line from Shakespeare.

User-Friendly

> *Many recipes call for flaming the coq au vin with cognac, but not this* ***user-friendly*** *version.*

Viable Option

> *His behavior in the next few days and weeks will have a significant effect on whether that becomes a* ***viable option****.*

Welcome To

Here's the formula for one of our era's most overused openings: (1) Describe some oddball scene. (2) Write "welcome to . . ." (3) Complete the sentence with an abstract characterization of the scene you just described.

> *Two middle-aged sports lay on the bank, passed out in a litter of beer bottles. Two trollers cross lines and curse each other in the middle of the lake. A teenager cuts loose with a tremendous cast and falls off the dock.*
>
> ***Welcome to*** *the opening day of trout season, Deep Lake style.*

Went South

> *. . . but the team* ***went south*** *against Yakima Valley with seven errors.*

> *A gasoline tax for improving roads* ***went south****, too.*

Work in Progress

> *The election of Silvio Berlusconi might have done more harm than good to the reform movement, which remains very much a* ***work in progress****.*

World-Class

> *Burnside Skate Park Is* ***World Class*** *and Ready for National Contests*

Years Young

> *She was 40* ***years young****.*

You've Come a Long Way, Baby

> *Exactly how far has Tobkin come?* ***A long way, baby****.*

The Chapter 10 Cheat Sheet

FIVE WAYS TO DEVELOP YOUR VOICE

1. **Write the way you talk.** Read your copy aloud. Does it sound like you? If not, try making your writing vocabulary more like your talking vocabulary. You want to be as appealing to readers as you are to face-to-face listeners.
2. **Execute the worst offenders.** Pick the three stuffiest words in your writing vocabulary and eliminate them. Likely suspects include "purchase" (buy), "reside" (live), "funds" (money), and "prior" (before).
3. **Think small.** The most meaningful words precisely target their real-world referents. "Dachshund" is better than "dog," and "dog" is better than "canine." Trend words and clichés, on the other hand, often are more vague than the words they displace. Hacks write "venue" instead of "gym," but effective writers look for the words that carve out the smallest possible categories. Precision helps create concrete images in the reader's mind.
4. **Start with the subject.** A sentence that begins with a long phrase smacks of journalese. ("Hoping to detain the worst offenders before any destructive acts could occur the law-enforcement agencies instituted a policy of checkpoints and random searches.") Figure out who's doing what to whom, and then describe it in just that order. ("Police set up checkpoints and conducted random searches, hoping to head off violence.")
5. **Let 'er rip.** Don't worry about clichés in your first draft, when you should be loose, fast, and accepting. When you've finished the draft, go back and figure out a fresh replacement for each cliché. Instead of "needle in a haystack," try some other metaphor for one hard-to-see thing in a vast universe: "Just another drop of oil on an asphalt parking lot."

11

Mechanics

Among artists, a writer's equipment is least out-of-reach—the language we all more or less use, a little patience at grammar and spelling, the common adventures of blundering mortals.
—John Updike

SWEATING THE SMALL STUFF

Any craftsman cares for his tools with professional pride. No good carpenter works with rusty saws and dull drill bits. No capable writer turns in finished copy marred by the errors that shout "amateur!"

Knowing something about mechanics can help you deal with subtler issues, too. How can you achieve sentence variety if you can't tell the difference between compound and complex sentences? How do you choose the most rhythmic alternative if you don't know that you usually can replace a subordinate clause with a participial, gerund, or infinitive phrase?

A *practical* understanding of mechanics is invaluable. So what follows is a quick review of the most common questions facing professional writers. Every one of the bad examples that follows comes from published work, and the space devoted to each subject is in rough proportion to the problem it poses in the real world.

If you want a more thorough grounding, try Joseph Blumenthal's *English 3200 with Writing Applications*, fourth edition. It's a programmed workbook that offers a complete tour of the language, and it's still in print after more than a quarter century. A few minutes each night for a month or so, and you'll have the solid grounding in grammar that you missed in school.

Webster's New World College Dictionary is the official dictionary in most newsrooms, and it's a great guide to standard questions on spelling and meaning. The preferred dictionary for book publishing is *Merriam-Webster's Collegiate Dictionary* When it comes to usage questions—the difference between "lectern" and "podium," or whether you can use "presently" to mean "now"—the *American Heritage Dictionary* with its unique usage panel, was quite useful until 2018, when the dictionary quit offering usage advice. *Merriam-Webster's Dictionary of English Usage* survives, however, and will answer most usage questions.

You turn to a stylebook to find out if it's 12-year-old boy or a twelve-year-old boy, whether you live at 246 W. 25th Street or 246 West Twenty-Fifth Street. Stylebooks may also set rules for usage (does "presently" mean "now" or "in a little while"?) and punctuation. They include forms for everything from election results to box scores.

Different publications employ different stylebooks. Newsrooms usually hew to the *Associated Press Stylebook* (246 W. 25th St.). For a book manuscript, I turn to the *Chicago Manual of Style* (246 West Twenty-Fifth Street) or the *MLA Handbook* (246 W. 25th Street). If those aren't enough options, the US Government Printing Office has its own style manual, and so do publications such as the *Economist* and *Wired*. Some magazines, such as the *New Yorker* combine more conventional style guidelines with their own idiosyncratic rules.

If you're writing for a publication that doesn't have an official stylebook, or if you aren't writing for publication, use the *AP Stylebook*. It's short, simple, and available online. It's not scripture, however. It dates back to only 1975, which is when UPI and AP combined stylebooks. And, as a relative latecomer, the *AP Stylebook* incorporates a number of questionable rules that are fairly recent arrivals. It insists on a distinction between "that" and "which," for example, and some editors seem to think that rule dates back to Chaucer. In fact, the Fowler brothers first proposed the current distinction in 1909. Thomas Jefferson ignored it. So did the translators of the King James Bible. So do many—perhaps most—current speakers and writers of English. So much for divine guidance.

If stylebooks contained revealed truth, they'd be consistent. In fact, they disagree on hundreds of points. The *AP Stylebook* insists that you drop the zeros for the times on the hour and that you write "a.m." and "p.m." in lowercase letters. So journalists write "4 p.m." The *Chicago Manual of Style* recommends retaining the zeros: "4:00 p.m."

And so it goes. . . . AP style uses numerals for numbers above nine, as does MLA style. Chicago style makes the break at ninety-nine. AP uses a single style of dash. Chicago calls for dashes in five different lengths, each with its own use.

Whichever you use, your stylebook will bring consistency to your English mechanics in the same way Dr. Johnson's dictionary brought consistency to English spelling. Consistency simplifies our decision making because we don't have to start from scratch every time we confront a style question. It no doubt helps our readers by making written English a little more predictable.

Adhering to style too strictly can have the opposite effect, producing odd constructions likely to baffle readers:

> *He also helps the river pilots to berth the ships that arrive at night, placing the multiton seagoing vessels within inches of their targets on the docks.*

What's a "multiton vessel"? What the writer meant was "multi-ton vessel." But the editor who handled the sentence was scrupulous about AP style, which says you don't hyphenate prefixes attached to words beginning with consonants. Hence "multiton," which has an odd, vaguely Greek look to it. Perhaps Achilles sailed to Troy in a multiton.

When style violates sense, you should violate style. Write it "multi-ton," and include a note to the editor indicating that you meant it that way.

Just make sure you never get hung up on language mechanics to the exclusion of more important things. Yes, your verbs should agree with your subjects, and you don't want an adjective where the rules call for an adverb. But larger issues such as tone, rhythm, and story structure matter far more. Don Murray, who practically invented the job of writing coach, once complained that "our newspapers are filled with poorly written stories in which no grammatical rule is bent and no word misspelled."

I. Grammar

It is not wise to violate the rules until you know how to observe them.
—T. S. Eliot

EARNING THE READER'S RESPECT

Back in the 1990s, long before politicians began attacking them for selling "fake news," journalists noted that their credibility was sinking. In a panic, news executives commissioned a major study to find out why. One result was especially surprising. According to the study, the No. 1 threat to the credibility of print journalism was that "the public sees too many factual errors and spelling and grammar mistakes. . . ."

Chris Urban, who directed the study, explained: "Even seemingly small errors feed public skepticism. . . . Each misspelled word, bad apostrophe, garbled grammatical construction, weird cutline, and mislabeled map erodes public confidence."

"They used to proofread," one focus group member said. "I don't know what they do now."

They sure don't proofread. Once upon a time, every newspaper story had to survive a rigorous round of proofing after it was set it type. That practice died eons ago. Now even the copyediting at most news organizations is minimal, although copy desks live on at many other publishers. But the threat that inept language mechanics poses to credibility remains. In fact, the instant comments by readers allowed by many online news sources makes the threat even larger. Which means the burden of making sure everything's correct weighs more heavily than ever on the writers themselves.

That—and simple pride in craft—should provide powerful motivation for taking a little time to deal with the most troublesome aspects of language mechanics . . .

KEYS TO GRAMMAR

Grammar concerns the functions performed by the parts of a sentence and the relationships between them. To understand it you have to grasp a few key ideas about the underlying structure of sentences:

Subject: That which performs the action. "*Jack* hit the ball."
Words that act as sentence subjects are in the nominative case.

Predicate: What the subject is or does. The predicate is the verb with any object or modifiers. "Jack *hit the ball.*"

Object: The thing receiving the action in a sentence with a transitive verb. "Jack hit *the ball.*"

Basic Statement: The fundamental components of a sentence. At a minimum, that means the subject and the predicate. "*Jack hit.*"

Phrase: A group of words functioning together. "*Over the ball*"; "*hitting hard.*"

Clause: A group of words containing a subject and a predicate. If the group can stand alone, it's an independent clause. "*Jack hit the ball.*" If the group can't stand alone because it depends on some other idea to give it full meaning, it's a dependent or subordinate clause. "*When Jack hit the ball . . .*"

REACHING AGREEMENT

Every literate person knows that predicates should agree in number with their subjects. You don't write that "the fans is filling the arena with noise" or that "the reason are difficult to discern."

Agreement failures are, nonetheless, one of the most common published grammatical faux pas:

The council's actions, concluding more than six hours of testimony on the matter, effectively nullifies a city hearings officer's decision. . . .

10 Days of Abortion Protests Winds Down

Errors in subject-predicate agreement happen because we dash through sentences and forget what the beginning said before we reach the end. Or because the phone rings in midsentence and breaks our train of thought. Or because we edit part of a sentence and don't read far enough to find that the new material doesn't agree with the old.

As is the case with many kinds of writing problems, one solution is to read your copy aloud before submitting it. Straight subject-predicate problems almost always produce a clang.

But most published subject-predicate errors aren't so obvious, and tricky constructions can trap the unwary into committing agreement errors. By far the worst of them is the confusion created when a prepositional phrase containing a plural noun appears between a singular subject and its predicate. For example:

*A **total** of five youths **were** arrested in both incidents. . . .*

*Early returns from rural areas indicated that **support** for the Communists **remain** strong.*

*A **group** of neighborhood volunteers **are** identifying these houses and forcing owners to fix them up or tear them down.*

"Total," "support," and "group" are all the simple subjects of their respective sentences. A prepositional phrase follows each of them. The objects of those prepositions—"youths," "areas," and "volunteers"—are all plural. The erroneous plural verbs follow those objects.

Most other subject-predicate problems stem from the writer's failure to recognize certain nouns as plural:

> *... but it contains genetic material and reproduces by division, as* ***does bacteria****.*

> Business **Data Waits** in Bookstore

> *His* ***criteria*** *for inclusion, he acknowledges,* ***was*** *vague.*

"Bacteria," "data," and "criteria" are all plural. So they all take the plural form of the verb.

The *AP Stylebook* does make one exception for "data." It says that you may use a singular noun when it describes something acting as a unit, as in "the data is sound." Making that determination, however, can involve some real hairsplitting. When in doubt, treat "data" as plural.

WHEN ONE IS TWO

> ***None*** *of Universal's permanent sound stages, made of concrete and steel and used for interior filming,* ***were*** *destroyed.*

"None" may be the trickiest of sentence subjects. It's a contraction for "not one." Logically, it takes a singular verb for the same reason that "one" takes a singular verb. But the *AP Stylebook* allows for exceptions when it appears with a prepositional phrase that gives the clear sense of "no two" or "no amount." "None of the consultants agree on the same approach." "None of the taxes have been paid."

When in doubt, go with a singular verb.

THE PARTS OF SPEECH

Making the right choices about language depends, in large part, on recognizing the role each word, phrase, and clause plays in the overall function of a sentence.

That means knowing the parts of speech.

If you just need a quick review, here it is:

verb:	A word that expresses action. "The cattle *ran* frantically down the dusty street."

Verbs converted to perform other functions become verbals, which come in three varieties. If you add "-ing" to a verb and use it as a noun ("*Running* caused the cattle to lose weight"), you have a **gerund**. Add "-ing" and use the verb as an adjective ("*Running* cattle scared the children") and you have a participle. Combine a verb with "to" and use it as a noun ("To *run* is to risk injury") and you have an infinitive.

noun:	A word that names a person, place, or thing. "The *cattle* ran down the *street*."
pronoun:	A word that stands in for a noun. "He," "his," "she," "her," "it," "they," and so forth. "*His* cattle ran down the street." The noun a pronoun refers to is its **antecedent.**
adjective:	A word that modifies a noun. "The *frantic* cattle ran down the *dusty* street."
adverb:	A word that modifies a verb, an adjective, or another adverb. "The cattle ran *frantically* down the *already* dusty street."
conjunction:	A word that connects other words or parts of a sentence. "The cattle ran frantically down the already dusty street *and* streamed into a park."

The six **coordinating conjunctions**, which join independent clauses, are "and," "for," "but," "nor," "or," and "yet." **Subordinating conjunctions**, which introduce subordinate clauses, include "because," "unless," "so that," "although," and the like.

article:	A word that introduces a noun. "*The* cattle ran frantically down *the* already dusty street and streamed into *a* park."

MIXED-UP MODIFIERS

A word's function often determines the form it takes, and the distinction between adverbs and adjectives is a case in point. Most adverbs end in "-ly." Most adjectives don't. All too often, we fail to distinguish the two.

Adjectives modify nouns. Most adverbs modify verbs, explaining something about how an action unfolds. That distinction is something the writer neglected in these two examples:

Roberts Moves Too Slow for Some on Measure 5

In these races . . . he could run slow enough that his injuries usually wouldn't bother him.

In both cases, "slow" modifies a verb—"move" in the first example and "run" in the second. The correct form of the modifiers is, therefore, "slowly."

The distinction can be more subtle. Anything that modifies an adjective or another adverb is an adverb, too. Violating that rule produced this error:

But high-skilled U.S. workers who make tractors, road-building equipment, . . . and capital goods for industry. . . .

"High" modifies the adjective "skilled," which makes it an adverb. The proper form is "highly skilled U.S. workers."

"Our players feel very badly," OSU coach Ralph Miller said.

Not likely. Miller's basketball players no doubt felt superbly. They were, after all, fine physical specimens. What he probably meant was that they felt bad after losing a big game.

Here's the rule: If you want to indicate that somebody's ill or emotionally low, you say he feels bad. If you want to say she has a lousy sense of touch—which is almost never the intended meaning—you say that she feels badly.

Here's the reasoning behind the distinction. Verbs such as "feel," "smell," "taste," and the various forms of "to be" often act as linking verbs. When they do, they merely state equivalences. So they take no objects, direct or indirect. A linking verb works like the equals sign in an equation. A = B is similar to A is like B, or A feels like B.

Because such sentences state equivalences instead of describing action, the words on the right side of the equation—those that appear after the linking verb—don't receive action. Instead of being in the objective case, in other words, they're in the nominative case. When a modifier appears in that position, it's a predicate adjective.

In our sample sentence, "bad" doesn't modify anything the players did. Instead, it describes their state of being. So it's a predicate adjective. It describes the players in the same way that words such as "quick" and "strong" describe them.

You wouldn't say that Miller's players "are quickly." And you wouldn't say that Miller's players "are strongly." Neither should you say that they "feel badly."

Ralph Miller did, of course, and that's the way he should have been quoted. But the same error often turns up outside of direct quotes. You can expect grammatical errors from basketball coaches. But you'll feel bad if you get caught making the same mistakes.

THE CASE OF THE WRONG PRONOUN

The most embarrassing pronoun errors concern case. Lots of readers who had the differences between she/her and who/whom permanently etched into their brains in elementary school take mighty offense at sentences such as these:

Bostwick . . . said the office working relationship between he and Penn had broken down.

Jimmy DeFrates . . . is clear about the problems caused by the rules that come between he and his wife.

Brothers said it was not a good situation for either he or Okken. . . .

Most of us would catch such obvious errors if we just read our copy aloud. Wrong-case pronouns just *sound* wrong. But we should understand the basic grammatical principle involved, too. You use "he," "she," and "they" in the nominative case—that is, when they are the subjects of the clause in which they appear. That's when they refer to a person or thing originating the action described. "*He* hit the ball." "*They* crushed the opposition."

Use "him," "her," and "them" for the objective case. "Objective" indicates that the person or thing described is receiving the action: ". . . to knock *him* and Davis Love III out of the lead."

Or, use the objective case when the pronoun is the object of a preposition: "Between *him* and his wife."

The same rule that guides choices between he/him and she/her determines the choice between who/whom and whoever/whomever: A pronoun's case is determined by the clause in which it appears.

Take this sentence: "Give the prize to whoever/whomever shows up first." Well, which is it? At first glance you might choose "whomever" because the pronoun looks like the object of the preposition "to." But the pronoun is the subject of the clause "whoever/whomever shows up first." So "whoever" is the correct choice.

Consider these published errors:

> *The kind of fan who opposing fans love to hate.*

> *You never know who you might run into at Powell Butte Nature Park. . . .*

> *She had a younger sister, Elizabeth, who she quickly overshadowed. . . .*

In the first example, ask yourself who's generating the action and who's receiving it. The opposing fans are the ones who love to hate; so "fans" is the subject of the clause. The single fan, the obnoxious one, is receiving that action. So the pronoun that stands for him should be "whom." In the next examples, the person run into at Powell Butte is receiving the action, as is the overshadowed younger sister. All should be identified with "whom."

One way to sort out such sentences is to turn them around. "Fans love to hate *whom?*" But watch out for this construction:

> *Montana, whom coach George Seifert said wouldn't need surgery, wasn't available. . . .*

You might think that "whom" is the object of "said," as in "said whom?" But "said" is simply part of an attribution: "Seifert said." The pronoun refers to Joe Montana, who is the subject of the clause in question: "who wouldn't need surgery."

SEPARATING THE WHICH FROM THE THAT

The relative pronoun "that" dates to Middle English. "Which" joined it as part of the language shortly afterward. We've been using the two terms interchangeably ever since, but that hasn't stopped various authorities, including the *AP Stylebook*, from insisting on a distinction.

The basic argument is that you reserve "that" for introducing restrictive clauses and "which" for introducing nonrestrictive clauses. To make the issue even cloudier, restrictive and nonrestrictive clauses are also known as, respectively, essential and nonessential clauses.

If you don't understand all this, you're in good company. Neither did Shakespeare, who apparently used "that" or "which" depending on what sounded best.

If you want to understand the modern rule, you have to distinguish between restrictive (essential) and nonrestrictive (nonessential) clauses.

A restrictive clause restricts meaning by setting the noun or pronoun it modifies apart from other members of its class. Take the sentence "This is the house that Jack built." The restrictive clause—"that Jack built"—modifies "house." It restricts that noun's meaning by setting it apart from other houses—the other members of the class to which it belongs.

You can't pull a restrictive clause from a sentence without altering the sentence's meaning. Hence the idea that such constructions are "essential clauses." Other examples:

Hand me the knife that's on the counter.

Check the calendar that hangs in the office.

The reindeer that head south stand a better chance of survival.

Nonrestrictive clauses, on the other hand, say something about all members of a class. They're also called nonessential clauses because you can drop them from a sentence without distorting the original meaning. Some examples:

Switchblade knives, which were outlawed as concealed weapons in 1954, have become collector's items.

Cheap printed wall calendars, which quickly became favored promotional items for American business, increased the demand for stock photography.

Reindeer, which the Laps domesticated in the twelfth century, form a staple of the tribal diet.

A simple rule of thumb helps distinguish between restrictive and nonrestrictive clauses. If you can set a clause off with commas without distorting the intended sense of the sentence, it's nonrestrictive. If you can't, it's restrictive.

Once you have that distinction firmly in mind, the rest is fairly simple. Prefer "that" for introducing restrictive clauses. Use "which" to introduce nonrestrictive clauses.

The rule of thumb for distinguishing the two types of clauses also helps you choose between the two relative pronouns. "Which" should almost always be preceded by a comma. "That," on the other hand, should never be preceded by a comma.

REMEMBERING WHERE AND WHEN

Keeping "which" and "that" straight hinges on your ability to distinguish restrictive and nonrestrictive clauses. But the language is filled with restrictive and nonrestrictive clauses introduced by relative pronouns such as "where," "when," "who," and "whom." Using the proper pronouns with such clauses isn't the issue—the choice is almost always obvious. The problem goes deeper than that.

Some of those clauses are restrictive. And some are nonrestrictive. The only way to distinguish the two is by how they're punctuated. So the writer's choice of punctuation can make a big difference in meaning.

The rule's simple: If you mean the clause to be nonrestrictive, you set it off with commas. If you mean it to be restrictive, you don't. Making the wrong choice can alter the meaning of a sentence. Consider this example:

> *The protesters who denounced the president then marched up Broadway.*

As written and punctuated, the subordinate clause—"who denounced the president"—is restrictive. It means that some, but not all, of the protesters denounced the president and marched up the street. If we were to set the clause off with commas, on the other hand, we'd change the meaning significantly. The commas would signal a nonrestrictive clause, meaning that all the protesters denounced the president and marched up the street.

> The protesters, who denounced the president, then marched up Broadway.

Usually the intended meaning is more obvious. But you still can look silly when you fail to set off nonrestrictive clauses with commas:

> *The . . . State Bar drops its probe of Jonathan Haub who prosecuted a migrant laborer.*

There's only one Jonathan Haub at issue. But the failure to set the subordinate clause off with commas suggests the writer was trying to distinguish this Jonathan Haub from another one.

PUZZLING PRONOUNS

Pronouns can lead you astray in a dozen ways. You can pick pronouns of the wrong case ("For Who the Bell Tolls"). You can pick pronouns that don't agree in number ("Everybody held on for their lives"). You can pick pronouns that don't match the predicate ("Each of the children were excited").

But another breed of pronoun problem can cost you not only credibility with readers, but clarity as well. Note this photo caption:

> *Police and others talk to a thirteen-year-old boy after he was held hostage briefly by a gunman who later shot his mother. . . .*

In fact, the gunman shot *the boy's* mother, not—as the caption would suggest—his own mother. The problem is that "his," the pronoun in question, follows "who," which follows "gunman." Pronouns should follow the nouns or pronouns they modify. If any confusion is possible, repeat the noun: ". . . a gunman who later shot *the boy's* mother."

A similar problem afflicts the lead of the same story:

> *A . . . police officer shot and killed a twenty-nine-year-old man Wednesday evening moments after he shot at and wounded a . . . woman whom he had held hostage in her home.*

The sentence suggests that it might have been the police officer who wounded the woman. Not so. The writer could have clarified by repeating the critical noun:

> A police officer shot and killed a twenty-nine-year-old man Wednesday evening moments after the man shot and wounded a woman he had held hostage in her home.

Misplaced pronouns caused the confusion in these sentences, too:

> *. . . said Marine 1st Lt. Kevin Anderson of Twenty-nine Palms, Calif, who was eating some crackers with his Third Battalion inside Kuwait . . . when he was struck in*

the face . . . by mortar shrapnel. He could feel his shirt fill with blood and saw his sergeant spinning around after he was hit.

The queen was widely reported to have attempted to persuade the duchess, the former Sarah Ferguson, to save the marriage, but she was unsuccessful.

Who was wounded, the lieutenant or the sergeant? Who was unsuccessful, the queen or the duchess? Again, pronouns appear after the wrong nouns. The "he" that should refer to the lieutenant appears after "sergeant." The "she" that should refer to the queen appears after "duchess."

A more extreme version of the problem is the pronoun that has no antecedent at all:

Jordan, a career 28.6 percent three-point shooter heading into this season, went long-range crazy Wednesday night, making six of them in the Chicago Bulls' 122–89 rout of the Portland Trail Blazers. . . .

What did Jordan make? Presumably, three-point shots. But the story never mentions three-point shots. So "them" has no antecedent.

All of which suggests three simple rules for pronoun clarity:

1. Keep pronouns adjacent to their antecedents.
2. Repeat nouns when necessary to avoid confusion.
3. Make sure each pronoun refers to a specific noun or pronoun.

DISAGREEABLE PRONOUNS

Sometimes a pronoun's antecedent is a noun. Sometimes it's another pronoun. In either event, the rule's the same. Plural pronouns go with plural antecedents. Singular pronouns go with singular antecedents.

Watch out for the following common disagreements:

1. SINGULAR NOUN . . . PLURAL PRONOUN

   If the student *lives at home before school starts . . . they can clear $3,325 after taxes.*

   . . . to make it look as if ***the person*** *is standing . . . on* ***their*** *head . . .*

If you refer to human beings with singular nouns, you must follow with singular pronouns. That means he/she or his/her. That's often awkward, but you can avoid the problem by using plural nouns: "If *the students* live at home . . . *they* . . ." ". . . to make it look as if *the subjects are* standing . . . on *their heads* . . ."

The one exception—according to the *AP Stylebook* and the *Chicago Manual of Style*—is when people who identify themselves as nonbinary express a preference for plural pronouns (they/them) in reference to themselves.

2. PLURAL NOUN . . . SINGULAR PRONOUN

__Women__, especially holding wine glass in one hand, cocktail napkin or plate in the other hand, and niftily plucking hors d' oeuvres off a passed silver tray, all the while clutching an elegant little purse under __her__ arm. . . .

Her birthday __parties__ went beyond most girls' wildest dreams. __It__ was a dress-up affair with mother in a cocktail dress. . . .

Plural nouns take "them," "they," and "their." "They were dress-up affairs with . . ."

3. EVERYBODY/NOBODY/EVERYONE/ANYONE AND THE LIKE

__Everybody__ has __their__ favorite parts of the American dream.

__Nobody__, they say, can return from a war zone . . . and remain the same person __they__ were.

. . . an open society in which __everyone__ could achieve __their__ full potential.

. . . a form of humor __anyone__ can make up for __themselves__.

Traditionally these terms have been considered singular and followed by a singular pronoun or by "his or her." As the language changes, however, many language experts and style manuals including AP and Chicago have endorsed limited use of the singular, non-gender-specific "they" in such situations. It's also possible, and often better, to rework the sentence.

Me, Myself, and I

Red Smith said, "'Myself' is the refuge of idiots taught early that 'me' is a dirty word." As in:

The cuffs went on Bozo, with the police standing between him, and myself, and Pam Snavely's father, Henry.

"Between" is a preposition. "Him" is the object of the preposition and is properly cast in the objective case. "Myself" occupies exactly the same position in the sentence. Therefore, the proper pronoun is the objective pronoun—"me."

The same sort of error takes several forms:

> *Harold Jank chain-smokes while talking about the Feb. 7 night a mudslide knocked his house, wife, and himself into the river.* (a photo caption)

The mudslide reporter should have followed Red Smith's advice by writing that the mudslide "knocked his house, wife, and *him* into the river."

There's not much debate on this question. And Red Smith isn't the only authority who says so. Ninety-five percent of the *American Heritage Dictionary* Usage Panel rejected the usage illustrated by the examples.

"Myself" is a personal pronoun that can function in the reflexive case ("I blame myself") or intensive case, adding a little extra when you want to emphasize something ("She wanted to help, but I did it myself"). But the simple rule of thumb is that if you can use normal nominative or objective forms, you should. So in this example . . .

> *Minsker also scoured the Internet, where he found other used-jean dealers like himself.*

. . . you can write "used-jean dealers like him." Therefore, you *should* write "used-jean dealers like him."

THE LANGUAGE OF THE UNREAL

Few grammatical distinctions confuse Americans as much as the differences among the subjunctive, indicative, and conditional moods.

Do you write "if I were older, I might consider it"? Or do you write "if I was older"? How about the same choice in this sentence?

> If a defendant *was/were* found liable for causing injury, another jury would hear a second trial to determine damages.

If you chose "were" for the first example and "was" for the second—and you know why you made the choice—you've figured it out. Go on to something more fun.

But chances are you missed the distinction between the two examples. The subjunctive mood is no different from the indicative in most English constructions, and few of us notice when it isn't. "So be it," for example, is a subjunctive construction that few of us think twice about. If we did, we'd recognize it as strange English indeed.

Fortunately, we almost never have to worry about such fine points. Our screwups deal almost exclusively with one situation—sentences that require us to choose between the true subjunctive and the merely conditional.

The subjunctive mood evolved to describe things contrary to fact, either because they were impossible or because they had not yet occurred. "Were" is the subjunctive form of "to be" in the present tense. So we write, "If I were king of the world." And "be" is the subjunctive form of "to be" in the future. "If he insists on cutting his own throat, then so be it."

But just because a clause begins with "if" doesn't mean it's describing an impossible or future condition. "If" also can describe one of two or more *possible* conditions. The result is a conditional statement, and to make it you use the ordinary (or indicative) mood of the verb. Here's an example:

> I promised to quit if the hill *was* higher than expected.

Use "were" after "if" when you're describing a condition contrary to present fact. Use "was" when you're describing something that could very well be the case. Here are some examples of how you shouldn't do it:

> *Nishida said he couldn't imagine coming back to school for his senior year if there **were** no music.*

The fact is, music *may* be taught during Nishida's senior year. So the writer wanted the conditional. The correct form is "if there *was* no music."

> *That stuff is important, but it isn't the whole job description. If it **was**, broadcasters and sportswriters would be regularly getting big-league managing contracts.*

Because that stuff isn't the whole job description, we are describing something contrary to fact. Therefore we want the subjunctive. "If it *were* . . ."

> *People treated me as if I **was** invisible. . . .*

But the writer wasn't invisible. So we need the subjunctive: "as if I *were* invisible."

II. Punctuation

I believe a story can be wrecked by . . . a mistake in paragraphing, even punctuation. Henry James is the maestro of the semi-colon. Hemingway is a first-rate paragrapher.
—Truman Capote

ROAD SIGNS

Punctuation marks are the road signs of prose, one of the main mechanisms for clarifying written thoughts. A carelessly placed comma can alter the whole meaning of a sentence, and writers who pay close attention to punctuation can convey subtle differences in meaning.

But punctuation marks are small things, and they sometimes seem to get attention proportional to their size.

Here are some of the more common errors:

> *No, I never had one, particular John Keating, but I had a few teachers who were inspirations to me. . . .*

It's easy to get confused about the need for commas in a series of modifiers. The easiest way to deal with the problem is to remember that the commas substitute for "and." You wouldn't say "one *and* particular John Keating." So you don't need the comma.

> *George Douglas looked out to the gently rolling grass-covered land from the window of his home on Sauvie Island. . . .*

On the other hand, you could say "gently rolling *and* grass-covered land." So you write, "gently rolling, grass-covered land."

> *If it costs money it's an uphill battle to win it.*

Always set introductory subordinate clauses off with commas. "If it costs money, it's an . . ."

> *. . . the judge could order that the six sentences be served consecutively meaning that Rogers wouldn't be able to even apply for parole in his lifetime.*

Set participial phrases off with commas. "The sentences will be served consecutively, meaning that . . ." Follow the same rule for any similar construction: "He invited the whole cast, including the stagehands." "The jalopy sat at the curb, billowing smoke." "Running down the sideline, he looked back over his shoulder."

THE VICE OF THE SPLICE

If you want to reproduce stream-of-consciousness thinking, à la James Joyce in *Ulysses*, you might have a case for writing run-on sentences. It's hard to imagine any other justification.

The basic rule is simple enough: You can't splice independent clauses with commas, as the writer did in this example:

> *"Daniel and I were very close, we shared a wicked sense of humor," Pumela Peacock said.*

The first part of the passage, the clause beginning with "Daniel and I," is independent. In other words, it's a complete thought by itself, and it can stand alone as a separate sentence. The same is true of the second clause—"we shared a wicked sense of humor." The fact that a comma improperly joins the two clauses explains why run-ons are also known as "comma splices."

You can eliminate a comma splice in a variety of ways. The most obvious is to treat the two clauses as separate sentences—end the first with a period and begin the second with a capital letter.

You also can join closely related clauses with a semicolon, a dash, or an ellipsis.

> *I was at home; she wasn't.*

> *I was at home—she wasn't.*

> *I was at home . . . she wasn't.*

For some reason, writers are especially prone to run-ons in direct quotations. So be especially alert with quoted material, making sure that it's punctuated with the same care as the rest of your copy.

"It didn't squawk at all, it was really quiet."

"This wasn't the thrill of victory, it was the relief of not causing defeat."

SEMI-RIGHT

Minimize the use of semicolons, limiting them to two clearly defined situations:

1. When you need to use additional commas within the elements of a series:

The victims included John Jones, an auto mechanic from Gresham; Sally Johnson, a Beaverton brain surgeon; and Helen Ing, a Hood River mountain-bike designer.

2. When you want to connect two closely related independent clauses:

The United States remains its No. 1 customer; Japan is second.

Do not use semicolons to separate independent clauses that appear in a normal series, as in this lengthy example:

They may have ground a few gears in the process; they may have lost once to Atlanta; they may have staged a circus of absurdity one night in Dallas; the newly acquired Shawn Kemp may have been little more than a vaguely curious sideshow; but they're up there and smiling, from Steve Smith after getting knocked to the floor to assistant coach Pippen over there at courtside in a sling—even if this isn't quite the summit because it's well, the East.

Simple commas do just fine in such situations. Commas also do just fine in most other instances where writers seem compelled to use semicolons. You do not, for example, need a semicolon in this construction:

They came from the people who didn't have to walk around crack addicts on the sidewalk; from people who hadn't seen their friends get shot and killed.

HYPHEN HASSLES

No punctuation problem causes more trouble than the question of when to hyphenate a compound modifier. On that issue, writers and editors are about as consistent as a slot machine.

The basic rule is straightforward. You hyphenate compound modifiers when they act as a unit, referring to the noun they modify in a collective way. You might refer to a hard-driving fullback or a blue-green couch.

The rule of thumb is that you use a hyphen when the individual elements in the compound won't stand alone without altering the meaning of the phrase. You probably wouldn't say "hard fullback," for example, or even "driving fullback." You might say "blue couch," but that's not the meaning intended in "blue-green couch."

That's simple enough. But it's only a small part of the story. The rule is rife with complications and exceptions. For one thing, you have to distinguish such compounds from modifiers that merely appear in series, modifying the noun in question independently. You wouldn't want a hyphen in "deep, dark woods."

You also must watch out for modifiers referring to all that follows. In the phrase "dirty white horse," for example, "dirty" modifies "white horse," rather than acting as a compound with "white." So it's not a dirty-white horse. It is a horse that is white and dirty.

Remember, too, that the *AP Stylebook* and the *Chicago Manual of Style* call for omitting the hyphen when one of the elements in the compound ends with "-ly." The logic is that the adverbial ending tips readers off, alerting them to the fact that the modifier is joined to the modifier that follows. So it's "closely watched trains," not "closely-watched trains."

You don't use hyphens in proper names, either. It's the Dred Scott decision, without a hyphen. And you don't use hyphens with compound modifiers that routinely appear together. You don't, for example, hyphenate "high school" in the phrase "high school dance," or "civil rights" in "civil rights leader."

Some copy editors take that exception one step further, omitting the hyphen in any compound that seems clear without one. By that logic, you'd write "criminal justice system." But you'd retain the hyphen in "man-eating shark."

III. Spelling

It's a damned poor mind that can think of only one way to spell a word.
—Andrew Jackson

MAKING SENSE OUT OF NONSENSE

My mother was a terrific speller. I was terrible.

When I took my doctoral prelims, the weeklong series of daylong closed-book tests that capped my coursework and determined whether I'd be allowed to proceed with my PhD dissertation, one professor graded an answer and wrote, "I guess he passes. But he spells like Will Rogers."

The comparison with Rogers, the folksy 1930s humorist who spelled phonetically as part of his comic routine, humiliated me. So the next time I was home, I asked Mom what made her a walking dictionary. Well, she said, she just followed the rules she learned in school. Rules! What rules? We sure never learned any rules when *I* was in school.

She still remembered a few of hers, though, and she passed a couple along. For the first time, I understood why "judgment" is spelled without an *e* after *g* and why "spaghetti" has a double t.

I started keeping a notebook filled with the words I looked up in the dictionary, and I studied it each night at bedtime. Then somebody turned me on to *Twenty Days to Better Spelling* by Norman Lewis. That little workbook changed my life. I faithfully did the exercises for a few minutes each day. And lo! There *were* rules!

I never became a perfect speller. But I got pretty good. I saved the hours and hours I used to spend looking words up in the dictionary (often the same words I'd looked up many times before). I embarrassed myself far less often. And even when computer spell-checkers came along, Mr. Lewis saved me oodles of time because I got things right the first time.

Besides, spell-checkers don't catch everything. They ignore, for example, many variant spellings that often catch my irritated eye. And they're no help at all on hand-lettered notes, labels, and the like.

A Spelling Rule That Works

The entrants from California cancelled.

. . . which will have its liquor license cancelled on July 1.

You constantly see it as "cancelled," but the preferred spelling is "canceled." You can avoid the error—and a lot of other common spelling boo-boos—by remembering a simple rule: When you add a suffix, you double the final consonant in the root word only when the spoken stress is on the last syllable.

The rule becomes clear when you consider a couple of examples:

Start with "cancel." The spoken stress is clearly on the first syllable. It's "CAN-sel." If you pronounced it with the stress on the second syllable, you'd pronounce that syllable the same way you pronounce "cell."

Because you don't pronounce it "can-CELL," you don't double the final consonant—the *l*—when you add the suffix "-ed." So it's "canceled," not "cancelled."

The same is true of "offer." The stress clearly is on the first syllable. It's "OFF-er," not "off-FER." So you don't double the final consonant when you add a suffix. The correct spelling is "offered," not "offerred." Ditto with "open" (OH-pen—"opening") and "worship" (WHIR-ship—"worshiped").

"Occur," on the other hand, takes its stress on the final syllable. It's pronounced "oh-CUR," rather than the way "ochre" is pronounced. So the correct spelling is "occurred." The same rule applies to "begin" (be-GIN—"beginning"). Ditto with "referred," "deterred," and "concurred."

The rule isn't absolute. Some dictionaries, such as *Webster's New World College Dictionary* do list spellings such as "kidnapped" and "programmed" as preferred. But they also list the one-consonant variety. And the Brits don't follow the rule at all. "Travelled" is a perfectly proper spelling in a British dictionary, as well as in some American publications such as the *New Yorker*, which affects some British spellings. But, by and large, the rule is a good guideline.

Here are some more published errors, each avoidable through its use:

> *. . . joked with him ate with him,* ***travelled*** *with him.*

It's not pronounced "tra-VELL." So the correct spelling is "traveled."

> *. . . the red blinking light from the Bligh Reef buoy* ***signalled*** *danger.*

It's "SIG-nal," not "sig-NAL." The correct spelling is "signaled."

TWO TRICKS

Problem: "noticeable" or "noticable"?
Rule: Does the word end in a soft *c* followed by *e*? Then keep the *e* when you add a suffix.

C sounds soft when it calls for a hissing sound, like *s*. So the *c*'s are soft in "censored" and "service." In "conceit" the first *c* is hard, and the second is soft.

The *c* is soft in "notice." So it's "noticeable." It's also soft in "serviceable," "embraceable," and "pronounceable."

The same rule applies to other suffixes, too: "pronouncement," "placement," "enforcement."

Problem: "changeable" or "changable"?
Rule: Does the word end in a soft *g* followed by *e*? Then keep the *e* when you add a suffix.

G sounds soft when it calls for the *j* sound in "junior" or "junket." So the *g* is soft in "general," "gypsum," and "gyration." It's hard in "gas," "guts," and "glory."

The *g* is soft in "change." So it's "changeable." Ditto with "manage" ("management") and "marriage" ("marriageable").

You generally don't need the *e* before "-ment" after a soft *g* if it's preceded by *d*. So it's "judgment" (often misspelled as "judgement") and "acknowledgment."

WHERE CHAOS REIGNS

In English, as in most languages, separate words routinely linked in daily use gradually grow together, first joined with hyphens and then merged into a single word. But no rational arbiter governs the process.

Even the major dictionaries often disagree. One staff of lexicographers will decide that it's time to join two formerly independent words with a hyphen or to make them one word. The other will wait for another ten or twenty years before taking the plunge. For example, *Webster's New World College Dictionary*, the official dictionary in most newsrooms, lists "offramp" as one word. The online version of the *Merriam-Webster's Collegiate Dictionary* lists it as "off-ramp."

All you can do is memorize the versions listed in your preferred dictionary or in a long list that appears in the *Chicago Manual of Style*. Here's a sampling of the most frequently botched combos, at least according to *Webster's*.

> *Double check the principal and interest you're paying now. . . .*

It's "double-check."

> *It was a thankyou letter.*

No, it was a "thank-you" letter, although my online dictionary now lists "thankyou" as an alternate spelling. No matter. You'll always want to go with the preferred spelling.

The Blazers got down only six of twenty-five shots in the second period and, suddenly, it was a ballgame.

Sportswriters see "ball" and "game" together often enough to start thinking of them as a single word. But they're not.

No question about it, when you take those tests and wear that badge and sign up for a career in policework, you're going to see some crazy things.

Including "policework" as one word, which it isn't.

YOU COULD LOOK IT UP

Many years ago the *Oregonian* ran a cute feature on some new street signs in the college town of Eugene, Oregon. BUSSES ONLY, the signs read.

"A kiss is still a kiss," went our lead, "but a bus is definitely not a buss." This led, as you might have expected, to a couple of gags about kissing in the street and an embarrassed apology from the contractor responsible for the sign.

Great fun. The only problem, as one of our readers pointed out, is that while "buses" is the preferred plural for "bus," "busses" is also an acceptable form in most dictionaries.

Furthermore, many older readers still think "busses" is the way to go. "I was taught to use this form while attending a strict, old-fashioned grade school during the 1930s," said a complainant, "and have always considered the subsequent use of the simplified form 'buses' to be substandard English."

At the least, we should have recognized all that in our story. This raises a fundamental point: If you're going to question somebody else's spelling (or if you have any doubts about your own), you should always look up the word in question.

IV. Snake Rules

Any fool can make a rule. And every fool will mind it.
—Henry David Thoreau

Don Fry, a newspaper writing coach, says he was visiting a large midwestern daily when newsroom discussion turned to a photo rejected for publication the previous Sunday. One editor explained the decision:

"We rejected that photo because of the lizard rule."

"No," said another editor, "that was the snake rule."

"No," said the third, "it was the reptile rule."

Despite the argument over nomenclature, the three agreed that the paper had an ancient rule banning the appearance of snakes on Sunday section fronts.

Fry investigated. He says the rule dated back to 1924, when the owner was offended by her discovery of a snake picture in the paper. The photo appeared on Sunday, a day when ladies with delicate sensibilities were especially likely to be reading. Hence, the snake rule.

Most publications have their own snake rules. Their origins are often murky. Someone in authority offers an unsubstantiated opinion, and it gets passed along. Or a message gets botched as it's passed from hand to hand. A new snake rule is born, and then passes down the generations because nobody bothers to consult the original source or to look the damned thing up.

It's time to eliminate a few of these slimy vipers. They cripple creativity, waste time, and cause unnecessary friction between writers and editors. So question everything. Never accept anybody's unsubstantiated "just-because" rule on writing.

SNAKE RULE NO. 1: DIRECT QUOTATIONS MUST APPEAR AS SEPARATE PARAGRAPHS

Where'd this one come from? True, journalists create a separate paragraph for the words of each speaker in a dialogue. But what does that have to do with direct quotes?

For the record, no rule dictates that you set off each direct quotation as a separate paragraph. Do so if you want, for emphasis. But if the quote flows naturally from the preceding introductory material, you'd be well advised to leave it in the same paragraph, like this:

> Brady leaned into the bar, cranked his head to the right, and spied the bartender twelve stools down. "Bring me a beer and a shot," he bellowed. "I'm not a patient man."

SNAKE RULE NO. 2: YOU CAN'T BEGIN A SENTENCE WITH "AND" OR "BUT"

Who says? "And" and "but" are coordinating conjunctions, just like "or," "yet," and "for." You can start a sentence with any of them.

The rule to the contrary is one of the most widespread myths in writing. It's been passed from editor to writer for generations, with absolutely no support from any of the authorities.

You can overuse "and" and "but" at the beginning of sentences, of course. So when you give your draft a final read, you might try dropping those introductory conjunctions. If you lose nothing by deleting, it's best to delete.

SNAKE RULE NO. 3: YOU CAN'T SPLIT AN INFINITIVE

The idea that such a thing as a "split infinitive" even existed in English didn't surface until the late nineteenth century. The ban on its use, according to *Webster's Dictionary of English Usage*, "has never had a rational basis."

Or much popular respect. *Star Trek* captains Kirk and Picard took their assignments "to boldly go" without much grammatical objection.

Webster's goes on to conclude that "the consensus in the twentieth century is that the awkward avoidance of the split infinitive has produced more bad writing than use of it."

SNAKE RULE NO. 4: YOU CAN'T END A SENTENCE WITH A PREPOSITION

The snake rule against ending sentences with prepositions—so-called dangling prepositions—began dying in my youth and has been moribund for years. Good thing, too. Sometimes you're better off with the preposition at the end. "She was the first actress he offered the part to" is more conversational than "She was the first actress to whom he offered the part."

On the other hand, prepositions don't usually function as particularly snappy kickers. You're better off avoiding dangling prepositions *and* stuffy alternatives: "He offered the part to her first."

SNAKE RULE NO. 5: ATTRIBUTIONS BELONG AT THE END OF DIRECT QUOTATIONS

This rule exists only in the heads of editors who heard it from editors who heard it from editors. The attribution for a direct quote belongs in the most natural position. Sometimes that's at the end, although even powerful quotations tend to trail off weakly with an attribution at the end. More often, the attribution works effectively at the beginning, which allows the last word of the quote itself to serve as a kicker for a sentence, paragraph, or story.

But the most rhythmic position for an attribution is usually at the quote's first natural pause. "We stopped their running game," he said, "and we shut down their passing, too."

Note, however, that placing the attribution at the first natural pause assumes that the quotation contains a natural pause. Avoid odd constructions such as "Four score," he said, "and seven years ago . . ."

SNAKE RULE NO. 6: DON'T SPLIT VERB PHRASES

Lord knows how many hours I wasted on this one. In my early years somebody told me that nothing should separate an auxiliary verb from a main verb. So, as I edited, I dutifully unraveled sentence after perfectly good sentence and then tried to put each back together again without the dreaded "split auxiliary."

"Was slowly swimming" became "was swimming slowly." "Should have been immediately apparent" became "should have been apparent immediately."

This, presumably, did no great damage, although editors should avoid casual disruption of the writer's intended rhythms.

But I, like other editors, was perfectly willing to follow this rule into new realms of nonsensical syntax. I would, for example, turn "will today introduce a next-generation microprocessor" into "will introduce today a next-generation microprocessor." And I had no qualms about turning "had carefully studied nicotine" into "had studied carefully nicotine."

The snake rule had become a snake language.

SNAKE RULE NO. 7: USE A QUOTATION EVERY THREE PARAGRAPHS

The snake in question here is journalistic. It is primarily newspapers and magazines that quote reflexively and excessively. Few snake rules have done more to dull up journalistic writing. Not that a good quote isn't a good thing. But what's the basis for the newsroom notion that you *have* to quote somebody every few paragraphs in every story?

SNAKE RULE NO. 8: YOU "SEE" WITH YOUR EYES AND "FEEL" WITH YOUR HANDS, AND YOU NEVER USE EITHER VERB IN ANY OTHER WAY

The rule ignores the fact that "I feel as though I should go" or "I see what you mean" are standard fare in American English. Odd, isn't it, how often snake rules ignore the standard speech and writing that potential readers use every day.

And ignore the language authorities. *Webster's New World College Dictionary* defines "feel" as "to think or believe, often for unanalyzed or emotional reasons."

The Chapter 11 Cheat Sheet

FIVE SHORTCUTS TO IMPROVING YOUR SPELLING, GRAMMAR, AND USAGE

1. **Find the basic statement.** You can answer many grammar questions if you identify the subject and predicate—the "basic statement"—at the heart of a sentence. For one thing, the predicate should agree in number with the subject. The basic statement "number has declined" is the core of this sentence: "The number of burglaries in the neighborhood has declined this year." That's why the proper verb is the singular "has declined" instead of the plural "have declined." If the sentence is "Burglaries have declined this year," you have a different basic statement—"burglaries have declined"—and a different verb.
2. **Use commas after the introduction; skip them before the conclusion.** You set a subordinate clause off with a comma when it comes at the beginning of a sentence. "If she shows up early, she'll just have to wait." But you don't set off clauses when they're at the end of the sentence. "She'll just have to wait if she shows up early."
3. **Do yourself a favor.** Never use reflexive pronouns such as "myself," "yourself," "himself," or "themselves" if plain old pronouns will do. If you can write "Fred and I volunteered," then don't write "Fred and myself volunteered." If you can write "He gave the assignment to Fred and me," don't write "He gave the assignment to Fred and myself."
4. **Try the modifiers separately.** Is it "the third largest crowd" or "the third-largest crowd"? If the modifiers can stand alone, you don't need a hyphen. If they must work as a unit, you do need a hyphen. It's not the "third crowd." And it's not the "largest crowd." Ergo, it's "the third-largest crowd."
5. **Listen for the accent.** If the accent's on the last syllable, double the final consonant when you add a suffix. It's "oc-CUR." Therefore, spell it "occurred." But it's "OFF-er." Therefore, spell it "offered." Ditto with words such as "cancel" ("canceled"), "open" ("opening"), "worship" ("worshiped"), and "travel" ("traveled").

12

Mastery

The lyf so short, the craft so long to lerne.
—Geoffrey Chaucer

WRITING AS AN EVERYDAY ENTERPRISE

Your goals in life will determine your writing goals, and as the one evolves, you can decide on the other. You don't master writing in a one-size-fits-all level of competence.

The vast majority of words churned out by the millions of hands that touch keyboards each day are generated without literary ambitions. Their authors simply want somebody to understand something clearly and to act accordingly. For most of us, writing is a means to an end.

The fact that most writing is largely functional in no way diminishes its importance. These days, fewer and fewer of us work with our hands alone, and less and less of our communication is face to face. Substituting brain work for grunt work and shifting our routine daily contacts out of earshot magnifies the importance of writing. We may spend a lot of time on cell phones, but most of us also devote huge amounts of our waking hours to turning out reports and memos, sending emails, blogging, and conducting online transactions. For that matter, even cell phones have text-messaging.

It follows that anybody who can write succinctly and powerfully, who can attract and hold interest with the written word, has an advantage in almost any field. The engineer whose written proposal makes a compelling case for a new structural system wins the design competition. The sales rep who writes the best marketing plan gets the account. The citizen who writes a persuasive letter gets her street paved.

So even if you view writing as a tool, it pays to think of it as one of the most valuable tools you have. As with all important tools, you'll want to invest in quality.

My father was career army, and for him a firearm was one of the most important tools he could imagine. He was also a duck hunter, and when I was a boy he occasionally took me along on early morning outings in a camouflaged rowboat. As I went away to college, he presented me with a fine shotgun. He had been a warrant officer, not a general, but he didn't stint on quality when he picked out that semiautomatic. Take good care of this, he told me, and you can give it to one of your sons. It looks as though I will. The old twelve-gauge is still in excellent shape, and after a hard day at the keyboard I take it out to the skeet range and happily blast away at clay targets. With each direct hit a little more frustration disappears in a satisfying puff of smoke.

Using writing as a tool depends on sound process. If you've learned how to generate a solid idea, find a focus, efficiently gather information, organize material, and quickly generate a workable rough draft, you have the working essentials that will, like the shotgun my father gave me, last a lifetime.

Of course, I've taken care of that shotgun. My father was in the Ordnance Corps, was a fanatic about maintaining tools, and passed his conscientiousness along to me. When I get home from the skeet range, I immediately dismantle the shotgun, swab the barrel with powder solvent, and coat every part with the best gun oil I can buy.

Plenty of nonprofessionals maintain the same kind of respect for the written word. I regularly hear from readers who, although they aren't full-time writers themselves, are keen students of the language. They debate points of usage, take note when a writer turns a fine phrase, and call foul when the editors allow clichés, confusing constructions, or cloudy thinking into print.

Taking part in that continuing conversation will keep your writing on the upswing. Throughout this book I've mentioned resources that can help with your language skills, and more are listed in the Selected Resources for Writers at the back. But beyond those, a lifelong curiosity about language and the writing process is your best guide.

The place to start is with analytical reading. This book offers a template for learning something from writers you admire. They don't have to be highfalutin literary types—you can profit by analyzing just about any writer's impact, clarity, rhythm, and color. I'm a fly fisherman, and I'm partial to fishing writer

John Gierach. When he makes me laugh out loud, I may reread the responsible passage, looking at the rhythms, levels of abstraction, and sentence forms. Gierach has a distinctive voice, and I'm alert to the techniques he uses to create the wry, self-deprecating persona I find so appealing.

Several online resources will help you stay tuned in to the writing conversation. Sites such as the Writing Cooperative can help substitute for a writers group, although when it comes to writing there's nothing like face-to face feedback. Googling "writing groups" just produced a list of nearly fifty such groups within twenty-five miles of my little island in Puget Sound. I could choose between the "West Seattle Writer's Block" group, the "Write On Writers," or—my favorite based on the name alone—"Shut Up and Write!" in nearby Tacoma.

As you might guess from the title of this book's sequel—*Storycraft*—I'm into narrative nonfiction. So I eagerly look forward to the weekly installments of *Nieman Storyboard*, Jacqui Banasznski's blog for the Nieman Foundation's Narrative Program at Harvard. Jacqui, an old friend and colleague, keeps me on my toes by challenging assumptions and introducing me to noteworthy new work in my field. Lane DeGregory, like Jacqui a winner of the feature-writing Pulitzer, and Maria Carrillo, her editor at the *Tampa Bay Times*, are key figures in *WriteLane*, a narrative nonfiction blog that links to a regular podcast. Another old friend, Chip Scanlan, is the honcho for *Chip on My Shoulder*, a writing blog HQed at the Poynter Institute, a midcareer school for journalists. Visit the website and you can sign up for *Chip in Your InBox*, a weekly newsletter on the craft of writing and reporting.

If those folks can't keep you on the road to mastery, nobody can.

And then there are all the books on writing and language. Keeping one on your nightstand is a good way to focus your thinking on the clarity and vigor of your own writing. The bedtime reading about writing I've enjoyed most in recent years includes Bill Bryson's *Made in America*, a history of American English, *Eats, Shoots & Leaves* by Lynne Truss, and Stephen King's *On Writing*.

If you appreciate good writing, you're far more likely to give it its due. An executive who has a high regard for words won't spend weeks on research for a product launch and leave only a day or two to write a hasty proposal that confuses her staff and fails to convince her board of directors. Instead, she'll set aside a reasonable amount of time so that she can write a theme statement and jot an outline, organize her material, draft easily, and polish the document into a readable, useful tool that does the job it was intended to do.

That same respect for the importance of writing will help you maintain the kind of habits that will keep you improving your own writing. Read your work aloud, listening carefully for sense, cadence, and clarity. Inveigle friends and colleagues and members of your writing group to read drafts of anything you write. Ask them to put diplomacy aside and underline anything that gives them pause—thoughts that seem incomplete, words that seem unnecessary or don't quite fit, sentences that require a second reading. An honest reader is your closest ally, a yardstick for measuring the only thing that matters—how effectively you produce the results you're aiming for in the minds of others. No two readers will have exactly the same response to a piece of work, but when every reader of a piece has a problem with a certain spot, your need for a revision is clear.

EASING INTO THE WRITING LIFE

One of the myths of writing is that the transition from amateur to pro is akin to stuntman Evel Knievel launching his motorcycle across the Grand Canyon. In fact, professionalism—like mastery—runs in a gentle continuum that reflects the goals of the writer.

You can dip a toe into professional writing in any number of ways. If the experience appeals to you, a gradual slope leads deeper and deeper into the writing life.

You may choose to satisfy some immediate goal with a quick sally into the writer's world. During the early days of personal computers, my brother, an amateur radio enthusiast, cooked up a device for translating the output of a primitive desktop computer into a teletype radio signal that could be decoded by a similar device at a distant location and displayed on a computer screen. He designed a kit for building the thing, which was a real breakthrough for its time, and enlisted my help in writing an article on it for a ham-radio magazine. The article did what it was intended to do—sell the kits—and my brother went back to his day job. As far as I know, he never had any ambitions as a professional writer.

If you do, the only requirement is an ironclad commitment to regular writing time. You can't build a career in writing, be it large or small, if you don't write in a disciplined way. When I still had a time-consuming and demanding day job, I was pretty good about wearing a little fuzz off the fabric of my home-office chair between eight and nine every weekday morning. For two years, that hour a day allowed me to dispose of about seven hundred cups of coffee, to watch the leaves fall off the trees in the park out my back window—twice—and to write this book.

If you're launching a professional writing career, start small. When I taught classes in beginning magazine writing, the term project always involved planning, marketing, and writing an article with the intent of actually getting it published. The majority of students started out thinking they'd submit something to one of the national slicks: the *New Yorker* maybe, or *Travel + Leisure*. How about the *Atlantic Monthly*? Or *Glamour*? Right. And how about taking the controls of a 747 on your first day of flight school?

About half the students, on average, do end up getting published, and quite a few make enough money to cover tuition for the course. But they find their way into print by discovering the twenty thousand or so specialty publications serving the almost unimaginable array of American occupations, crafts, and private passions, many of them listed in guides such as *Writer's Market*. Once they find magazines that pique their interest, they request writers' guidelines and sample copies. They analyze their target publication's article lengths, tone and style, preferred topics, and freelance policies. They learn how to write professional query letters and bounce ideas off editors who welcome thoughtful approaches. As a result, they've lost their publishing virginity in magazines for opticians, powerboating enthusiasts, quilters, sailboarders, miniature-horse breeders, and organic gardeners, markets that are often obscure to the point of invisibility. But those magazines pay hard cash. And, more important, they produce clippings that prove you're a published pro. The clips can lead to more successful queries in bigger markets.

You may be thinking that you don't have time for all that. But one of the conversational threads in a writing blog I used to follow was about how to squeeze regular writing into otherwise busy lives. I've kept a post from Ana Marie Rodriguez, an Argentine-born biologist who became a research scientist in Houston. Ana Marie started her writing in scientific journals, but then she volunteered for a science-by-mail program sponsored by Boston's Museum of Science. Kids conducted scientific experiments, sent their reports to Ana, and she wrote back to them with comments and suggestions. That got her interested in writing about science for children. But she had her own children at home, and she had very little time.

"I decided to begin small, literally," she said in her post. "I decided to write short science articles for kids. I could document and write a good science article, between 300 and 800 words long, every month, sometimes one every two months. The articles would be shorter than adult articles, but, believe me, not easier to write. But the shorter length matched the time I had available."

She collected a few rejections, but eventually started selling to *Super-Science*,

Yes Mag and other juvenile science periodicals, eventually selling more than fifty articles aimed at children. She woke up two hours before her own children so that she could read and write without interruption. She took correspondence courses on writing for kids. She was on the road to mastery.

"I did not notice it at first," she recalled, "but after a few years, my articles were getting better and needed less editing. When one of my editors, one I knew for three or four years, told me without my asking that she had noticed how my writing had improved, I sat down and wept."

If you to set out on a similar course, check out the dozens of conferences that offer inspiration for fiction writers, poets, essayists, journalists, and writers of every stripe. Big-name speakers often serve as crowd-pleasers while agents suggest practical ways for breaking into print. For additional fees, some conferences also supply manuscript criticism from professionals.

Writing workshops are a great way to squeeze some instruction into a crowded life. I once taught weeklong courses for the Haystack Summer Program in the Arts, a workshop that operated in a picturesque little town on the Oregon coast. Students in my narrative journalism class may have been professional writers interested in expanding their repertoire, but they often were teachers, lawyers, engineers, or other nonwriters who chose to spend vacation time learning an avocation. After a day in class, they could take their evening's reading assignment to the beach.

Writing colonies and camps give harried writers a quiet place—maybe a cabin in the woods or a room in a remote lodge—where they can confront a screen without distractions. In the evening, they gather with like-minded souls for supper and conversation. Unlike workshops, however, camps tend to be for more experienced and literary writers, who are selected via competitions. On the other hand, they tend to be funded by grants that pay a participant's way.

The Association of Writers & Writing Programs website offers numerous programs. The AWP's online *Directory of Conferences & Centers* lists hundreds of possibilities, searchable by type of conference, writing genre, and region. You can even find out if a program offers scholarships.

If you're out to give your writing a booster shot, there's no shortage of resources.

Once you start easing into the professional writing world, you'll have your first encounters with editors. They'll be crucial to your success, something I learned from an especially revealing perspective many years ago when I was named editor of *Northwest*, my newspaper's Sunday magazine.

Northwest piggybacked on the *Oregonian*'s Sunday circulation of 450,000 and paid the highest freelance rates in the region, so it attracted more than two hundred queries a week, ranging from the rankest amateur to national-quality pros. As an inexperienced editor, I was intimidated when I first worked with established writers who'd sold to some of the best-known magazines in America.

But the real professionals were always the easiest to work with. They met deadlines and never quibbled over the small stuff. They weren't lapdogs—if I or one of the other editors suggested changes that introduced inaccuracies, they were quick to object. But mere changes in wording never bothered them, and if we needed to cut for space, they'd whack away at their own words without blinking. One of my favorite writers always took my rewrite suggestions and checked off each one as he adjusted his manuscript in response to it, explaining in a note just what he'd changed.

I learned that the real pros also kept good records, posted reminders on their calendars, cashed their checks promptly, filed the appropriate tax information at the appropriate time, and were generally well organized. Naturally, we came to rely on a stable of such regulars for our cover stories and major departments. Because they had mastered the process, they were able to open the gate to a huge regional audience for their writing. Several of them parlayed that exposure into successful national writing careers.

My stint at *Northwest* taught me about editors not only as gatekeepers, but also as teachers. We worked with a lot of writers who didn't know much about magazine style, and local freelancers weren't conversant with the kind of narrative storytelling we preferred. So we took time to work with our contributors, both at the idea stage and during editing. The writers who progressed fastest and farthest took advantage of that, asking questions, carefully responding to suggestions, and avoiding any defensiveness about editing.

Not every editor has time for the extensive manuscript markups *Northwest*'s editors routinely produced—many publications will take a freelancer's submission and simply rewrite. But every editor nonetheless offers every writer a chance to move along the road to mastery. At the very least, a writer can make a word-for-word comparison of a final draft with the published version. What did the editor change, with what result? What was cut? What was lost? What was gained?

The point is to keep learning, even if you're writing just as a sideline. Mastery flows from many incremental improvements. After fly-fishing for forty years, I find that not a season passes without my discovering something new about casting, fly selection, or the habits of the wily cutthroat trout. As with writing, there's too much to know for any one lifetime, and the challenge of constant learning is half the sport.

TAKING THE PLUNGE

You've dipped your toe in. Maybe you've even waded in waist-deep, freelancing some magazine articles or selling a couple of short stories. The water seems fine, and you've decided on a full-immersion writing career. What's next?

That depends, of course, on what kind of career you're planning, how far along you are, what kind of resources you have at hand, and any number of other variables. If you're a high school senior and you want to be a novelist, you'll be making different choices from a forty-year-old mother of three who's decided to take up technical writing.

As a newsman who spent years teaching journalism, I'm most familiar with the educational options open to nonfiction writers. Hundreds of universities and community colleges offer some kind of instruction in journalism, broadcast writing, advertising, public relations, and technical writing, including more than one hundred full-fledged degree programs certified by the national journalism accrediting agency. If you want to attend a J-school, you won't have trouble finding one.

There is a long-running debate about the value of a journalism degree versus a liberal-arts degree in something such as history or political science. If you want to write and you're thinking about college, don't worry about it. The liberal-arts partisans are right that education across the curriculum that teaches you to think is the best preparation for a writing career. But the notion that you can't get that in a good journalism school is bogus. Accredited J-schools have distribution requirements that spread coursework across the liberal-arts curriculum; so journalism majors often get a more diverse education than some majors in traditional liberal arts. How good that education is depends on the school, of course. But if you're charting your education for a writing career, I wouldn't pay much attention to the liberal arts versus professional school argument.

Do pay attention to a school's professional emphasis. Journalism schools such as Northwestern and the University of Missouri attract faculty members with strong track records as writers or editors at the best online newsrooms, magazines, newspapers, and broadcast outlets. If I were picking a J-school today, the first thing I'd do is check the faculty biographies in a printed catalog or online. Where did the writing professors work, and what did they edit or write? Then I'd run their names through Google and LexisNexis. What have they written lately?

I'd apply the same logic to plotting my education as a novelist, poet, or short-story writer. Look for professionally oriented programs with proven records. AWP's website lists undergraduate creative-writing programs by state and offers sound advice on evaluating them. If you see one that interests you, give the faculty the same going-over I recommend for J-school professors.

Whichever route to undergraduate education you choose, here's a tip from someone who conducted job interviews with dozens and dozens of college graduates. When you get on campus, you'll spend your time worrying about classes, assignments, and grades. But when you show up for an interview with me, my main interest will be in how you think, report, and write. I'll ask you how you organize your notes, find your focus, and work your way through a rough draft. I'll look for the passion it takes to carry you through a lifetime chasing big stories and writing under tight deadlines. I'll read your published clippings like a Joyce scholar analyzing *Ulysses*.

If you have a terrific GPA, so much the better. But a Pulitzer Prize winner recently told me how beside the point his undergraduate obsession with grades now seems. And not long ago I ran across the name of a classmate who spent most of his undergraduate days on academic probation because he spent all his time writing and editing for our college newspaper. He recently retired at the end of a long and distinguished career as an arts writer at a major metropolitan daily.

Seize every opportunity to write and to learn about writing. If you want to be a journalist, stop by the campus newsroom on the first day of your first term and sign up. Work for the campus magazine, or volunteer to be a sports stringer for the local daily. If you want to write fiction, get acquainted with the staff of the campus literary publication or send short stories to literary journals and other accessible markets. Start a novel and offer babysitting or lawn mowing to a respected local writer in exchange for reading your manuscript and giving you some tips.

If you're older, you can still find your way into full-time writing. The fact that you have some life experience may give you a leg up—you're more likely to know what interests you and where your writing talents lie.

Many toe-dippers simply take on more and more freelance work until one day they feel confident enough to give up their day jobs. Or they build up an impressive file of published clippings—what we used to call a string book—and use that to land a full-time staff writing job. But today's writing world is filled with midcareer educational opportunities, too.

If you can somehow take a break of two or three years from wages and family, you'll find plenty of midcareer master's degree programs in journalism, creative nonfiction, public relations, advertising, or various technical-writing specialties.

The master's program at Columbia University in New York City emphasizes print-journalism skills and gives students real-world experience in the world's largest media market. You probably wouldn't choose Columbia if you already had an undergrad degree in journalism because you would already have taken courses in basic skills. But Columbia's program or one like it makes great sense for someone with, say, a history BA, a few years of work in an unsatisfying career, and a burning desire to write for newspapers or magazines or online.

Similar programs serve any number of interests. The University of Oregon offers a master's degree to students attracted to literary journalism. MIT, Johns Hopkins, and several other schools have grad programs for students who want to specialize in science writing. Other programs emphasize technical writing, business writing, medical writing, and any number of other specialties.

Programs abound on the creative-writing side, too, and the AWP offers a comprehensive list. The Iowa Writers' Workshop is the prototype for fiction, poetry, and creative-nonfiction degree programs, with roots reaching back into the nineteenth century and a dozen graduates who've won a Pulitzer Prize. On the West Coast, the most successful counterpart is probably the Stanford Creative Writing Program, created by Wallace Stegner and responsible for graduates such as Ken Kesey and Scott Turow.

By midcareer, however, most lives are too hectic for a full-time master's program. Interest in writing careers keeps growing, though, and that time-squeezed demand no doubt accounts for the growth of "low-residency" MFA programs in writing. Warren Wilson, a small college outside Asheville, North Carolina, hosts the country's oldest, and its innovative structure has inspired more than thirty similar programs nationwide. The entire Warren Wilson curriculum generally takes four semesters. Every six months students gather on campus for ten days of classes and workshops, as well as sessions with a professional writer who serves as their mentor and who helps them plan the next semester's work. Then they return home, where they're expected to spend a minimum of twenty-five hours a week on new material that they mail to their mentor every three weeks for review and comment.

Low-residency programs in creative writing exist everywhere from Bennington College in Vermont to Antioch University in Los Angeles. Baltimore's Goucher College offers a low-residency MFA in nonfiction. It has tracks in memoir and the personal essay of the sort that are commonly associated with English departments, but it also draws on newspaper, magazine, and journalistic book traditions such as travel, nature, and science writing, as well as profiles and biography. Faculty mentors have included stars of literary journalism such as John McPhee, Susan Orlean, and Tom French.

MAKING COMMON CAUSE WITH CRAFT

The long road to writing mastery crosses many of the same hills and valleys whether it's traveled by a business executive or an architect, a playwright or a science writer, an ad copywriter or a newshound.

Several years ago I happened to be teaching a workshop at a big East Coast conference for narrative nonfiction writers. I dropped into another session to hear Ira Glass, the imaginative impresario of National Public Radio's *This American Life*. He stood at a radio control panel, cueing music and interview tapes while he talked about the principles of storytelling that guided his programming. They were exactly the same, I realized, as the principles I followed when I coached long-form narrative stories in print.

Increasingly, we live in a world where writers operate successfully in any number of genres. Jim Lynch left my newsroom to write his first novel, and published *The Highest Tide* to terrific reviews. He went on to a long, successful career as a novelist who, at latest count, had thirteen titles to his credit.

Mark Bowden, the longtime police reporter at the *Philadelphia Inquirer*, always saw his beat as more than a string of spot-news crime stories. So he had a strong track record that helped him talk his editors into a newspaper series on the disastrous 1993 American intervention in Somalia. Bowden wrote the hell out of the story, and the *Inquirer*'s editors did a terrific job of presenting it on the internet, attracting national attention. The author soon had a book contract, and *Black Hawk Down* became a Ridley Scott feature film that opened across the country. Bowden's great writing and storytelling defied all boundaries, leaping from newsprint to the Web to hard- and soft-cover book publication to the movies. Bowden himself went on to become a national correspondent for the *Atlantic* and to write more than a dozen nonfiction books.

My dear longtime friend and fishing buddy, the late Larry Bowen, who taught hundreds of University of Washington students how to write advertising copy, said his specialty was really just "storytelling for commerce."

Another thing you'll hear from almost any successful writer, regardless of genre, is that you gradually earn writing mastery by learning one set of skills and using them as a jumping-off place for the next. I remember feeling inadequate when I read about another top editor or star reporter who started by mimeographing a neighborhood newsletter at the age of eight. My first brush with journalism was during my junior year of college.

No matter. Norman Maclean didn't publish his first novel, *A River Runs through It*, until he retired from a distinguished teaching career at the University of Chicago. His last book, *Young Men and Fire*, was a challenging nonfiction work with an innovative structure that I've never seen duplicated. In his eighties, Maclean was still building on his body of work.

Walt Harrington, who wrote the revealing profile of Rita Dove I quoted in chapter 9, advises fellow writers: "Never do the same thing twice. Anything that's rote is going to become stale." Walt has been his own best example. His *Washington Post Magazine* profiles were all different, each one a fresh approach to getting inside the skin of a unique human being.

Of course, if you never do the same thing twice, you won't always succeed. The untried always involves risk. The first-time skier is fated to fall.

But if you hope to master the mountain, you can't let the inevitability of a mishap or two intimidate you. In writing, the greatest obstacle is fear of failure, a timidity that forces retreat into the tried and tired. Every journalist knows colleagues who never attempt anything new, who back into the same formulaic news stories day after day, year after year. The equivalent occurs wherever writers face an empty computer screen. The timid, predictable writing they produce may get published, broadcast, or sent out online. They may collect their paychecks, advances, or royalties. But they never truly live as writers.

Writing doesn't have to be frightening *or* formulaic. Writers who learn a workable process and a set of practical skills can create low-anxiety prose that's full of rhythm and color, rich in humanity, and high in impact. As with houses or handcrafted furniture, the preliminary stages may not look like much. But writers who know what they're doing will work through a familiar drill to produce something that, at its best, can rise to the level of art.

Mastery is not some closely guarded mystery, but the step-by-step conquest of craft.

Acknowledgments

Special thanks go to Mary Laur, senior editor at the University of Chicago Press, for that 2019 dinner at one of Portland's best restaurants. Not only was the food delicious, but Mary really listened when, over dessert, I suggested resuscitating my first writing book.

Mary, bless her heart, liked the whole idea, especially when it included a parallel update of *Storycraft*. She asked if I could get the rights back to *A Writer's Coach*. I said I'd try, and my crack literary agent, Caitlin Blasdell at Liza Dawson and Associates, went to work on that. When she succeeded, she cleared the way for *Wordcraft*, the University of Chicago Press edition.

I owe my friend Bill Blundell's *The Art and Craft of Feature Writing* credit for opening my eyes to much of what leads to good writing, and for coining the term "wordcraft" to discuss the kind of issues covered in this book. William Zinsser's *On Writing Well* was another source of inspiration. Walt Harrington, the *Washington Post Magazine* writer and University of Illinois educator, was an especially generous friend and mentor. Two other pals, independent writing coach Don Fry and Poynter Institute senior scholar Roy Peter Clark, deserve acknowledgment for doing so much to create and to develop the idea of the writing coach, at newspapers and throughout the writing world. Their *Coaching Writers: Editors and Writers Working Together across Media Platforms* is the definitive guidebook for collaborative editing. Chip Scanlan, the former head of the Poynter writing program, has been another stalwart comrade in the writing-improvement crusade that the Poynter Institute spearheaded.

Don Murray was influential in calling attention to the importance of the writing process, and Bob Baker explained the process as it played out in the daily lives of reporters. Their work changed the way I wrote, edited, and coached. I wish Don and Bob were still here to thank.

I also am in debt to my colleagues in the community of narrative journalists. Jon Franklin's *Writing for Story* showed us all how it could be done. Jacqui Banaszynski, Bruce DeSilva, Tom French, the late Ken Fuson, Anne Hull, Mark Kramer, John McPhee, Susan Orlean, Barry Siegel, and Stuart Warner were all inspirational. Dozens of other fine nonfiction writers have shown how far beyond the inverted-pyramid news story the creative side of journalism can stretch.

My special thanks go to the three writers—Pulitzer winners all—who worked most closely with me day in and day out at the *Oregonian*. Rich Read, now a national correspondent for the *Los Angeles Times*, routinely demonstrated how calm, productive, and insightful a reporter who is in command of his writing process can be. Tom Hallman Jr., who's still at our old newspaper, consistently found a rich, human vein in his feature writing. And Julie Sullivan, who moved on to a rewarding career in public relations, turned out powerfully emotional work as the living embodiment of Robert Frost's observation that if there are no tears in the writer, there will be no tears in the reader.

I also want to credit all the magazine and book writers, columnists, editorial writers, reporters, and other writers whose work I've snipped and clipped to illustrate one point or another. Many of them are dear former colleagues at the *Oregonian*, who indulged my nit-picking for decades. Nobody's more obnoxious than somebody who corrects your English. Thank you all for resisting any murderous impulses in return.

And I can't say enough in the way of thanks to Karen Albaugh, my significant other for more than thirty years. She saw me through defeat and discouragement that would have undercut my grand plans without her unwavering support. Thanks, Toots. Pardon the cliché, but it couldn't be more true than in this case: I really couldn't have done it without you.

Selected Resources for Writers

BOOKS ON WRITING, REPORTING, AND LANGUAGE SKILLS

Baker, Bob. *Newsthinking: The Secret of Making Your Facts Fall into Place*. Boston: Allyn and Bacon, 2001.

Berner, Thomas. *Language Skills for Journalists*. Eugene, OR: Wipf and Stock, 2003.

Bernstein, Theodore. *The Careful Writer: A Modern Guide to English Usage*. New York: Simon and Schuster, 1995.

Blumenthal, Joseph. *English 3200, with Writing Applications: A Programmed Course in Grammar and Usage*. New York: Heinle and Heinle, 1994.

Blundell, William E. *The Art and Craft of Feature Writing*. New York: Plume, 1988.

Brady, John. *The Craft of Interviewing*. New York: Random House, 1977.

Burroway, Janet. *Writing Fiction*. 10th edition. Chicago: University of Chicago Press, 2019.

Clark, Roy Peter. *The Art of X-Ray Reading: How the Secrets of 25 Great Works of Literature Will Improve Your Writing*. New York: Little Brown, 2016.

Clark, Roy Peter. *Writing Tools: 50 Essential Strategies for Every Writer*. New York: Little Brown, 2006.

Conover, Ted. *Immersion: A Writer's Guide to Going Deep*. Chicago: University of Chicago Press, 2016.

Egri, Lajos. *The Art of Dramatic Writing*. New York: Simon and Schuster, 1972.

Fedler, Fred, John Bender, Lucinda Davenport, and Michael Drager. *Reporting for the Media*. Oxford: Oxford University Press, 2004.

Field, Syd. *Screenplay: The Foundations of Screenwriting*. New York: Bantam Dell, 2005.

Fisher, Lionel. *The Craft of Corporate Journalism*. Oceanside, WA: Lionel Fisher, 2009.

Franklin, Jon. *Writing for Story*. New York: Mentor Books/New American Library, 1986.

Gardner, John. *The Art of Fiction: Notes on Craft for Young Writers*. New York: Vintage Books, 1991.

Gerard, Philip. *Creative Nonfiction: Researching and Crafting Stories of Real Life*. 2nd edition. Long Grove, IL: Waveland, 2017.

Harrington, Walt. *Intimate Journalism: The Art and Craft of Reporting on Everyday Life*. Thousand Oaks, CA: Sage, 1997.

King, Stephen. *On Writing: A Memoir of the Craft*. New York: Scribner, 2010.

Kramer, Mark, and Wendy Call, eds. *Telling True Stories: A Nonfiction Writers' Guide*. New York: Plume, 2007.

Lanson, Gerald, and Mitchell Stephens. *Writing and Reporting the News*. New York: Oxford University Press, 1994.

Lewis, Norman. *Twenty Days to Better Spelling*. New York: Signet, 1989.

Macauley, Robie, and George Lanning. *Technique in Fiction*. 2nd edition. New York: St. Martin's, 1987.

McKee, Robert. *Story: Substance, Structure, Style, and the Principles of Screenwriting*. New York: HarperCollins, 1997.

Metzler, Ken. *Creative Interviewing*. Boston: Allyn and Bacon, 1997.

Murray, Donald. *Writing for Your Readers*. Portsmouth, NH: Heinemann, 2000.

Murray, Donald. *Writing to Deadline*. Chester, CT: Globe Pequot, 1983.

Phillips, Larry, ed. *Ernest Hemingway on Writing*. New York: Scribner, 2004.

Rhodes, Richard. *How to Write*. New York: HarperCollins, 1995.

Rich, Carole. *Writing and Reporting the News: A Coaching Method*. Boston: Cengage Learning, 2016.

Scanlan, Christopher. *Reporting and Writing: Basics for the Twenty-First Century*. Oxford: Oxford University Press, 1999.

Stewart, James. *Follow the Story*. New York: Touchstone, 1998.

Strunk, William, and E. B. White. *The Elements of Style*. San Luis Obispo, CA: Spectrum Ink Publishing, 2017.

Wolfe, Tom. *The New Journalism*. New York: Picador, 1975.

Zinsser, William. *On Writing Well*. New York: HarperCollins, 2006.

COLLECTIONS OF GREAT WRITING

The Best American Essays. Boston and New York: Houghton Mifflin, Harcourt. Annual publication.

The Best American Short Stories. Boston and New York: Houghton Mifflin, Harcourt. Annual publication.

Clark, Roy Peter, and Christopher Scanlan, eds. *Best Newspaper Writing: A Collection of ASNE Prizewinners*. New York: Bedford St. Martins, 2005.

Furman, Laura, ed. *The O. Henry Prize Stories*. New York: Vintage Anchor. Annual publication.

Henderson, Bill, and the Pushcart Prize Editors, eds. *The Pushcart Prize: Best of the Small Presses*. Wainscott, NY: Pushcart Press. Annual publication.

Kerrane, Kevin, and Ben Yagoda, eds. *The Art of Fact: A Historical Anthology of Literary Journalism*. New York: Touchstone, 1998.

Klement, Alice, and Carolyn Matalene. *Telling Stories, Taking Risks*. Belmont, CA: Wadsworth, 1998.

Sims, Norman, and Mark Kramer, eds. *Literary Journalism: A New Collection of the Best American Nonfiction*. New York: Ballantine, 1995.

Snyder, Louis, and Richard B. Morris, eds. *A Treasury of Great Reporting*. New York: Simon and Schuster, 1975.

STYLEBOOKS

Associated Press Stylebook and Briefing on Media Law 2019. New York: Associated Press, 2019.

Chicago Manual of Style. 17th edition. Chicago: University of Chicago Press, 2017.

MLA Handbook. 8th edition. New York: Modern Language Association, 2016.

ONLINE EDUCATION RESOURCES FOR WRITERS

ACEJMC Accredited Programs. All 117 university journalism programs accredited by the American Council on Education in Journalism and Mass Communication, listed by state and including all degree programs, with contact information,

Association of Writers & Writing Programs. The most comprehensive guide to creative-writing degree programs (graduate and undergraduate), writing conventions, workshops, camps, and colonies, as well as publications of interest to writers.

Index